THE
ENVIRONMENT OF
HUMAN SETTLEMENTS

Human Well-being in Cities

Volume 1

Supplement No. 1 to the International Journal HABITAT

THE
ENVIRONMENT OF
HUMAN SETTLEMENTS

Human Well-being in Cities

Proceedings of the Conference held in
Brussels, Belgium, April 1976

Volume 1

Editor in Chief

P. LACONTE
University of Louvain, Belgium

Editors

G.EPSTEIN
Shepheard,Epstein and Hunter, London

J.E.GIBSON
School of Engineering and Applied Sciences,
University of Virginia

P.H.JONES
Institute of Environmental Sciences,
University of Toronto

U.LUOTO
Ekono Consulting Engineers, Helsinki

PERGAMON PRESS

OXFORD · NEW YORK · TORONTO · SYDNEY · PARIS · FRANKFURT

U.K.	Pergamon Press Ltd., Headington Hill Hall, Oxford OX3 0BW, England
U.S.A.	Pergamon Press Inc., Maxwell House, Fairview Park, Elmsford, New York 10523, U.S.A.
CANADA	Pergamon of Canada Ltd., P.O. Box 9600, Don Mills M3C 2T9, Ontario, Canada
AUSTRALIA	Pergamon Press (Aust.) Pty. Ltd., 19a Boundary Street, Rushcutters Bay, N.S.W. 2011, Australia
FRANCE	Pergamon Press SARL, 24 rue des Ecoles, 75240 Paris, Cedex 05, France
WEST GERMANY	Pergamon Press GmbH, 6242 Kronberg-Taunus, Pferdstrasse 1, Frankfurt-am-Main, West Germany

First edition 1976

Library of Congress Catalog Card No. 76-5192

In order to make this volume available as economically and rapidly as possible the author's typescript has been reproduced in its original form. This method unfortunately has its typographical limitations but it is hoped that they in no way distract the reader.

Printed in Great Britain by Express Litho Service, Oxford
ISBN 0 08 020978 5

CONTENTS

Contents

Contents

IV — DESIGN AS AN AID TO SOLVING URBAN PROBLEMS

V — WELL-BEING IN CITIES AND THE FUTURE

The present book is dedicated to MR J. DE SAEGER, *Minister of Public Health and Family of Belgium, who has consistently expressed his concern about a practical approach of the problems of Environment and Health.*

We thank the Committee which has supported the activity of WERC and in particular its President, MR N. HILGERS, *Deputy Cabinet Chief.*

INTRODUCTION

For the first time in history, the world population will double in thirty
years. In the year 2000 our planet will number 6500 million inhabitants, of
whom more than 3500 million will live in urban settlements. The largest
human conglomerates are the fastest to expand. This is resulting in a series
of problems affecting the quality of life and "human well-being in cities",
which was chosen as the theme of the Brussels Conference.

This conference has been commissioned for the World Environment and Resources
Council (W.E.R.C.) by the Belgian Government, in order to provide input to
its participation in the United Nations Conference on Human Settlements
(Vancouver, May-June 1976).

The primary objective of WERC is to encourage discussions between and meetings
of engineers, scientists and decision-makers concerned with local, national,
regional and global environmental problems and to assist appropriately
qualified non-governmental national bodies (professional, scientific societies,
organizations of concerned citizens, etc.) in coordinating their activities
at national and international levels.

WERC sponsored among others, the successful First International Conference
on the Conversion of Refuse to Energy (Montreux, November 3-5, 1975) and the
International Congress of Scientists on the Human Environment (Kyoto,
November 16-26, 1975).

The technical scope of the conference has tried to cover four main headings:

   Modern technology for cities of today (including a special workshop
   on water resources).

   Decision-making for human well-being in cities (including political,
   legal and economic considerations).

Introduction

Urban and land-use planning (including a session on citizen participation).
Design as a component in urban policy.

It has also been intended to illustrate the theme of the conference by visits
to the old city of Bruges and the urban development of Louvain-la-Neuve
(Ottignies) which were chosen as the two contributions of Belgium to the
United Nations Conference.

To cover this technical scope, the executive committee of WERC has appointed
the following board of editors: Mr. U. Luoto, Ekono Consulting Engineers,
Helsinki, Finland; Dr. P.H. Jones, Institute of Environmental Sciences,
University of Toronto, Canada; Dr. J.E. Gibson, School of Engineering and
Applied Sciences, University of Virginia, USA; Arch. C. Epstein, Shepheard,
Epstein and Hunter, London, UK; Dr. P. Laconte, University of Louvain, B1348
Louvain-la-Neuve, Belgium.

The other members of the Programme Committee were: Dr. Yacov Haimes, Case
Western Reserve University, Cleveland, Ohio; Dr. Harold Chestnut, General
Electric Company, Schenectady, USA; Dr. E.A. Wolff, National Aeronautic and
Space Administration, Greenbelt, Maryland, USA.

On the basis of a general call for papers and personal contacts with authors,
the board of editors has selected about fifty papers covering the four main
headings.

The papers which were accepted and could be edited in time to be distributed
at the Conference in a printed form were included in Volume I.

Volume II will include the text of the keynote speeches, the other papers
presented at the conference and a report on the discussions.

It is our personal pleasure to thank all those who contributed to the
preparation of this Conference besides the executive committee of WERC and
the Programme Committee, in particular the secretary of the conference,
Mr. M. Minet and Mrs. R. Baridaens-Hawlena and the press officer, Mr. M.
Dubrulle. Special reference is made to the staff of the International Council
of Societies of Industrial Design (I.C.S.I.D.) who took the responsibility of
preparing the Bruges session.

ONTARIO'S RESOURCE RECOVERY PROGRAMME

Wesley Williamson
Ontario Ministry of the Environment, Toronto, Ontario.

ABSTRACT

By 1974, it had already become apparent that a broader approach
to solid waste management was necessary than legislative controls
directed primarily to prevent pollution of the natural environment and to eliminate health hazards. Preventive planning, the
total human environment and positive measures for improvement required greater emphasis, and the urgent need to conserve material
and energy resources was recognised.

Most of the larger municipalities in Ontario already faced critical problems in obtaining adequate disposal facilities, and
these problems were increasing. Although action had been initiated on some of the general approaches necessary for a complete
solution, further government action was necessary to integrate
and extend these into a comprehensive provincial program.

An outline of the program, and its objectives in each of 3 five
year stages, is provided; the organisation set up to develop and
implement the program is described; and the implications of present program policies in relation to municipalities, industry and
the public are examined.

GENERAL BACKGROUND

Ontario, by 1974, had already made very substantial progress in
almost every aspect of waste management since the province assumed
certain responsibilities in the field by the Waste Management Act
of 1970. However, also by 1974, the role of the Ontario Ministry
of the Environment, in this and other issues, was recognized as
requiring a broader approach than simply to prevent further contamination of the three elements of the natural environment; air,
land and water. Greater emphasis had to be placed on preventive
planning, on the total human environment, and on positive measures
for improvement. Particularly, the urgent need to conserve, to
the greatest degree possible, resources both of materials and
energy was recognised.

The Provincial Resource Recovery Program derives directly from
these wider concerns.

PROBLEMS

One of the most critical problems facing municipalities at this
time is the disposal of the waste materials produced by our afflu-
ent society.

1

Legislation to control the handling and disposal of waste may ensure the basic protection of the environment and the public, but
the enforcement of such legislation reduces the disposal options
available to municipalities and results in substantially increased
costs.

Even more important, since space for the landfill of wastes is
rarely available now within the municipalities own boundaries, disposal sites must be sought in adjacent rural areas. The resulting
confrontations are invariably highly emotional, bitter, and prolonged, and whatever the outcome exacerbate the social tensions
already in existence and imperil the resolution of other pressing
municipal problems totally unrelated to this issue.

Moreover, it is essential that energy and material resources be
conserved to the greatest degree possible. The reduction of waste,
and the recovery of resources from waste, are not only desirable
in themselves, but symbolic of a committment to such conservation.

SOLUTION APPROACHES

It is recognized that a complete solution will require a number of
different basic approaches which must be pursued in parallel to
achieve success. Summarily, these approaches are:

1. reduction in the quantity of material produced which is likely
to result in waste;

2. changes in the method of manufacture or types of material
used to simplify the separation and reclamation of the wastes produced;

3. separation of some elements of the waste at source, either
at the household, commercial or industrial level;

4. planned, coordinated, waste management systems;

5. central resource recovery plants;

6. possible additional processing facilities for materials separated at the central plants;

7. encouragement for the re-use of reclaimed material, and the
development of new uses for this material.

Action had already been taken, or was being planned, by the Government of Ontario to investigate and develop programs covering some
of these approaches. Two of these programs are of particular significance.

Area Planning Studies
One very significant program initiated in 1972 was the encouragement of waste management area planning studies by the provision of
a fifty per cent provincial grant. Sixteen of these studies are
now completed or in progress, generally covering entire counties
or regions of the province. When implemented they will result in

in a marked reduction in the total number of landfill disposal
sites, principally due to the consolidation of a large number of
small sites into a few central treatment facilities, which can be
improved in stages, as reclamation processes and equipment become
practicable, to resource recovery rather than merely disposal
sites.

Experimental Reclamation Plant
Another, vital, step was taken with the decision to construct a
full scale reclamation plant.

The technology for the separation and further processing of the
components of waste to produce reusable materials or fuel has not
yet been fully developed. The application of this technology to
the design of working plants is even less advanced, and the economics of the various possible processes, which essentially depend upon the marketing of reclaimed materials, is uncertain.

While certainly some working plants are now in operation in the
U.S. and Europe using various processes, it is extremely difficult
to make a reliable assessment of their long term effectiveness,
real cost, or to determine the marketability of products. It is
even more difficult to make a critical comparison between different processes, to determine which might be more suitable in a
given application.

It was for these reasons that the Ministry decided to construct a
full scale working plant, which would provide the capability of
testing in practice any existing or new processes which appeared
feasible. Equally important, such a plant would provide a reliable
supply of reclaimed material for testing by industry, to determine
its marketability, or to develop new markets.

This plant, of two hundred ton per day capacity capable of servicing a population of about one hundred thousand, is now under construction in Toronto, Ontario, and is scheduled to commence operations in the summer of 1976.

In addition to corrugated paper, bundled newsprint and ferrous
metals, glass and non-ferrous metals will also be recovered.

A fraction comprising shredded paper and film plastic will be
separated, and part utilized for plant heating in a module designed to provide data on its possible use as a fuel in industrial
boilers. This fraction will also be available to, for example,
the cement industry for testing as a fuel, and to the paper industry to examine the further processing required before reuse as
paper.

Another fraction, consisting mainly of organic material, will be
processed with sewage sludge in a mechanical composting module.

The plant has been designed upon this modular concept, which will
enable at a later stage the addition of a plastics recovery module, a pyrolysis or hydro-gasification module, and units for
other processes which may be developed.

Very extensive facilities have been provided for monitoring the
waste stream throughout the plant so that accurate data on all aspects of the processes will for the first time be made available.

The plant will also be used as a training school for operators of
other plants to be built under the program, and has been designed
so that it can be accessible to the public without risk or interference with plant operations.

This is a most important development and is the keystone of the
comprehensive resource recovery program.

COMPREHENSIVE PROVINCIAL PROGRAM

The provincial program covers three, five-year stages;

Stage 1
During stage one, between 1975 and 1980, waste management systems
will be improved so that the majority of existing disposal sites
in a particular area will be eliminated, and disposal operations
concentrated in a few large sophisticated facilities.

At some major population centres where transfer stations are already necessary, front end processing plants will be constructed.
The front end process includes the manual separation of readily
recoverable materials such as corrugated and bundled newsprint,
the remainder of the waste being shredded and ferrous metal removed magnetically. It is important to note that the front end
processes have many advantages, even if the material produced is
subsequently land filled, or incinerated for the production of
energy, as an interim measure. Nuisance effects are almost eliminated, the cost of disposal is reduced, and a proportion of
marketable materials can be recovered immediately. This staged
approach is sufficiently flexible that immediate advantage can be
taken of new processes and equipment as they are developed and
proven at the experimental plant.

During this period also, certain large scale demonstration projects
may be supported as an interim measure providing that they are
compatible with the objectives of the provincial program, and are
sufficiently flexible to be incorporated within the program eventually.

The 'Watts from Waste' project, which is essentially a front end
plant using the separated light fraction as a fuel in an existing
electrical generating station, is a typical example of such a project.

Stage 2
During stage two, between 1980 and 1985, the provision of transfer
stations and transportation networks should be completed throughout the province. This will enable the remainder of the front end
plants to be constructed.

The full development of this concept, however, may be contingent
upon the improvement of long haul transportation of waste, by the

use of rail haul for example.

During this stage, also, sufficient progress should have been
made in process technology and market development to enable work
to begin on the installation of proven back end recovery processes.

Stage 3
Finally, in the third stage between 1985 and 1990, it should be
possible to complete the program by the installation of complete
resource recovery processes serving ninety per cent of the population of the province.

ONTARIO CENTRE FOR RESOURCE RECOVERY

The administration of the program is based on the concept of an
Ontario Centre for Resource Recovery, as a focus for all activities bearing upon the conservation and recovery of resources related to solid waste.

The Centre includes essentially an executive group, and research
and experimental facilities. An independent advisory group is
also associated with some of the Centre's functions.

The goal of the Centre, formally stated, is "to develop and implement a comprehensive waste management program for the conservation
and recovery of resources", which may be made clearer by consideration of the five specific objectives which have been established:

1. to minimise unnecessary waste by encouraging the more efficient
use of material resources;

2. to provide guidance and assistance in the economic development of integrated waste management systems;

3. to recover to the greatest degree practicable the energy and
material resources in solid waste;

4. to foster the development of markets for the full utilisation
of the energy and materials recovered;

5. to reduce to a minimum the use of land for solid waste disposal.

A Resource Recovery Branch has been established in the Utility
and Laboratory Services Division of the Ministry of the Environment and made responsible for the execution of the provincial program.

The experimental plant already described will form the principal,
though not of course the only facility, at which research and
development activities will be carried out.

An independent body, the Waste Management Advisory Board, reporting directly to the Minister of the Environment, has been established, generally to assist in an advisory role in the management of waste and the development of resource recovery from waste,

but specifically to investigate and make recommendations on means of achieving the first goal, to minimise unnecessary waste.

PROGRAM POLICIES

In this completely new field, where both technology and management techniques are in their infancy, and with little experience elsewhere in the world to draw on, a keynote of the program must be flexibility.

The staged program described provides that flexibility for the utilisation of new technology developed or proven at the Ontario Centre for Resource Recovery, in conjunction with the development of markets for recovered material and energy.

It is equally important that the same capability to adapt to changing circumstances should be built into the administrative and financial policies of the program at this stage.

A major program of this type will have both direct and indirect effects, and in some cases very significant effects, on municipalities; on the various segments of industry - secondary material brokers and processors, material and energy producers and users, road and rail transport and private waste management companies; on other Government agencies; and of course on the general public.

Municipalities
Municipalities in Ontario have the entire responsibility for solid waste arising in their community.

For present purposes, we can separate this general waste management system into four separate functions; collection services; waste handling systems; resource recovery plants; and residue disposal sites.

Municipal collection.
Collection services must remain the sole responsibility of the local municipality. The provincial role will generally be restricted to a research and advisory function, to assist in the development and acceptance of more effective and economic collection systems and equipment. This restriction is also applicable to possible residential source separation and separate collection projects.

Indirectly, of course, the provincial program will assist in both these areas, for example, in reducing cost by limiting the haul distance of collection vehicles by the establishment of transfer station, and by providing additional outlets and more stable markets for source separated material.

Municipal waste handling system.
Waste handling systems can be defined as all waste management functions except collection to the point where the waste is delivered to the processing or disposal facility. In areas without municipal collection services, it would include a rural container system to which the individual delivers his own waste.

The development of improved waste handling systems is a necessary prior step to the establishment of resource recovery plants, apart from the limited number of areas with a concentration of population high enough to justify the establishment of a major transfer station in any event.

The provincial role in this area is two-fold.

To develop a provincial system within which local systems can be integrated; and to assist in the development of such local systems.

Proposed subsidy program. It is recognised that in general, the development of improved local systems will impose additional costs particularly on the smaller municipalities, even if waste management costs are equalised throughout a particular administrative area, especially in the early stages of the program.

However, although the need for provincial assistance has been accepted in principle, we have found significant problems to be surmounted in developing a practicable, and equitable, program of subsidization which have delayed its development.

Resource recovery plants. With respect to resource recovery plants, two facilities, the experimental plant in North York and the 'Watts from Waste' demonstration project were initiated prior to the development of the comprehensive provincial program, and their financial and administrative arrangements vary in some ways from those adopted for the remainder of the program.

With respect to the other facilities to be constructed in the first stage of the program, the province is prepared to provide the entire capital funding for the construction of such transfer stations and front end resource recovery plants, though fifty per cent of this cost will be recovered as an annual charge amortised over forty years.

During at least the first stage of the program, the ownership and control of these plants will be retained by the province. This policy is dictated by the need to ensure that the long term efficiency which can only be obtained by a fully integrated provincial system is achieved.

The decision, of course, whether to participate in the program or not remains entirely within the jurisdiction of the municipalities involved.

Full municipal participation is ensured by setting up technical coordinating committees, with membership shared by the province and the municipalities involved, to supervise the study.

Residue disposal sites. Turning to the controversial problem of landfill disposal sites, it must be emphasized that even though the provincial program fully meets its objectives within the fifteen year period proposed, the need will still remain for landfill disposal. However, the area of land required will be progressively reduced, and over the period the emphasis will be changed from the use of land for waste disposal, to the use of processed waste for land reclamation and improvement.

In view of this progressive change in requirements, and the urgency with which the need to preserve undisturbed land is viewed a policy on the use of such land was announced in April, 1975. This policy essentially stated that where there is any feasible alternative, the use of any undisturbed land for the disposal of waste is not in the public interest.

Industry
In the case of industries which are prospective clients for separated materials, or a processed fuel fraction, the question of guaranteed supply and guaranteed quality is paramount if the industry is to be involved in a further processing operation, involving committments in plant modification or expansion, or is to be entirely dependent on this source of supply.

Conversely, it would be imprudent in the early stages of the program to make large scale long term committments to any industry for the supply of waste products, particularly if alternative uses, or alternative processing methods, appeared promising.

Private waste management companies range from small companies providing a collection service to commercial establishments and smaller municipalities to very large companies offering a wide range of services, and which, in some cases own and operate their own landfill disposal sites.

The trend in Canada, as in the U.S. has led to the amalgamation of many of the smaller companies into large conglomerates, with a strong trend to monopolisation of the market in certain areas, particularly where they own disposal facilities.

Policies established at this stage are not intended to limit the participation by industry generally or private waste management companies in the provincial program. However, until technology and market development are further advanced, the Ministry's position is that sufficient information is not available to permit funding of any particular proprietory process.

There remains, of course, even in the first stage of the program, a major role to be played by private industry in the operation of waste management systems and processing plants under contract with municipalities or the Ministry.

General Public
There are essentially three different levels of involvement by the general public in the provincial program.

First there is the very specific involvement of residents in areas where processing plants or residue disposal sites are located. Any project under this program or associated with it will undergo an environmental assessment process, including a public participation program commencing at the earliest planning stage possible.

Second, the efforts of the Waste Management Advisory Board in achieving a reduction in the quantity of waste produced hinge on whether the individual consumer will be prepared to take a degree of responsibility herself or even himself in accepting some degree of restriction of complete freedom of choice; in using more selective purchasing practices; or even by boycotting particularly wasteful goods.

And, generally, this program can only achieve its objectives if there is full public support of those objectives and the primary reason for setting them - to conserve irreplaceable resources of materials, of energy, of land itself for future generations.

ACCESSIBILITY FOR GOODS AND PEOPLE

Wilfred Owen
The Brookings Institution, Washington, D. C., U. S. A.

TOWARD SUCCESSFUL HUMAN SETTLEMENTS

Since human settlements function as meeting places and places for the exchange of goods and ideas, the quality of their transportation, and communication plays a key role in their viability and performance.

Historically transportation determined the size, shape, and density of urban settlements. When transportation was mostly on foot, the radius of the town was restricted to a few miles, and the area to perhaps a dozen square miles. Population was limited by the space available, and by the capacity of transport to feed and supply the community. But recent advances in technology have increased the radius of the metropolis by many miles, the urbanized area by hundreds of square miles, and the supportable level of population by many millions.

As a result of these changes, the conventional practice of allowing transport technology to dictate the character of the city has been challenged. Transport is no longer a constraint, and modern transport technologies can support almost any degree of concentration or sprawl. If urban communities follow blindly whatever growth patterns the technology of transportation makes possible, they will grow to completely unmanageable sizes and shapes. Urban man is called upon to decide the kind of city he wants, and then to use technology to help achieve it.

Imaginative efforts to overcome the problems of the conventional city has been launched in many parts of the world through major urban redevelopment projects and the creation of planned new cities. The objective is to create attractive communities for human beings on sites that combine jobs, dwellings, shops, schools, community services, recreation and open space. The new city and the renewed old city feature area-wide bicycle paths and pedestrian walkway systems, the separation of people and vehicles, and mixed land uses that substitute easier access for greater mobility. Streets can often be eliminated by the clustering of housing, and the land vacated by street abandonments can be used for recreation and community facilities. Unnecessary use of the automobile is avoided by supplying each neighborhood with convenience shopping and a variety of social services that include clinics, child day-care centers, schools and meeting places.

The idea of a car-free city and therefore an energy conserving city has thus far received limited attention. Instead, most cities have placed heavy reliance on the automobile, and efforts to supply mobility have resulted in ignoring the pedestrian and making easy access impossible. There is much to be said for guiding urban growth into more manageable sub-communities, where the location and arrangement of buildings and activities in an acceptable

environment can reduce travel and avoid congestion. Roads should be used to
enclose and insulate neighborhoods, streets can be used to provide exclusive
bus routes, and city life can be organized in designs to the advantage of
everybody.

Better communities also need to be part of a national or regional urbanization plan that establishes where development is to take place and where it
is not. In the regional city of the future continuous urban spread would be
replaced by the city of many centers, divided into units of manageable size
and dispersed to make open space easily accessible and to help revitalize the
countryside. Mobility would make every place easily accessible to permit the
region to function as a unit. Space in existing cities could be created by
thinning out the old city center, with growth and overspill accommodated in
surrounding cities and towns through their planned expansion.

IF THE TRENDS CONTINUE

The trend toward living in cities and riding in automobiles has resulted in
spatial and environmental conflicts that have detracted from the quality of
urban life nearly everywhere. Many of the world's cities, already overcrowded
and suffering critical shortages of housing and public services, will double
their population by the end of this decade and triple their ownership of
automobiles. While motorization has led to important economic and social
change, the unwanted side effects have been substantial and they will be
further intensifying today's urban problems. Traffic congestion in the
largest cities has reached staggering proportions, the air has become increasingly polluted, public transit is grossly inadequate, and pressures
are mounting for costly expressways and subways that divert resources from
other more basic urban needs and cannot be counted on to relieve congestion.

The efficiency of the city and the contribution of urbanization to development
will depend to an important degree on how the problems of mobility are resolved. A key factor will be the degree to which the motor vehicle can be
accommodated or contained in the interest of a satisfactory total transportation system. The growth of car ownership and use on the Western pattern
should not be considered inevitable. It is also possible to make public
transit work and to link urban growth policies and community designs to
reduce the causes of congestion.

POTENTIAL IMPROVEMENTS IN ACCESSIBILITY

Different sizes, shapes and densities of urban places have differing needs
for transportation, and solutions lie in a variety of compromises between
pedestrians and riders, car owners and the carless, among different technologies, between new capital investment and better management, and between
solutions that focus on the supply of transportation and those that influence
the demand.

Improving Bus Transit

New investment in public transportation focuses attention on the bus. In
most cities of the world bus transportation is of poor quality and needs to
be freed from the traffic congestion created by other uses of the street.

What is needed is an integrated approach to the highway and vehicle elements of the bus transport system so that a complete public transport service is provided. Focussing on the equipment alone, and overlooking roadway requirements and the management of bus operations, have prevented the creation of an effective system.

A space-saving and energy-conserving transport solution for developing countries that could decongest traffic at reasonable cost might be the enlargement of bus fleets and the creation of a city-wide network of all-bus or exclusive bus and taxi streets. The possible effects of such a program appear to be well worth the cost. For example, it is estimated that in 1970 about 270 million people were living in cities of over 500,000 population in developing countries.* The equipment in their bus fleets is estimated at 135,000 units (assuming 500 vehicles per million people). Doubling this fleet to 270,000 units at a cost of $30,000 per bus would require a capital outlay of $4 billion. This is about equal to the investment required for eight subway systems comparable to the Mexico City Metro. The additional buses (assuming 1,000 passengers are carried per bus per day) could move 135 million passengers daily compared to a total capacity of 10 million passengers for the eight subway systems. For an immediate increase in urban travel capabilities, therefore, an expansion of bus fleets plus preferential treatment for buses on city streets appears to offer considerable promise.

The Public Automobile

Urban traffic patterns show that the group-riding taxi, or public automobile, is increasing in popularity, and that in many cases the bus has already lost considerable ground to the more convenient jitney taxi. The trends reflect the fact that the taxi offers a relatively unexploited means of supplying public transport service. If extensive and better organized public automobile fleets were used as a supplement to the bus, or as a substitute, they would supply service comparable to that of the automobile, would eliminate parking problems, and would reduce the social gap that separates car owners from the carless by providing all urban residents with physically comparable equipment. A special advantage of the jitney taxi is its ability to maintain high average speeds that are not much lower than that of the automobile. From the standpoint of employment, taxis that work around the clock provide jobs for a large number of drivers and for workers in the shops and assembly plants.

Based on experience in Teheran, Manila and other cities, a moderate-sized fleet of group-riding taxis could provide high quality transport at low cost if operated in zones freed of private automobiles. If a bus costing $32,000 can carry an average of 1,200 passengers per day, 8 public automobiles priced at $4,000 apiece and carrying 150 persons per day could perform the same transportation task for the same cost. The jitney taxi would provide a seat for all, frequent scheduling, and nearly door to door service. And compared to a private car, assuming 8 people are carried per day (4 trips with an average of 2 people) the public automobile could do 15 times as much work. The services of 100,000 private cars could be accomplished with 6,600 public cars.

---

*Based on United Nations population estimates contained in "Urbanization: Development Policies and Planning," International Social Development Review, No. 1, 1968, p. 19.

Rail Rapid Transit

An obvious drawback to rail rapid transit solutions is that costs are high: $24 million a mile for San Francisco, $45 million for Washington, and $50 million for Rio de Janeiro. It follows, therefore, that an extensive network capable of serving a large metropolitan area involves high total outlays. Operating deficits are also mounting and even these costs are more than can be covered by fares. Substantial amounts per ride will have to be made available out of general taxes to pay the bill. Rapid transit thus competes with other urgent needs such as housing, health and education, and low-income inner-city residents appear to benefit least. For short trips typical of urban travel needs, the bus is likely to provide a better service.

If rapid transit and the high densities they make possible permit large cost reductions through the scale and organization of economic activity, then the rail system with its high costs may be warranted. It may not be the high cost of rail transportation relative to other transport solutions that is critical, but rather the total costs and benefits of alternative urban settlements that can be supported by various transportation solutions.

If the city were to agree to abandon all automobiles in favor of rapid transit, and if the amounts spent for private cars were to be used instead for public transit, then a metro system complete with bus and taxi feeder services could perhaps be afforded. But in that eventuality, with automobiles removed from the streets, it would no longer be necessary to build transit underground, for good surface transit could be supplied on the vacated streets. Actually the only practical compromise seems to be a mix of automobile and surface transit in which the two methods are separated.

Managing Transport Systems

The use of the streets and the prices charged for such use indicate a kind of global perversity that rewards those who waste space and discourages those who conserve it. The facts have been well documented, but the recommended solutions are often politically unacceptable.

Methods of limiting traffic include three types: restraints, such as pricing urban street use and charging motorists more for parking restrictions, such as the designation of vehicle-free zones; and avoidance, such as designing urban activity systems that reduce the need for vehicle movement.*

Pricing urban road services, banning street parking, and reflecting social costs in the fees paid by motorists could all help reduce congestion quickly, with relatively minor investments in buses or other public transport. Pricing policy could act as a rationing device that would reduce the peaks and shift some travel from private cars to public vehicles. One approach would be to use the proceeds of the social costs paid by the motorist to subsidize transit in recognition of its social benefits. By keeping transit fares low, or eliminating them altogether, it might be possible to minimize the total transportation bill.

---

*J. Michael Thomson, "Methods of Traffic Limitation in Urban Areas," Working Paper No. 3, OECD, Paris, 1972.

At the present time automobiles are generally able to park on the streets
without charge. They are not paying the social costs of air pollution,
accidents, and environmental destruction.   In addition, automobile user
charges are uniform regardless of where and when the travel is performed,
so that peak-hour commuters are being subsidized by off-peak drivers. The
simplest remedy appears to be the banning of free parking, which is a burden
on the city, and the introduction of parking charges for off-street facilities that reflect both the cost of parking and the costs incurred for peak-
hour driving.*

Another low-cost remedy for traffic congestion is the banning of automobile
traffic in limited areas of the city, and dedication of selected streets to
pedestrian traffic. About 100 vehicle-free zones and pedestrian shopping
streets have been created in European cities with moderate financial commitment and physical change, often by simply paving over streets and installing
lights and landscaping. An ambitious proposal has been made in Vienna to
ban automobiles from the entire central area (enclosed by the inner ring
road). Other means of regulating vehicle use have been introduced in Goteborg,
Sweden, where the division of the city into separate sectors and the prohibi-
tion of direct movement of cars from one sector to another has had favorable
effects on traffic flow and on the environment.

Unfortunately there is not much appeal to traffic engineering and management
solutions, and the greater visibility of expressways and subways gives these
high-cost remedies greater acceptance. Yet an integrated traffic management
strategy could have impressive results. It would include pricing policies
that charged the motorist his full costs, preferential treatment for buses,
computerized signal systems and other uses of electronics, street parking
prohibitions, pedestrian zones, strict enforcement of traffic rules, routing
of through traffic away from the center, staggered work hours and staggered
days of work. Such a strategy could be reinforced by investments in bus and
taxi equipment, grade-separation of selected highway intersections, relocation of bus and truck terminals, and off-street truck loading and unloading
facilities. Thus far no city has set about to design and carry out a comprehensive strategy of this kind.

Emerging New Design Concepts

The planned cities of the world, granted their many shortcomings, have
introduced new concepts of urban form that help us visualize how existing
cities might be redesigned to work better and to provide a more satisfactory
environment. These same concepts suggest how future growth might be channeled
into more orderly settlements. The lessons are provided by the successes
and failures of British new towns, Singapore, Brasilia, Chandigarh, Tema and
many others. Judging from the best features of attempts to build whole
communities, it is apparent that efforts to improve accessibility in existing
cities will have to focus to a greater extent on how things are located and
arranged. Neighborhoods should be as free as possible from the intrusions of

---

*For a fuller discussion of automobile and transit subsidies and user charges,
see The Metropolitan Transportation Problem, (Brookings Institution, 1966),
pp. 142-164, and The Accessible City, (Brookings Institution, 1972), pp. 46-
48.

through traffic, and housing made accessible to jobs, shops, services and recreation.

Mobility is not the only aim, for mobility is only a means of making accessible what the city has to offer, and what individuals seek to do in the community. A series of clustered activities that provide easy access by local transport or pedestrian pathways to neighborhood markets or centers, and that are provided with nearby employment opportunities and recreation, seems preferable to a planless and often disorderly pattern of urban growth. In the latter case disorder and inaccessibility must be overcome by excessive investments in movement. But this compensatory transport, if carried to extremes, drains resources from other needed services and often detracts from the quality of urban life. Efforts to reach a compromise between mobility and accessibility hold the key to more satisfying communities.

Singapore is probably the best illustration of how a series of satellite urban clusters and center city redevelopment are creating a regional city of many centers in place of the conventional solid urban build-up. Singapore satellites are moving people out of the congestion to help provide them with good housing and neighborhoods. Instead of paying the high cost of transportation needed to cope with a single center, steps are being taken to organize urban activity in subcenters that contain built-in transportation solutions. Transportation is then supplied along well-defined corridors to interconnect the clusters.

But Singapore is a special case, with no rural hinterland that threatens to pour millions of rural migrants into an attractive redesigned city. Is it possible to solve problems of accessibility in other cities where rural to urban migration continues to add new population? An affirmative answer is suggested by two current examples of urban planning and redevelopment: Bogota and Karachi.

A United Nations-World Bank study of Bogota was designed to explore how the social and physical development of the city might be altered to preserve the best features of the existing city, to make way for further growth, but to do so in a way that would conserve the city's resources and eradicate the slums. The essense of the recommended development plan is to build three "new cities in the city" to accommodate growth and to restructure the downtown for both living and working. In addition, approximately 100,000 jobs that do not need to be downtown would be removed from the central business district and relocated in the new satellites, where they would be within easy access of housing.

Unlike many other cities, Bogota has not included a subway in its plans, but has opted for surface rail or bus lines from the city center to the satellites, plus a rationalization of the bus system. Part of the plan is to re-route buses passing through the center but having destinations elsewhere, which may eliminate thirty to forty percent of the bus traffic now congesting the center. Measures recommended to control the automobile include the creation of auto-free zones in the city's historic center, restrictions on downtown parking, designation of exclusive bus lanes and bus streets, and higher taxes on peak hour use of private cars.

The situation in Karachi, Pakistan, also dramatizes the scale of the remedies required. Karachi is a port city of 3.5 million people which could conceivably have a population of 12 to 15 million thirty years from now.   This possibility leads to serious concern over the adequacy of water supply, sewage facilities, housing, and transportation, for it is impossible with limited budgets to satisfy the basic needs of even the existing population. Karachi faces a financial crisis as development funds fall short and costs continue to rise, and as the benefits of rising land values are realized by the private sector rather than the community. Some 100,000 workers are now unemployed, but if jobs were made available in the construction of new communities, these people would be capable of creating values nearly as great as the entire Pakistan five-year plan allocation for slum improvements and low cost housing.

The growth plan proposed by a United Nations study is to create a series of "metrovilles" or compact partially self-contained and accessible communities of 40,000 to 50,000 people.* Four metrovilles are scheduled in the initial program. This planned growth effort is designed to interest people in building their own homes, to provide nearby work places, and to provide adequate transport connections to the center. The metrovilles would plow back into the community the profits from the rising values of land publicly held, and would rely on the clustering of urban activities and services to improve access and reduce travel.

In summary, the problems of mobility for urban settlements involve both the technologies and systems of management that supply transportation and the design and location of community activities that generate the demand for transportation. On the supply side the focus should be on low-cost solutions that organize existing facilities more effectively and rely primarily on surface public transit, with exclusive rights of way where necessary. On the demand side the essential factors are national urban growth plans that influence the general patterns of job location, and local community improvement programs that combine transportation with other aspects of urban development in a comprehensive city-building approach. Viewed in these ways, transportation is not primarily a problem but a powerful means of building more satisfying human settlements.

---

*PADCO, Karachi Master Plan Project, 1974.

AN EXPLORATION OF INTERSTATE HIGHWAY INTERCHANGE COMMUNITIES AS SITES OF FUTURE SETTLEMENTS

Raymond W. Eyerly, Assistant Professor
Department of Business Logistics, College of
Business Administration, The Pennsylvania State
University, United States

ABSTRACT

The presence of an Interstate highway interchange in a community
is generally expected to confer substantial impacts on the local
economy because of restructured linkages between local and distant
land uses. Maps of real estate values were prepared by a computer
plotting method to show the pattern of land use development of
four rural interchange communities. Isovalue lines plotted at
1,000 dollar intervals of real estate values depicted the extent
and intensity of development in the interchange communities.
Most of the patterns on the maps showed development that occurred
prior to the construction of the Interstate highway and this
development was related to the already existing road system.
Although it was expected that interchanges would be the focal
points of patterns of development, only one development nodule
centered on an interchange. An industrial park was located at
this interchange. Perhaps the time span, five years after the
interchanges opened, was too short a period for discernible
growth to occur. Studies of longer duration are recommended.

INTRODUCTION

In much of the literature on the location of economic activity
and, in particular, the location of human settlements such as
villages, towns, and cities, emphasis is placed upon the uniqueness
of transportation available at that site. Examples usually given
are a port located where a large river leading to the interior
empties into a large body of water such as a lake, bay or ocean,
settlements located at the confluence of two navigable rivers,
settlements located at intersections of natural pathways for
overland travel, and the more recent phenomena of urban places
developed at hubs of railroad networks. Transportation provides
accessibility by linking a land resource with other land resources
that serve as markets or sources of raw materials and thereby
promotes regional and interregional growth (Kraft et al., 1971:
1-5).

In this century, the internal combustion engine has given man
freedom to move over landforms in rubber wheeled vehicles. The
limitations of previous transportation systems based on natural

19

features were overcome. In order to facilitate the movement of
motor vehicles over landforms, networks of roadways have been
built having an essential purpose of connecting places where resources are consumed with places where resources are produced or
available. Large numbers of people and great quantities of goods
are now moving over these roadway systems.

The nearly complete 41,000 mile Interstate Highway System has
altered the existing transportation system by providing highspeed,
limited-access highways connecting the major cities of the United
States of America. These highways traveled by the motor vehicle
with its inherent advantage of accessibility to land uses coupled
with speed that reduces the time for movement between land uses,
thereby reducing the size of inventory in motion, have altered
traditional travel and goods distribution patterns, have generated
changes in the characteristics of existing developed land and have
opened up undeveloped land to new uses (Eyerly, 1972) (Stein,
1969) (Corsi, 1974) (Twark, 1967).

At various points along the Interstate system, access is provided
to local and regional road systems. The interchange is a crucial
segment for it is the interface of the Interstate Highway System
with the local transportation system. The interchange is designed
to maintain flows of traffic on both the Interstate highway and
the feeder highway system while facilitating on and off flows of
traffic. Because the Interstate connects local areas with regional,
state, and national resources and markets, it is in the land areas
in the vicinities of interchanges of the Interstates and the feeder
road systems that the most significant visible impacts of the
Interstate highways are occurring (Eyerly, 1972) (Twark, 1967).
These land areas are expected to become nodes of growth for the
local economies.

This paper proposes that interchanges in rural or semi-rural areas
could form the nuclei of future urban places similar to past developments of urban places at transportation route intersections.
In cases where the Interstate provides improved access to a
larger, already developed urban place, new settlements at or near
the interchange are likely to develop. Humphrey and Sell (1972)
found population growth of minor civil divisions having access to
an interchange and located less than 25 miles from a metropolitan
area was augmented by the improved access. This paper will describe a case study of land use patterns at interchanges that were
located in rural areas but that were close to a small city.

TRANSPORTATION AND LOCATION OF ECONOMIC ACTIVITY

The location of a physical facility of an economic unit is a land
use that resulted from a decision-making process which analyzed
many factors to decide on a region, a local area, and finally the
specific site. The location chosen should optimize profits from
a feasible combination of factors entering into a decision-making
process. As transportation is believed to be a key variable in
ordering spatial distribution of economic units (Isard, 1965:
77-125) (Miller, 1962: 9) and as the development of the Interstate

System offered a new alternative that restructured accessibility
and therefore transportation costs, economic units must certainly
give weight to the effects of the Interstate highways on their
internal cost structure and include this variable in spatial
location decisions.

Most current theory of the effect of spatial location on land
utilization stems from von Thunen's conceptual model of concentric zones of agricultural land use development (Barlowe, 1972:
34-7) (Webber, 1972: 50-60). Differences in land use were
attributed directly to transportation costs. Lands close to the
market city were to be intensively farmed to produce products
that were highly perishable or heavy and bulky and costly to
transport. Lands located at increasing distances from the city
would suffer increasing economic handicaps because transportation
cost was proportional to distance and would therefore be used for
more extensive production of products having lower transportation
costs. Different zones of production possibilities evolved as
concentric circles around the city. Relaxation and adjustments
of the basic model and application to urban situations by later
authors (Webber, 1972: 60-67) have not shaken the importance of
von Thunen's original emphasis on transportation costs as the
bases for ordering land uses (Barlowe, 1972: 37).

THE INTERCHANGE AS A DEVELOPMENT NODULE

The model applied to the interchange situation must relax the
original assumptions based on agriculture but keys in on the
location and distance (transportation costs) to the interchange
to determine the order of land use. The interchange which provides access to region, state, and national markets and raw
material sources thus becomes the local market or urban central
place toward which land uses are oriented.

Uses of land are characterized as being ordered from lower uses
(extensive uses such as farmland, forests, parkland, vacant lots,
wasteland, etc.) through various ascending levels such as single
family housing to higher uses (intensive uses such as office
buildings, high-rise apartments, contiguous residences, manufacturing plants, retail complexes, etc.). The transition from
undeveloped rural areas to highly developed urban areas is a
transition from a pattern of lower order uses to a pattern of
higher order land uses. Clawson (1974) discusses the land conversion process in suburbia and notes that it is a large and
complex subject.

It was assumed that the most intensive, highest order land uses
would group around the interchange because of the access function
and that as distance to the interchange increased progressively
more extensive, lower order land uses would occur. Further
assumptions were that the micro-region or interchange community
was isolated from other communities except by access through the
interchange and that all locations had a uniform means of access
or transportation to the interchange. Figure 1 portrays the
pattern that would be expected to evolve when prior development

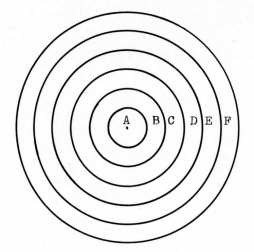

Fig. 1. Concentric Zones of Land Use Development

or nucleation of higher order uses was not present in the interchange community. Similar to Burgess' diagram of a city (Chapin,
1965: 14-17) (Webber, 1972: 65-6), concentric zones would
develop portraying the effect of distance and transportation costs
on the relative order of land use. Zone A would indicate the
highest order of land uses while Zone F would indicate the lowest
order uses. The progression from Zone A to Zone F would be
through successive zones of diminishing orders of land use.

In actual interchange community situations, the variations in
topography and road systems would alter the relative location and
transportation costs of sites equidistant to the interchange.
Isard (1965: 276-7) depicts such alterations to the von Thunen
rings. Also, development nodules of higher order land uses might
have formed in areas away from the interchange prior to the construction of the Interstate highway.

THE CASE STUDY

This study attempted to graphically display patterns of land use
development. Preliminary surveys indicated that a circle with a
two mile radius would adequately encompass the principal area of
an interchange community. The four communities studied were
rural in nature, but showed some prior development and some
development associated with the interchange. There was a small
city located in the region.

Theoretically, the area of each interchange community was 12.56
square miles or 8,038 acres. All properties within or partially
within the circle were included in the study. The inclusion of
whole properties and allowances for geographical and political
features gave a distorted shape to the interchange community
rather than forming a true circle.

Real estate value was assumed to be reflective of land use, i.e. higher order uses had higher real estate values per acre than lower order uses.* Dollar values thus provided a common denominator and a surrogate of land use patterns.

Real estate values were mapped using a grid system based on the U. S. Geological Survey Maps. Each grid was 2,500 feet on a side, enclosing an area of 6,250,000 square feet or 143.48 acres. Each property in an interchange community was assigned the code number of the grid zone in which it was located. For properties located in more than one grid zone, the property was assigned to the grid zone in which the largest portion of the property was located.

For each grid zone the real estate values and acreages of the assigned properties were totaled and the real estate value per acre was derived. This value was imputed to the center point of the grid zone. The values used were for the fifth year after the Interstate highway was fully opened. Contours of value per acre or iso-value lines were plotted at intervals of one thousand dollars of real estate value per acre by a computerized method.

Clear plastic sheets on which the road networks and boundaries of the individual communities were portrayed were laid over the computer printouts and were photographically reduced for analysis. The boundaries of the study areas on the plastic overlays appeared on the photoreductions as thick gray lines. The Interstate highway appeared as two thick, dark, parallel lines that ran from south (the bottoms of the maps) to north (the tops of the maps). The interchanges were located at approximately the centers of the maps and were shown with short ramps connecting to the cross-routes. A single, thick, dark line running north to south on each map represented an older primary highway servicing the region. The other roads appeared with thinner lines, the major ones being dark and the minor ones being light.

Analysis of the maps revealed large areas of undeveloped land in the communities. Most of the higher use or value patterns were of areas developed prior to the construction of the Interstate highway and were verified by field inspection. Only one pattern centered on an interchange and was considered to have resulted from the interchange. An industrial park constructed since the opening of the Interstate increased the average values per acre to more than $10,000. The iso-value lines of this nodule exhibited the concentric pattern that was expected according to the model. This community is presented in Figure 2.

_____

*Chapin (1965: 11-4) reports Knos found an inverse relationship between land values and distance to city center for Topeka, Kansas and that land values influence intensity of land use. Chapin reports also that from Hoyt's work in Chicago and Knos' work "it is clear that the patterns of uses, intensities, and values are all three strongly intercorrelated." (Chapin, 1965: 13)

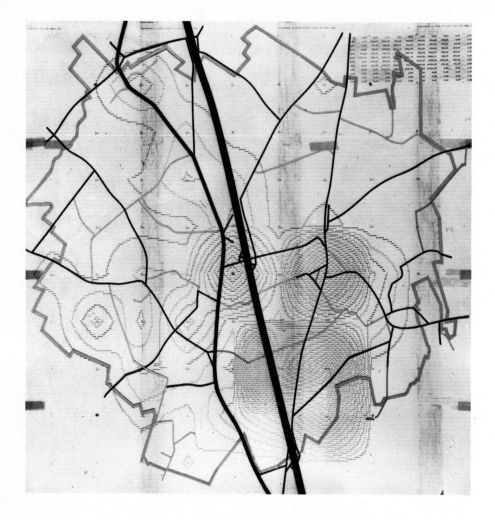

Fig. 2.   Iso-value Map of Real Estate Values Plotted
at 1,000 Dollar Intervals in an Interchange
Community

Because of the nature of the method used in developing grid zone
values, the center point of a grid zone included values as much
as one-fourth mile away. The point that formed the center of the
nodular pattern on the map therefore might be slightly off-center
from the actual point of highest values. In this case, the central
point of the nodule was slightly southwest of the interchange.
However, the initial development of the industrial park did take
place in the southwestern quadrant of the interchange. Another
reason for the center point of this particular pattern to be
pulled away from the interchange location might have been that
the prior land use developments that existed along the older primary highway were included in some of the grid zone values of the
immediate interchange area.

Going north from the interchange area, a pattern of value emerged
that seemed to be the result of older development. There were
some residential areas scattered among open space uses west of
the primary highway which created several small nodular patterns.

East of the interchange was an older secondary road and an old
town producing a heavily patterned nodule with a center point
value of nearly $26,000 per acre. An industrial park was located
here, to be close to the Interstate but also to have a railroad
siding. Going south on the secondary highway, the area was highly
developed in residential and commercial uses and values ranged up
to $42,702 per acre, mainly as the result of closely spaced
residences in the suburban areas of a small city. Heavy iso-
value patterns of closely spaced lines were shown for these areas
which comprised the southeastern section of the interchange community. The northeastern section of the community was relatively
undeveloped as shown by the relative lack of nodular patterns in
this area.

SUMMARY AND RECOMMENDATIONS

The mapping of real estate value by plotting iso-value lines did
not show the type of development but it did show the intensity
and extent of the development by the patterns of iso-value lines,
although not necessarily concentric circular zones, outlining the
development nodules. Most of the patterns that did emerge seemed
to be related to the highway network that existed prior to the
development of the Interstate highway. The older developed areas
located in the interchange communities showed up very well on the
maps. Only one interchange community had a definite nodule
centered on the interchange and this was portrayed by iso-value
patterns that closely resembled the basic land use development
model.

The Interstate highway did appear to be located in areas that
were of lower real estate value. This was apparent from field
inspection and from the iso-value line patterns of the real estate
values plotted by the computer. This method might have applica-
bility to future transportation corridor locations in that computer
value mapping could aid in selecting route locations that would
have lower acquisition costs. Possibly, effects on the environment

in the form of lower social costs of air and noise pollution
could be minimized by locations in less developed areas that
could be found by computer iso-value mapping.

The computer mapping method could be expanded to show the areas
where changes in the community are taking place by comparing
measurements at two different times. Economic and social data
could be depicted, possibly by formulation and comparison of
index values. Many possibilities exist for the use of the computer mapping method and they need to be explored because it
reduces sometimes complicated verbal and tabular presentations
of data to more meaningful visual displays that are understood
by many people.

Although it is expected that interchanges will become nuclei or
focal points of land use developments in rural areas, five years
after the Interstate opened might have been too short a period
for growth to occur. Clawson (1974: 50-1) has remarked that the
shadow of a city extends far into the countryside to include
small town and rural residents who daily commute to work in the
urban area. As an Interstate radiating from a city changes the
time-distance access function, the shadow may be elongated along
such corridors. A study of mature interchanges in existence for
15 or 20 years may yield more definite results as to long-term
changes in the land use - land value patterns of interchange
communities in reasonable proximity to established urban places.

In rural areas lacking proximity, land use - land value changes
may take a longer time span to evolve. However, if governmental
policies such as set forth in the Rural Development Act of 1972*
are carried out, the time span for change in rural areas having
Interstate interchanges may shorten as new rural jobs are created
and population shifts from rural to urban areas are averted or
reversed. Such interchanges may become focal points for local
settlement patterns.

Investigations into long-run growth possibilities need to be conducted before valuable planning and other resources are committed
to interchange communities. Perhaps they evidence differentiating
growth possibilities and time lags. Understanding the growth
mechanism would allow commitments of planning talent and monies
only when needed.

ACKNOWLEDGEMENTS

This research was supported by The Pennsylvania State University
and predecessor agencies of The Pennsylvania Department of Transportation and the Federal Highway Administration, U. S. Dept. of
Transportation.

---

*"Rural development means the planning, development and expansion
 of business and industry in non-metropolitan areas in order to
 provide increased employment and income."

REFERENCES

Barlowe, R., Land Resource Economics: The Economics of Real Property, 2nd. Ed., Prentice-Hall, Englewood Cliffs, N. J., 1972.

Corsi, T. M., A Multivariate Analysis of Land Use Change: Ohio Turnpike Interchanges, Land Economics L, 3: 232-41 (1974).

Eyerly, R. W., Economic Impacts of an Interstate Highway on Four Selected Pennsylvania Interchange Communities, Ph.D. Dissertation, The Pennsylvania State University, 1972.

Humphrey, C. R. and Sell, R. R., The Impact of Controlled Access Highways on Population Growth in Pennsylvania Nonmetropolitan Communities, 1940-1970, Rural Sociology 40, 3: 332-43 (1975).

Isard, W., Location and Space-Economy, MIT Press, Cambridge, Mass., 1965.

Kraft, G., Meyer, J. R. and Valette, J. P., The Role of Transportation in Regional Economic Development, Lexington Books, Lexington, Mass., 1971.

Miller, E. W., A Geography of Manufacturing, Prentice-Hall, Englewood Cliffs, N. J., 1962.

Stein, M. M., Highway Interchange Area Development - Some Recent Findings, Public Roads 35, 11: 241-50, 264 (1969).

Twark, R. D., A Predictive Model of Economic Development at Non-Urban Interchange Sites on Pennsylvania Interstate Highways, Ph.D. Dissertation, The Pennsylvania State University, 1967.

Webber, M. J., Impact of Uncertainty on Location, MIT Press, Cambridge, Mass., 1972.

WERC BRUSSELS CONFERENCE ON THE ENVIRONMENT OF HUMAN SETTLEMENTS: IMPLEMENTATION: POLITICAL DECISION-MAKING

The Honourable Margaret Scrivener
M.P.P., Riding of St. David, Toronto
Chairman, Noise Control Group
Institute for Environmental Studies
University of Toronto, Canada

A. DESCRIPTION OF A SUCCESSFUL HUMAN SETTLEMENT

1. The element of change is the only certain non-variable of a human settlement. Like people, towns and cities are born with the passage of time; they mature, grow old, sicken and die or become no longer inhabited.

2. Decision-makers can be likened to doctors, diagnosing and treating the corpus of the settlement. They identify and respond to its needs, nurture its growth, dress it up and change its habit and diet as it grows, nurse its ailments, and try to restore its health by whatever effective remedies they can devise.

3. Each action taken by the urban physician constitutes a decision. Thousands of individual decisions made daily determine the character and well-being of the city. While most of the decisions are made, not by government, but by residents, builders and businessmen who inhabit the city, many other decisions affecting the city are made by government, either to prepare the city for its future, or (to continue the medical analogy) to prescribe remedies for its malfunctions.

4. Ideally, the government decision-maker would prescribe only those laws and public programs necessary

   (a) to maintain a healthy balance between the private decisions influencing a city's development, and the public works, services, facilities and amenities sustaining that development; and,

   (b) to establish an economic base for the support of the public programs which will be required by the city's future development.

5. In practical terms, this balance is never achieved: the city's future needs never seem to be perceived or understood clearly enough by the community collectively (represented by government) to provide the support for the corrective or remedial decisions which government has to make.

B. LIKELY FUTURE STATE OF HUMAN SETTLEMENTS

1. There seems to be broad understanding of the fact that decline
    may be an inherent feature of urban growth, or, in other words,
    that urban development may be for the worse as well as for the
    better.

2. The inhabitants of many cities are being accused by environ-
    mentalists, planners and community leaders of "fouling their
    own nests", contrary to nature.

3. On the other hand, the builders of cities--including their
    governments--sometimes appear to be unaware of, or indifferent
    to, the impact their respective decisions may have on the
    general well-being of a human settlement. This is demonstrated

    (a) when the human needs of that settlement are over-
         looked, or ignored, in order to exploit a commercial
         opportunity; or

    (b) when they ignore the potential negative which is
         implicit when certain special interest groups--
         social, political or industrial--are favoured in
         a decision at the expense of the settlement as a
         whole, in order to maintain the decision-maker's
         power base; or

    (c) when the type of decision is employed which
         anticipates that the negative impact of a poor
         decision will not be experienced within the tenure
         of the decision-maker's rule; or

    (d) when occasionally, shockingly, egomania impels the
         decision-maker towards a deliberately-made wrong
         decision, in order to provide opportunities for
         him to take effective remedial action, thereby
         enhancing his own reputation; or

    (e) when regrettably, but understandably, the right to
         ownership of land is confused with the privilege
         of using it as the owner sees fit, notwithstanding
         the negative impact on the community as a whole; or

    (f) when the decision-maker may be greedy, or ignorant,
         or both.

4. The presence of any of these decision-making conditions
    inevitably damages in varying degrees the fabric of a human
    settlement. Trends are created which become very difficult,
    if not impossible, to reverse.

    (a) If such conditions are prolonged, a city's develop-
         ment could be warped and distorted to such scale
         and complexity that no good understanding of how
         it works can ever be obtained and, therefore, no
         effective action taken to recognize and strengthen
         a weakness before it ruptures.

(b) Further, these negative decision-making conditions can
     lead to a city whose development is out of the control
     of its inhabitants and requires the intervention of
     increasingly remote decision-makers, persons who may
     themselves encourage the conditions which cause
     deterioration in the fabric of the settlement.

(c) Alternatively, such conditions could result in abandon-
     ment of the city and the enormous investment in its
     social, cultural, environmental and economic structure,
     in favour of relocation within simpler urban
     institutions which are more easily understood and are
     governed by the inhabitants themselves.

(d) Predictably, public disgust arising from negative forms
     of decision-making could create a demand for an
     imposition of a norm, or standard, of behaviour and
     ethical business conduct, which would reduce the
     effective range of private decision-making. This
     would tend to establish a rigid conformity in the
     life of the community, virtually ensuring its ultimate
     decline and ruin.

C. POTENTIAL IMPROVEMENTS IN HUMAN SETTLEMENTS

1. The trends described are taking place most dramatically in the
    metropolises and megalopolises of the world; but the smaller
    communities are not free of the symptoms of decline or
    ineptitude in the decisions taken to reverse decline.

2. These symptoms have been commonly recognized--not the least
    at the WERC Brussels Conference. They can be identified as

    (a) the failure of the decision-makers to initiate
         effective land use planning, environmental manage-
         ment, and social and economic development programs to
         make best possible use of known technology as a means
         of relieving the symptoms and making a cure, or
         investing in the research and development of new
         technology to resolve anticipated future problems.

    (b) the disaster inherent in the assumption that the
         manifestations of urban decline are phenomena most
         directly related to urban development (particularly
         to urban growth) without acknowledging that the real
         cause of the decline may rest in the quality and
         weaknesses of the decisions guiding urban develop-
         ment, rather than in those manifestations of poor
         decisions. For instance, the critics of urban
         development may be investigating and proposing
         remedies merely to treat the symptoms--not the
         causes--of urban decline, and, in doing so, neglect
         and even contribute to the greatest cause--the poor
         quality of the decision-making process.

3. The process itself is worthy of considerably more study and
    research than has been attempted in the past, if government

decision-makers are to be better qualified to make the
decisions required of them for the environmental improvement
of human settlements.

4. Under Canadian constitutional law, the governments of the ten
    provinces have exclusive responsibility for the management of
    municipal affairs and, therefore, for the quality of municipal
    decisions which affect the urban environment.

5. To the greatest extent possible, the Government of Ontario has
    delegated such management to popularly elected municipal
    councils. Where urban problems have assumed proportions
    greater than can easily be handled by such councils, the
    Government of Ontario has responded by introducing new
    municipal decision-making and management apparatuses, in order
    to sustain and improve the quality of decision-making at the
    local municipal level. (e.g. Metropolitan Toronto, Regional
    Municipalities, Restructured Counties.)

6. At the same time, the Government of Ontario has developed new
    machinery to improve the quality of its own decisions,
    including those which provide for better local government
    decisions.

    (a) These mechanisms are aimed primarily at developing a
         better and more accurate understanding and
         identification of the nature of urban problems.

    (b) They are also used to devise alternative ways
         of responding to identified problems and under-
         standing the strengths and weaknesses--both short
         term and long range--of each alternative.

    (c) And, finally, they can be employed in anticipating,
         designing and coordinating the public programs
         required to improve the quality of the urban
         environment according to a pre-selected alternative
         course of action based on properly identified need
         and pre-determined probable effect.

7. Admittedly, these mechanisms are still imperfect. However,
    they are in constant process of improvement as a matter of
    Provincial Government policy, and their necessity has been
    acknowledged.

8. The failure to understand and appreciate this need for re-
    evaluation of the decision-making process and the necessary
    mechanisms for its implementation, is perhaps the greatest
    single contributing factor to the poor quality of decisions
    relating to urban environmental improvement.

EFFECTS OF HIGHWAY NOISE IN RESIDENTIAL COMMUNITIES*

Hays B. Gamble and Owen H. Sauerlender
Institute for Research on Land and Water Resources
The Pennsylvania State University, United States

ABSTRACT

Four residential communities bisected by interstate highways were
examined to determine the effects of highway generated disturbances on property values. Disturbances instrumentally measured
within each community included noise, carbon monoxide, oxides of
nitrogen, hydrocarbons, and particulates. Data on traffic mix,
volume and speed were obtained simultaneously. Residents were
interviewed to determine their perceptions of the intensity of
highway disturbance and other pertinent information. Data were
gathered for all valid property sales from 1969-1971. There was
a high degree of correlation between measured noise (NPL) and perceived noise.

Residents objected to noise more than to any other highway originating disturbance. The relationship of NPL (Noise Pollution
Level), distance from the highway, and property value loss was
determined. The NPL regression coefficient was found to be significant in explaining variation in residential property values in
all communities, and showed an average loss of $2050 per highway
abutting property. This was approximately 6.6 percent of the
average price of properties in the four study areas.

INTRODUCTION

Land value theory hypothesizes that residential property values
tend to capture or reflect negative externalities that may adversely affect the level or quality of housing services anticipated by
prospective purchasers. Various researchers have conducted studies
which show the effects of air pollutants and of aircraft noise in
the vicinity of airports on residential property values. For example, Nelson (1975), Dygert (1973), and Emerson (1969) studied
the effects of aircraft noise on property values in the vicinity
of Washington, D.C. National Airport, San Francisco International
Airport, and the Minneapolis Airport, respectively. All three
studies had remarkably similar results in that the capitalized
damages for noise ranged from $100 to $140 per unit change in the

---

*The research reported here was financially supported by the Fed-
eral Highway Administration, Department of Transportation,
Contract DOT-FH-11-7800.

Noise Exposure Forecast. Thus a property located near one of these airports would be worth about 10 percent less (or about $3,000 less for the average dwelling) than a property not located in the area affected by the noise, other things equal.

The studies cited above, as well as a few others, show quite conclusively that a technological development such as jet power for aircraft do have some adverse effects on people in cities and that these adverse effects become translated in part into lower residential property values. However, it should be pointed out that there has been considerable discussion in the recent literature over the proper interpretation of the results, although the basic conclusions are not altered.[1] This paper reports on the first major attempt to measure the effects of _highway_ generated noise on nearby residential property values.[2]

One of the outgrowths of the "environmental movement" of recent years has been legislation to reduce or abate highway noise. However, the resulting benefits and costs of such legislation have not been adequately considered, primarily because so little is known about them. The benefits to society from noise reduction include, in part, the reductions in the direct and indirect costs associated with noise. Estimates of these costs are necessary in order to determine the extent to which abatement programs should be optimally carried out and to select the kinds of abatement or regulatory programs that would be most suitable.

Not all the benefits from noise reduction can be measured, of course, because some are of an aesthetic or psychic nature for which no data exist. But although there is no market per se for quiet, it is highly probable that households will express a preference for amenities such as clean air and quiet and, all other factors being equal, pay more for quiet neighborhoods. Conversely, households are likely to pay less for noisy housing locations, such as those abutting or close to major highways. Thus, it is possible that a portion of the economic and social costs (damages) associated with highway noise are capitalized in residential property values.

Specifically, the authors' hypothesize that improvements in transportation technology, such as modern vehicles and limited access highways, generate adverse environmental side effects that accompany their many beneficial effects, and that people's reactions to these adverse effects are expressed in different ways. Although some of these adverse effects can be empirically measured (for example, air pollutants in ppm or noise in decibels), such measures do not of themselves reflect their relative importance or cost to society. However, people do express their preferences for goods and services in the market place. Thus, people's annoyance or dissatisfaction from noise generated by highways becomes "transferred" to the housing market and finds empirical expression in terms of lower prices for houses close to such highways. In a

---

[1]For example see Feller and Nelson (1973).
[2]For a complete report of this study, see Gamble, et al. 1974.

very real sense, these differential residential property values
may be viewed as at least one objective measure of the degree to
which society is adversely affected by noise pollution.

STUDY AREAS AND DATA INPUTS

Four residential communities in the eastern part of the United
States were selected for study. All of the communities were in
the suburbs of major metropolitan areas and all were bixected by
a major interstate highway. Average daily vehicular traffic volume in 1970 varied from 54,500 on one of the highways to 73,400
on another, with the proportion of trucks varying from 9 to 18
percent. Population in the four communities varied from 7,700 to
27,400 in 1970, while the average value of housing ranged from
$24,800 in the "poorest" community to $33,300 in the "wealthiest".

Data on highway generated air and noise pollutants; traffic volume,
speed, and mix; property values; and household characteristics were
gathered in 1971 and 1972. Noise measurements were recorded at
different locations within each study area at various times of the
day and on different days of the week. Direct sampling of traffic
volume, mix (proportion of cars and trucks), and speed was done
concurrently with the noise sampling. The noise pollution level
NPL, as developed by Robinson (1971), was the objective measure of
noise used in the study. NPL, measured on the dBA scale, relates
very well to perceived annoyance from noise and provides a higher
correlation with human responses to fluctuating noise intensities
than do other measures. Noise levels were then computed for varying distances from the highway. Table 1 shows the maximum and minimum (ambient) NPL levels in each study area and the distance from
the highways at which the NPL is reduced to ambient.

TABLE 1   Noise Pollution Levels and Distances from Highway at which the NPL is Reduced to Ambient

Study Area	NPL (dBA)		Distance (meters)	
	Maximum	Ambient	Minimum	Maximum
Bogota, N.J.	80	70	30	183
North Springfield, Va.	85	55	274	351
Rosedale, Md.	90	60	244	366
Towson, Md.	85	55	168	274

A questionnaire was administered to 1,114 households in the study
areas and elicited information on the attitudes of residents toward
highway pollutants, their response to highway effects in terms of
house and activities alterations, their social interactions in the
community, and their use of the highway for various trip purposes.
Property value data gathered were the bona-fide real estate trans-
actions for 324 residential properties in the four communities for
the years 1970-1971 as obtained from public records in the respective county court houses.

MARGINAL CAPITALIZED DAMAGE ESTIMATES

Step-wise multiple regression was the principal statistical tool
used to determine the relationship between property values and
highway generated pollutants. Because many factors other than
highway related variables influence the value of residential property, a total of 93 independent variables were used in the many
regression equations tested to improve the explanation of variations in property values, the dependent variable.

Highway related variables included such things as measures of
noise levels, measures of air pollutants, changes made to a house
in response to highway effects (such as adding insulation to reduce noise), location of the house relative to the highway (distance, direction), and residents' perceptions of highway effects.

Non-highway related variables included characteristics of the land
and improvements, such as age of house, lot size, style of house,
size of house, number of bathrooms, corner lot, number of floors,
finished basement, construction materials, etc.; demographic and
socio-economic descriptors of household occupanta (income, age,
previously lived near a major highway, etc.) and outdoor facilities and outdoor use made of property.

Because each study area was relatively homogeneous within its
boundaries, no descriptors or variables were entered for community
facilities, accessibility to the major highway, distance to central
city, or other community characteristics. The objective of the
study required analysis of highway effects upon property values
within each of the four study areas separately, and then analysis
between the study areas. Because the variables that would be helpful in explaining property value differences between study areas
have identical values for each observation within a single study
area, the analysis between study areas was reduced statistically
to adding a dummy variable for each study area.

Of the several highway related variables that were significant in
some of the preliminary regression equations, the NPL noise variable was most frequently statistically significant. Moreover,
noise was the highway disturbance most frequently cited by people
during the household survey. For these reasons, and to avoid the
high degree of multi-collinearity between highway pollutant variables, the NPL variable was selected as the highway related variable. The final regression equation for all areas combined had an
R^2 corrected value of .60 and showed six variables as being statistically significant at at least the 10 percent level.[3] Three of
these variables were: number of rooms in house, number of bathrooms, and NPL. In addition there were three dummy variables

_____

[3] R^2 values up to .85 were achieved with some of the regression
equations, but because of multicollinearity the coefficients
of some of the variables were difficult to explain. For example, the simple correlation between NPL and the carbon monoxide (CO) variable in one equation was .88.

indicating central air conditioning, finished basement, and Rose-
dale (one of the study communities).

The regression coefficient for NPL shows that for each increase of
1 dBA of noise the value of property decreased $82. This is the
marginal capitalized damage estimate due primarily to noise, but
reflects also damages from vehicular air pollutants. The difference between the lowest ambient noise level (55 dBA) and the
highest (80 dBA) in the sample of properties tested was 25 dBA.
This difference times the coefficient of -82, or $2,050, is the
estimated amount by which the average price of properties abutting
the highways in the study areas was affected primarily by vehicular
noise. This value represents a decrease of approximately 6.6 percent below the average price of properties in the four study areas.
The decrease in NPL is not linearly related to distance from the
highway; rather, the rate of decrease in noise lessens as one
moves farther from the highway. Consequently the relationship
between property damages and distance from the highway is curvi-
linear in nature; i.e., the rate of increase in damages is higher
as one gets closer to the highway. These relationships are shown
in Table 2.

TABLE 2   Damage Estimates to Residential Property Related
to dBA's of Noise Above Ambient Noise Level and
Distance from Highway

NPL Above Ambient (dBA)	Average Property Loss (Dollars)	Distance from Highway to Ambient Zone (Meters)
25	2050	244
24	1968	239
22	1804	230
20	1640	219
18	1476	207
16	1312	194
14	1148	178
12	984	162
10	820	143
8	656	125
6	492	101
4	328	73
2	164	40

Analysis of data from the household questionnaire showed that noise
outdoors is the single most important source of annoyance from the
highways. People while indoors are annoyed about to the same
degree by noise as by dust on windowsills. Odors from the highway
are not important sources of annoyance to people while either indoors or outdoors. In all four communities, 58 percent of the
abutters were annoyed by highway disturbances while only 12 percent
of the non-abutters indicated annoyance.

Statistical analysis was performed on the relationship between perceived noise as reported by residents in the four highway commu-

nities and noise as measured by instrumentation and reported as
NPL. The regression coefficients for the above relationships were
highly significant in almost all cases. The close agreement between measured noise and perceived noise substantiates the usefulness of the noise pollution level (NPL) measure as an indicator of
human disturbance from highway generated noise.

Because noise from a source such as a highway could only affect
property values when it is at levels higher than the ambient or
background levels, there is no simple generally applicable relationship between property value losses and distance from a highway.
The areas used in this study illustrate this point. One community
had high levels of highway generated noise but also had high
ambient noise levels so that traffic noise could not be detected
as highway originating when only a comparatively short distance
away. In contrast, two other communities had ambient levels much
lower, but highway generated noise at about the same level. As a
result, highway noise was heard at a much farther distance from
the highway in the two quieter communities. For this reason, any
relationship showing damages to property values as a result of
highway noise and distances must take into account the ambient
noise level.

The estimates of property damages do not necessarily indicate the
total cost or loss from adverse highway environmental effects. To
the extent that some households may make expenditures to reduce
noise, such as by insulating the home or installing storm windows,
these costs are not included. Moreover, there may be a consumer
surplus involved which can be regarded as an additional social
cost not accounted for in the estimates given above. There are
also nonmeasurable aesthetic and psychic costs involved. It must
be emphasized that these are estimates of gross losses, not net
losses, since the beneficial effects of highways on property
values, primarily those associated with improved accessibility,
have not been shown. In most highway oriented communities highway
accessibility benefits are conferred on all properties, not just
properties located close to the highway. Because so many more
properties are beneficially affected by highway accessibility than
damaged by highway pollutants (including noise), the net highway
effects for the entire community are quite likely to be positive.

CONCLUSIONS

This study shows conclusively that the adverse environmental
effects, primarily noise, of a major limited access highway are
reflected in lower values for residential properties near the highway as compared to properties more distant from the highway. Significant reductions in noise generated by highway traffic may do
much to reduce the objections now raised by many people living in
highway communities or neighborhoods through which proposed highways are to pass. This suggests that a greater separation of people
and highway traffic is necessary. Future residential development
within about 250 meters of most major highways should be controlled.
Land uses that are not adversely affected by highway noise, such as
commercial and industrial uses, could be permitted on lands close
to highways. But residential, recreational, and other activities

where quiet is desired could be restricted to sites in the ambient zone of the community.

For already developed communities, reductions in noise levels will have to be achieved through vehicular modification to reduce noise at its source, through highway design and the provision of noise barriers, or through modification to existing structures. Vehicular modification would include improvements in engine design, exhaust systems, and tire design. Coupled with improvements in pavement surfaces and the utilization of existing natural barriers such as hills and woods, noise levels to nearby residences could be reduced. Erection of fences to serve as noise barriers or depressing a highway below grade through a community also attenuates the noise. Modifications to existing structures, such as adding insulation or storm windows and providing air conditioning, can improve noise conditions. All of these measures, of course, require funding, and one useful aspect of this study is that it shows that property values do provide a means whereby damages can be estimated, estimates that are needed so that public agencies can determine the extent to which abatement programs should be optimally carried out. Much more research is needed, however, to determine the kind and range of land use which will reflect the negative externalities of highways.

An important finding of the study was that the level of noise above the average ambient noise level for a community is more important than the actual noise pollution level itself in the impact zone. Where costs of noise abatement are borne by the same society that would benefit from such noise abatement, it would not be optimum in the economic sense to use a uniform noise level standard for all residential areas. A standard that takes into account the ambient noise level would be more efficient.

Earlier studies were unable to uncover adverse impacts of highways on property values. This might be due, at least in part, to the fact that the demand for a better environment has only recently become a popular concern. This, together with the success of this research in uncovering and measuring the extent of the impact in four study areas, suggests that the social cost of highway generated nuisances may be increasing over time. As efforts to improve the overall quality of the environment become more and more successful there will be more insistent demands that most remaining highway generated nuisances be eliminated. Increasingly strong objections to highway nuisances occur. The tendency will be to increase the social benefits derived from the removal or avoidance of such nuisances. This in turn, may justify the higher cost that will be required if the higher social benefits are to be realized.

REFERENCES

Dygert, P.K. 1973. Estimation of the Cost of Aircraft Noise to Residential Activities. Ph.D. Dissertation, University of Michigan, Ann Arbor.

Emerson, F.C. 1969. The Determinants of Residential Value with Special Reference to the Effects of Aircraft Nuisance and

other Environmental Features. Ph.D. Dissertation, University
of Minnesota, Minneapolis.

Feller, I. and J.P. Nelson. 1973. Economic Aspects of Noise
    Pollution. Institute for Research on Human Resources and
    The Center for the Study of Science Policy. The Pennsylvania
    State University, University Park, Pa.

Gamble, H.B., C.J. Langley, Jr., R.D. Pashek, O.H. Sauerlender,
    R.D. Twark, and R.H. Downing. 1974. The Influence of High-
    way Environmental Effects of Residential Property Values.
    Research Pub. No. 78, Institute for Research on Land and
    Water Resources, The Pennsylvania State University, Univer-
    sity Park, Pa.

Nelson, J.P. 1975. The Effects of Mobile-Source Air and Noise
    Pollution on Residential Property Values. U.S. Department
    Transportation, Washington, D.C.

Robinson, D.W. 1971. "Towards a Unified System of Noise Assess-
    ment." Jrn. of Sound Vibration. Vol. 14.

THE GREAT AMERICAN BICENTENNIAL URBAN PRESERVE

Richard J. L. Martin
Stanford Research Institute, Menlo Park, California, USA

Do you remember D.C.? Do you remember when cities were lit by Direct Current electricity? When there was a tower in the center of town with an electric light that lit up the whole city?

Certainly not! Never happened. Must be a myth. Surely nobody remembers anything like that. Let's see, there <u>were</u> gas lights as we all know from the movies, but that's for nostalgia buffs. I remember street cars, don't you? They're no myth. Why you can even see their tracks in some cities today. (I understand in some places they still have them but I'm sure they're just for tourists--like in San Francisco.)

Do you remember Downtown?

Sure, that's where the big banks and offices are. We don't go there much anymore--not safe, you know.

But I mean the real Downtown, like in the Good Old Days. Where all the <u>good</u> stores were. Where you dressed up to spend the day. Where all the crowds were. Where you walked into the theater and looked in store windows. Where it was exciting and fun at night. Where you went to look at Christmas displays and the city was proud.

Well, of course we remember. It wasn't <u>that</u> long ago, but as I said, we don't go there much anymore. We prefer the suburbs. We have all the conveniences. There's no real reason to go downtown if you don't have to.

Our children will never have to go Downtown. They won't get to see the old buildings, the old people, and have the old memories we have. They'll get to remember the suburbs. I wonder how the suburbs will age? What will it be like when they get old--like Downtown? Will the memories be fond ones like we have of Downtown? You know, Downtown meant something once. We need to remember what it was like--so we can develop a perspective on where we are going--you know what I mean?

Now if we could only preserve Downtown--keep it for the memories--that would be important.

Maybe we could preserve a section of Downtown (we wouldn't want to keep it all, and of couse, we wouldn't want to keep the banks and large offices from rebuilding). Then we would have it to see--we really wouldn't have to use it. After all, Downtown is part of our heritage, like the plains and mountains and forests are. We preserve them, don't we? We have our national parts, historic monuments and wildlife preserves. Why not an Urban Preserve?

We could set aside the old part of the city and keep it as is. Put it under the control and operation of the National Parks Service. Make it a kind of urban park. The world's first urban park. Operate it just as we do our wilderness parks. Protect the natural habitat. No renovation. Just maintain the status quo. Allow the processes of urban decay to continue just as we let the forces of nature continue in our forest parks. After all, the suburban generation is entitled to see buildings fall into disrepair; to see the grass grow up through sidewalks; to see how the indigenous inhabitants of the central city adjust to their surroundings.

We could set up the Urban Preserve so the National Parks Service could conduct tours through it. We could map out special "urban walks" like "nature walks" and have people in campaign hats guide the tourists through. We could allow "grandfather rights" for property owners in the Preserve so they would not be denied their opportunities. In time, just as in our national forests, their property would become an integral part of the Preserve.

In practice, the idea would work this way: The city designates an unproductive portion of itself as the Urban Preserve--that fully developed part of the city which still demands considerable municipal services. Because of deterioration, the movement of residents to suburbs, traffic congestion and all the other factors we now associate with Downtown, the Preserve land has a declining tax base. It is no longer self-supporting, even though we traditionally--almost without thinking--look to it to support the rest of the city.

After designating the Urban Preserve, the city cuts off all municipal services except those necessary to operate the Preserve. This relieves the city of most of its Downtown service cost burden (which is greater than tax revenues). The city then ends all taxation in the Preserve by creating a special municipal improvement district. This dual elimination of taxes and services relieves the city of its responsibility to maintain the area on one hand, and allows the "grandfather rights" landowners to operate in a true free enterprise fashion on the other hand. This new breed of urban pioneer would have to provide his own water, power, transit facilities, and waste disposal services. After all, conventional wisdom has it that he can do it for less than the city did. In addition, he could pocket the tax money he no longer has to pay. Those who lack the pioneer spirit of this new urban frontier could sell out to the Preserve operators for "fair market value."

What an impact! The individual property owner, in a re-awakening of individual spirit, has the opportunity to re-make his community for himself

without shouldering the tax burden for the rest of the city. City government, for its part, could direct itself to healthier sections of the city
without being saddled by this atrophied part of itself. For the public,
inspirational guidance would be gained from tours and lectures on Urban
Decay and "do-it-yourself-government" by Rangers from the National Park
Service. Imagine, observing rugged individualists carving out their city
in the Urban Preserve, much as their forefathers did on the great prairies
and forests of a promised land!

Now don't misunderstand, the Urban Preserve is a serious idea. It's just
not a serious proposal...yet. It's a future alternative--maybe the only
workable one--to the present plight of our cities. Suburban sprawl, in
draining the economic base away from city centers, has left a great number
of cities near bankruptcy. Many publicized efforts to renew central cities
have required enormous capital investments--investments that compete with
the ongoing patterns of city development.

Evidence of that competition shows when cities rely on the central government money to finance downtown renewal projects rather than local money.
Cities argue that massive central-city redevelopment costs too much for
local purses. Yet strangely, these same cities seem always willing to foot
the bill for suburban development. For example: The City of Omaha,
Nebraska swelled its bonded indebtedness by more than $30 million by assum-
ing annexed neighboring municipal districts' bonds in the late 60's and early
70's to accommodate suburban growth. Why couldn't downtown renewal have
been financed incrementally, staged over the years without great front-end
capital requirements, like the suburbs were? Why does the city need outside
money to revitalize its heart when local funds abound for developing its
extremities?

Whatever the reasons, the facts are that the advantages for some in suburbia
have become a municipal cost for the rest of us. Because while the individual can move in search of a better environment, the city cannot. The
city cannot abandon itself.

The U.S. Army Corps of Engineers, in their publication "This Land is Your
Land" a study of water resources in the Omaha metropolitan area, pointed out
that the city of Omaha had grown from 45.6 square miles and a 260,000 population in 1956, to 83.05 square miles and about 350,000 population in 1975.
Only 34 percent more people on 83 percent more land. At the same time, the
Corps noted, "During the accelerated period of westward growth, the central
part of Omaha has been losing housing units at a rate of approximately 2.5
per cent annually, while housing units in the balance of the city increased
at a rate of 2.4 per cent annually."

Suburban sprawl supported an almost one-for-one transfer of population,
leaving behind an abandoned inner city. Omaha, like so many other cities,
has grown by feeding on itself. A relatively static population paying

services for mushrooming fringe development, left behind an inner city where dwindling taxes won't pay for services.

News item: In January of 1975 a blizzard cost the city of Omaha approximately $1 million to clear roads of snow on that expansive 83.05 square miles. Not that the $1 million could have been better used if all the square miles hadn't been added. But rather, that the city couldn't avoid its responsibilities for something even as temporal as a blizzard. Grow as it wants, the city must still nourish its entire body politic—even to shoveling the snow.

If cities are to reverse the trend to sprawl and consolidate growth, they must recognize the magnitude of the task. The city must re-direct its citizens' attitudes. It must encourage employers to locate in growth areas that serve the whole city. It must, above all, provide alternatives to sprawl that are recognized by the average citizen as well as dreamt of by the planner. If it can do this, renewal could perhaps develop naturally and with popular approval. The private developer could find his market and the public could realize its alternatives.

This evolutionary process is enormously difficult. It requires a consensus toward a common goal of urban betterment at the expense of individual advantage. Such a redirected consensus is part of the American community spirit, but it is contrary to the American dream of individual gain.

In Omaha, the Riverfront Development Program, an experiment by the U.S. government to promote redirected growth alternatives, was met with national excitement, heavy federal funding and considerable local ennue. The local consensus was not there. The City of Omaha, building on the Riverfront planning experience, has proposed continuing programs to redevelop the inner city. The fight is uphill. Perhaps these programs have appeared to most people to close out too much of the present development pattern without giving them a satisfactory alternative from which they can also benefit.

In any case, whether publicly endorsed or not, growth alternatives call for action. They require clear decision. But clear decisions have political and economic consequences which usually mean inaction. And inaction means continued urban decay and municipal bankruptcy. There must be another way. A way to cut our losses without upsetting the status quo...A way to avoid responsibilities and abandon the areas of greatest cost and risk.

The Urban Preserve!

Come with us now, to those thrilling days of yesteryear, when out of the west...and so on.

DECISION-MAKING PROCESS IN THE CANADIAN URBAN SOCIAL-CULTURAL ENVIRONMENT

Bhoo P. Agarwal

B.P. Policy Advisor, Ministry of State for Urban Affairs, Ottawa, Canada

Too long have the workers of the world waited for some MOSES to lead them out of bondage. He has not come; he never will come. I would not lead you but if I could; for if you could be led out, you could be lead back again. I would have you make up your minds that there is nothing you cannot do for yourselves. (Hal Draper in "The Two Souls of Socialism")

This paper is written in light of the Canadian experience in "participatory democracy" and as such is locationally specific to Canada's Social Cultural Environment. Due to the limitation imposed on the length of papers it has not been possible to fully expand the ideas and as such some thoughts are left undeveloped and may seem to "hang in the air".

The various sections of this paper are: general introduction to citizen participation, The Just Society, Decision-Makers Process, Types and Levels of Decision-Making and Conclusions/ Recommendations.

Many of us, or our parents, were born into a relatively small, simple and stable community: Most of its inhabitants knew each other, wanted the same general goals and sought them in much the same way. There was usually little need to assist the customary means of communication and decision-making.

Recently, we find ourselves living in larger, more complex urban communities, with a rapid rate of social and cultural change. Human relationships, instead of being largely close and direct,

have become more remote, fragmented and indirect. We find ourselves referring to most people as "they" and not "we", as
Alvin Toffler indicates in <u>Future Shock</u>.[1]   This leads to an
increasing sense of powerlessness, alienation and frustration;
increasingly, people feel themselves the victims of fate instead of the masters of their own destiny.

There is little doubt that the demand for citizen participation will continue to grow with these basic forces at work.
So too will the tendency to criticize the process of decision-
making in government, if the process appears to be inaccess-
ible. Moreover, this criticism of the underlying process will
increase to some extent independently of actual experience
with the process, if there continues to be major disagreement
over the content of public decisions (which seems likely as
the complexity of problems for public decision-making
increases).

Such an inference from the quality of decisions to the process of decision-making may to some extent be unwarrented.
Process of public decision-making may well be significantly
improved over what they were a generation ago, not only in
terms of their increased technical sophistication but also in
terms of their responsiveness. However, if the problems for
public decision-making are increasing at a faster rate than
improvements in the policy process, then it may seem that no
such improvements are occurring at all.

General

Constructive citizen participation is a systematic process
which provides an opportunity for citizens, planners, elected
representatives and members of relevant area agencies to share
their experience, knowledge and goals, and to combine their
energy to create a plan in order to participate in the social-
cultural environment. This plan can then reflect their know-

[1]A. Toffler, <u>Future Shock</u>, New York: Bantum Books.

ledge and best judgment at the time and will be understood and
actively supported by most of those affected by it.

Constructive citizen participation is happening when:

* decision-makers listen to residents;
* citizens find early and convenient opportunities to make
  positive contributions;
* citizens learn from planners and others a broader and
  deeper knowledge and understanding of their environment;
* individuals, interest groups and agencies are identifying
  with each other;

Constructive citizen participation is NOT:

* selling a pre-determined solution by public relations
  techniques;
* planning behind closed doors when information can be
  shared;
* one-way communication, e.g. planners telling people what
  is best for them;
* public confrontations between "people power" and the
  bureaucracy;
* bypassing elected representatives or impairing their
  freedom to exercise their decision-making responsibilities.

The Just Society

This leads to perhaps the most problematic aspect of the
demand for greater direct citizen participation, namely,
that it has been experienced so often at the late stages of
public planning and decision-making on specific issues,
and without a systematic relation to indirect forms of participation in the election process. This has been aptly referred to as citizen participation which is "too little, too
negative, and too late". The prolonged delays and reversals
of public decisions which often result add considerably to
the cost of government activity, and further strain already
tenuous relations of trust between citizen and government on
which our political system is ultimately based. Moreover, at
these late stages of planning and decision-making, there have
usually been no alternatives on which to base constructive
debate, and no time left in dealing with given problems to
rethink relevant objectives and assumptions.

It is unlikely that we can tolerate much of an increase in these "disruptions" in public planning and policy processes. In might well be concluded that our ability to reach important decisions collectively, will require more effective and continuous citizen participation than at present.

The scope and extent of government programs have increased to such an extent that those people who were formerly sources of help and assistance to their fellow citizens are often themselves inadequately informed. This problem arises with particular urgency in the larger cities of the country and among those citizen who are most in need of information -- the poor and those who are otherwise disadvantaged. Our research suggests that...the gulf between the educated thinkers who participate in ruling the country and the more poorly educated, who are ruled, is still very much in existence in Canada. The government information services do not appear to have helped close this gap, and the way things have been, and the way they remain, is that all those people who have the deepest need for the services of the federal government are exactly those people who are least likely to know anything at all about these same services. They are the least sure of where to find information and, at the same time, the most timid or reluctant to seek it. When it comes to exploiting their full rights as citizens of Canada, they have a potentially powerful handicap.

The new theory of democratic government has been stated as being:

> ...one which defines 'participation' as the central
> right of all citizens. By this is meant the involve-
> ment of the individual in the design and policy proces-
> ses of organizations to which he belongs as well as
> other policy processes which affect his or her future,
> regardless of formal memberships. Voting in any form,
> does not meet any meaningful definition of 'participa-
> tion' and, over time, electoral processes will diminish
> in importance...The fundamental unit of organizational
> activity in analysis, so it seems now, will be a coll-
> egial, non-hierarchical, face-to-face problem-solving

group large enough to include the perspectives and
expertise necessary to deal with the problem at hand,
but small enough to assure each participant that his or
her contribution is substantial, meaningful, and indispensable to the process.[2]

We are increasingly aware that democratic society must favour
maximum citizen participation in the decisions that determine
the development of communal life and, thus, the structure and
content of the individual life as well. How can this be
achieved? Certainly, Canadian society has not yet come close
to perfection in this field. It is encouraging to note that
many people are becoming as anxious over the apathy of a
growing proportion of citizens toward the source of decisions
as they are over the desparate and destructive character of
certain forms of participation. The discouraging complexity
of social and political institutions, contributing to what
is commonly summed up as "alienation" - the obverse of participation is undoubtedly at the root of both social withdrawal and, probably violent protest.

The minimum responsibility of the public authorities in the
area of participation by citizens is to furnish them not
only with good information and services that meet their needs,
but also with an input structure that encourages participation
in all its forms.

In summary due to a breakdown of the conventional channels of
communication between citizen and government, and due to
rapid urbanization, the communication between governments and
their citizens has severly deteriorated. The need for some
kind of communication is particularly acute for the people
occupying the lowest strata of society. These people, in need
of and eligible for services provided by the government, have
inadequate means of getting to know about them and thereby
obtaining them. The difficulty is compounded by the fact

[2]F.C. Thayer, Participation and Liberal Democratic Government,
    Toronto: Committee on Governmental Productivity, 1971,
    pp.3-4.

that the multiplicity of services is spread out over three
levels of government (municipal, provincial, federal).
The important components in the social-cultural environment
over which their governments have control include the location of recreational and cultural activities, the location
of work, educational, and other urban facilities and amenities;
housing, transportation systems, welfare, health, legal assistance, and the citizen's role in the entire urban decision
making process. The social and cultural environment must
be considered in inter-action and inter-dependence with the
psychological environment (values, beliefs, attitudes, habits,
desires and needs), the institutional environment (from the
family to the federal government), and the physical environment
(energy, air, water, land and other components ranging from
architecture to archeology). It is noted here that all the
private actions of urbanites within these complement the outputs not only of the social and cultural organizations but
also of all those of governments, of businesses and in fact
of all the institutions and organizations in the city. In
converse, the decisions of various role players e.g. company
managers, public administrators, politicians, do control or
influence the behaviors of urbanites and groups via the
deliveries of the urban organizations they are part of.

Decision-Making Process
Decision-making itself is a social process that deals in
symbols; it is, however, just one step removed from implementation, the communication of controlling signals to the units
and the application of power. Thus, the inputs into a decision (which, in this sense, precedes implementation) include:
the knowledge of the actor, used to chart alternative routes
and to explore their expected consequences; the actor's
consciousness of himself and of others, of the genetic and
synchronic bonds and links which affect the degree to which
he actively uses his knowledge in making decisions; and the
actor's general commitment, the normative context of his
decisions, the vague and general values and goals to be

specified in the decision-making process. Implementation
"follows" the decision-making process in that here decisions
are communicated and power is applied to enforce them. It is
that process thru which an idea moves from conceptualization
to actualization, including the provision for feedback.

Decision-making, thus viewed, is a synthesizing process of
the controlling centres in which knowledge and commitment
are fused and related to considerations of implementation.
It is also the point at which the element of choice (and,
in that sense, of freedom) is most explicit; decision-
making is the most deliberate and voluntaristic aspect of
societal conduct. This might be better illustrated by borrowing the following diagram.

<u>Types and Levels of Decision-Making[3]</u>

	HIGH UNDERSTANDING	
QUADRANT 2		QUADRANT 1
SOME ADMINISTRATIVE AND "TECHNICAL" DECISION-MAKING		REVOLUTIONARY AND UTOPIAN DECISION-MAKING
ANALYTICAL METHOD: SYNOPTIC		ANALYTICAL METHOD: NONE
INCREMENTAL CHANGE		LARGE CHANGE
QUADRANT 3		QUADRANT 4
INCREMENTAL POLITICS		WARS, REVOLUTIONS, CRISES, AND GRAND OPPORTUNITIES
ANALYTICAL METHOD: DISJOINTED INCREMENTALISM (AMONG OTHERS)		ANALYTICAL METHOD: NOT FORMALIZED OR WELL UNDERSTOOD
	LOW UNDERSTANDING	

[3]D. Braybrooke & C. E. Lindblom. A Strategy of Decision:
Policy Evaluation as a Social Process. New York: Free Press,
1970, p. 78

A)   General

Participation can be viewed as consultation with decision-
makers, and a two-way information flow. Thus, we have various
decision-makers at all levels of government consulting the
relevant policy constituents in public meetings before making
a final decision. Many in government would argue that participation is effective in this sense if the relevant constitu-
ency (people affected by the policy decision) are consulted
before the decision is made. Many "participants" seem to
feel that they have been "co-opting in such a situation,
although, the degree and forms of consultation vary substantially.

Others see participating as the ability to influence the
decision-making process. Thus, we observe citizen and
community groups attempting to influence city council decisions
at a local level, and representatives of these groups on local
government decision-making bodies (e.g. traffic commissions,
planning commissions, etc.). Participating is effective in
this sense if the participants have had an influence on the
ultimate policy decision.

It is at this point that the problem of relating direct and
indirect forms of participation becomes a serious one, and
the role of the elected representative is crucial and problematic. Approaches which substantially increase direct citizen.
participation in the policy process can easily circumvent
attempts to improve our representative institutions at various
government levels. On the other hand, many feel that participation primarily or solely based on the act of voting is
inadequate. It would seem that some new balance of indirect
and direct forms of participating may be required and that
neither should be dealt with to the exclusion of the other.

B)   Jurisdictional

In Canada, urban settlements are organizationally and consitu-
tionally the creations of the provinces. This power of the
provinces over the muncipalities carries with it responsibilities
for their fiscal and institutional well-being.

As the city achieves ever greater importance in the national
and international network of cities, the province tends to lose
relevance for the city's most pressing needs, and pressure builds
up for direct relationships between the cities and the federal
government. In fact, the new and increasing importance of the
largest cities leads to an evolving national structure of city-
states, containing the major levers of population, wealth,
commerce, communication and culture.

At issue is the division of both responsibility and power
between these three, and often four, levels of government, as
well as the collection and distribution of fiscal means to meet
these responsibilities. Equally important is the degree of
responsiveness of these governments to the needs of the urban
citizenry. The issue is the power of local political institutions
to resolve local problems according to local life-style preferences, within a larger context of equalization of urban services
and amenities, and a national ·redistribution of wealth, job
opportunities and infrastructure investment.

C)   Functional

Not so long ago, municipal governments were concerned with tasks
mostly administrative in nature. City officials were there to
ensure the proper delivery of a limited number of services at
the least possible cost to the property tax payers. At the same

time, the concept of municipal citizenship was limited to those
who owned property. The extentions of the right to vote to all
citizens has been only a partial move towards the democrati-
zation of the municipal governing process. Indeed, there has
been steadily growing pressure for municipal government to
"open up". Through better education, the mass media and polit-
ization, citizens are better aware of their rights to good
housing, better transport, more recreational and cultural
facilities, more protection for their children. They are able
to express their preoccupations about the quality of life in
cities, and more than ever before expect to be heard. Emerging
social groups are no longer willing to accept the frustrations
of seeing their environment changed and destroyed without having
any say in the process. The appearances of more militant and
activist groups can be related to the actual incapacity of
municipal structures to deal with people.

Governments are not readily prepared to give up their autonomous -
and sometimes discretionary - decision-making powers. The
information flow from municipal management to citizenery is thin,
when it exists at all. Reports and studies are seldom available
before final programs are proposed and legislation passed.
Individuals and groups are ill-equipped to present their problems
to city hall: they lack the proper funds, physical resources
and skills to reach consensus among themselves and present their
case to government.

New channels are needed to resolve these conflicting situations.
While provisions for appeal can be seen as a possibility, a more
positive approach is that of making city and people work together.
There are indeed, in the community, considerable human resources
that need only to be tapped. Not only is it important for
citizens to involve themselves in their own community, but it is
also essential that politicians establish communication channels
which will enable them to get constant feedback from the electorate.

Among the <u>benefits</u> to be obtained through public participation
are the following:

   <u>Data on goals, attitudes, values</u>, preferences and priorities
are a crucial input to the planning process. Their only valid
sources are the citizens affected.

   <u>Creative capacity</u>, for perceiving solutions to problems is
not a prerogative of technical experts. Concerned laymen can
often see sound alternatives which experts do not. e.g. A
technically sound alternative route for Highway No. 417 in
Ottawa was identified by a Citizens' Group; many teams of
specialists had considered the problems for years without reporting this technically sound and widely acceptable solution.

   <u>Additional data</u>, important to planners, can be provided by
persons who often have decades of year-round experience of
the environment.

   <u>Technical expertise</u>, in the key subjects of the project is
often possessed by residents of the area. They can contribute
this valuable resource in support of the project or if alienated,
can conspire powerfully against it.

   <u>Involvement in planning</u>, is demanded by increasing number of
citizens who want to experience the process of creation as well
as its product. Often they have a substantial sense of ownership in their part of the environment -- to ignore this is
insulting.

   <u>Managerial solutions</u>, for environmental problems (as opposed
to purely structural solutions), require changes in people's
behaviour. The likelihood and ease of citizens changing their
behaviour is greatly increased if they systematically become
aware, interested, informed and thus convinced that new behaviour
is needed. Placing new recommendations into traditional
mentalities increased the need for regulatory legislation, enforcement procedures and a needless proliferation of a law and
order society. Who needs it?

Betterment of <u>delivery</u> and use of services.

Fulfill <u>democratic</u> ideals.

<u>Accountability</u> of programs to clients.

<u>Equalizer</u> distribution of political power.

Greater concern for environmental approach or societal approach.

Setting of priorities for the development of services.

Participation generally involves a long process, and as such it has several disadvantages, especially when compromise is involved (time required); savings occur however in the implementation stages, as objections from citizens are less likely to occur, and because the projects have already acquired some momentum (expense is minimized).

From a political point of view, the participatory approach to urban governing and planning is very positive in that it promotes mutual trust. It permits useful feedback from citizens to the political structure and thus minimizes unpredictable situations. It can have negative consequences however, if manipulation is used to serve political ends.

The non-participatory approach offers political autonomy but it does present difficulties when it comes to predicting the electorate's move, and it promises costly changes in the case of policies which prove unpopular. It can bring about systematic obstruction from individuals and pressure groups when program implementation is undertaken due to:

a) Conflicts between client and organization in terms of values, interests, goals, needs and expectations.

b) Conflict in the technology utilized.

c)   Conflict regarding the process or means of input.

d)   Territorial or geocentric conflicts.

e)   Conflicts on the perception of future needs.

CONCLUSION

It is in the city, where the greatest concentration of goods, services, opportunities and people exists, that there exists also the gaps in opportunities, the lacunae in services and the possibility of unimaginable loneliness and alienation that constitutes the lives of quiet desperation of many citizens. All levels of government attempt to offer programmes to combat these problems, skirting gingerly contentious jurisdictional and fiscal areas.

There exists clearly considerable overlap in the type and range of services offered and a considerable number of unmet needs. One of the difficulties of a federal system of government and the centralization implied throughout the political structures is the "top-down" nature of problem-solving and decision-making. The enormous (and growing) bureaucracies of civil servants at all levels create a certain ponderousness, an inertia which inhibits quick or direct response to a particular problem. It takes a considerable time for the perception of a problem to percolate up through the hierarchy and for a response to come down again. During this time lag, it is possible that the problem may have solved itself, or conversely, become worse, and that the solutions proposed for it may thus be irrelevant.

This is not to suggest that there is no longer a place for these institutionalized social measures. In fact, it is essential to continue the various negotiations to rationalize and in some

cases extend the services. But, as evidenced by the success of
such programs as "Opportunities for Youth" and "Local Initiatives"
there exists a substantial need for short-term, ad hoc, immediate
responses to local problems, locally perceived. Without the
necessity of cutting through various levels of red tape, and
without creating a bureaucracy with the remarkable bureaucratic
propensity for gathering strength and momentum, possibly after
its usefulness is at an end, small scale interventions can get
to work quickly to meet a local need. On the other hand, it is
conceivable that such an intervention might serve as the agent
of reform for an existing structure or as the basis of a new
structure within the system.

THE ROLE OF REMOTE SENSING IN HABITAT

Henry Hidalgo* and Samuel Musa*
Institute for Defense Analyses, Arlington, Virginia, USA

ABSTRACT

The potential role of remote sensing in promoting the well-being
of human settlements is identified. This was accomplished by
formulating a closed loop system for habitat, wherein it requires
a continuous feedback between the flow of information derived
from remote sensing and the consequences of managerial decisions
to control the basic characteristics of the human settlements,
e.g., its environment, utilization of resources, early warning of
natural hazards, etc. In addition, applications of remote sensing in both global scale and mesoscale for habitat are documented.

INTRODUCTION

This paper is based on the considerations of the potential role
of remote sensing in habitat as perceived by a panel of technologists during a recent workshop by the U.S. Environment and Resources Council (USERC) on Environment, Resources, and Urban
Development (Ref 1). The remote sensing panel was part of a
larger one dealing with the broader role of technology in the
promotion of the well-being of human settlements in developed
countries such as the United States. The objective of this paper
is to present to a multidisciplinary audience a general overview
of the utility of remote sensing in human settlements.

A distinguishing characteristic of remote sensing is the measurement of variables that describe physical phenomena through the
utilization of sensors placed on platforms that are not in direct
contact with such phenomena. Some examples of remote sensing are
as follows: (a) the indirect determination of atmospheric variables (e.g., temperature vertical profiles) from measurements of
terrestrial radiation emitted to space by sensors on orbiting
satellites, (b) images of clouds and atmospheric phenomena (e.g.,
fronts, hurricanes, etc.) from meteorological satellites, (c)
images of the earth's surface from aircraft, etc. The scope of
the data obtainable from remote sensing is defined by *instantaneous* measurements over a very wide range of space scales. Remote sensing has thus had a significant impact on the improvement
of weather forecasts and the tracking of mesoscale phenomena such

---

*Members of the Research Staff. Although assistance in preparing
this manuscript was provided as a professional courtesy to the
authors, the Institute for Defense Analyses was not involved in
the work reported here and responsibility for the contents of
this paper rests entirely with the authors.

as hurricanes. Other unique applications of remote sensing have
involved the use of earth-resources satellites to map large urban
and rural areas.

The role of remote sensing in habitat is thus limited to the description of physical characteristics of interest to human settlements over a wide range of space scales. The need for an accurate description of such physical characteristics is acquiring
increased importance for the effective management of human settlements not only in a regional but global basis.

APPLICATIONS OF REMOTE SENSING IN A GLOBAL SCALE

An illustration of the potential importance of remote sensing in
a global scale for habitat is the preservation of the ozone shield
against solar ultraviolet radiation. Ozone (O_3) is a gas present
in the atmosphere in very small amounts, with typical concentrations of a few parts per million relative to that of air. Ozone
is abundant in the stratosphere, i.e., at altitudes between 50 km
and the tropopause, which is at about 16 km at the equator and 8
km at the poles. Ozone has the important property of absorbing
ultraviolet radiation, a property that shields the biosphere from
overdoses of ultraviolet radiation. The strength of this shield
depends on the amount of ozone; thus, any decrease of ozone would
increase the amount of ultraviolet radiation reaching the earth's
surface. This increase in ultraviolet radiation could have then
significant impacts on the whole spectrum of habitat.

The amount of ozone in the stratosphere is controlled by interactions among the absorption of solar ultraviolet radiation, the
ozone chemical reactions generated by the solar ultraviolet radiation, and the motions of stratospheric air as induced by its heating from the absorption of solar radiation by ozone. The ozone
chemistry in the stratosphere can thus be affected by the injection of catalytic chemicals, i.e., reactants that are preserved
during reactions with ozone. These injections can be introduced
in the stratosphere either directly by the engine exhausts of aircraft flying in the stratosphere or indirectly from the use of
chemicals at the earth's surface. It has been shown, for example,
that the nitrogen oxides in the engine exhaust of stratospheric
aircraft would react catalytically with ozone. The net effect
would then be a decrease of the ozone shield (e.g., Ref 2). Likewise, the nitrous oxides from the use of fertilizers at the
earth's surface are diffused upward to the stratosphere, where
they would react catalytically with ozone. The net effect would
again be a decrease of the ozone shield (e.g., Ref 3). These
effects produced by the direct or indirect injection of nitrogen
oxides in the stratosphere would reach maximum values in time
scales of a decade. Another example of an indirect injection of
chemical reactants in the stratosphere is the widespread use of
aerosol products and refrigerants at the earth's surface, which
produce a source of fluorocarbons at the ground. Again, these
fluorocarbons eventually reach the stratosphere, where they destroy ozone catalytically. The decrease of the ozone shield from
the indirect injection of fluorocarbons at the ground would reach
maximum values in time scales of a century (e.g., Ref 4).

The preservation of the ozone shield is a problem of global dimensions and of interest to human settlements in an international scale. The reason for this effect is given by the physical characteristics of the stratosphere. Any material injected in the stratosphere would reside there for a long time (a few years), a fact that is a result of the temperature inversion (i.e., the increase in air temperature with increasing altitude) from the heating of stratospheric air by the absorption of solar radiation in the ozone chemistry. The injected material is then dispersed globally by the general circulation of air in the stratosphere. Because of the global scale of the ozone decrease, remote sensing can then play a significant role in the worldwide monitoring of the stratospheric constituents such as ozone, nitrogen oxides, etc.

The role of remote sensing to preserve the well-being of human settlements can be illustrated by recent studies concerning the potential regulations of the emissions of nitrogen oxides in the engine exhausts of aircraft flying in the stratosphere. The Climatic Impact Assessment Program (CIAP) of the U.S. Department of Transportation has studied the physical processes involved in the destruction of the ozone shield (Refs 5-8) and the consequences on man, animals, and plants of the resulting increase in the ultraviolet dose at the earth's surface (Refs 9-10). This study has also identified the use of remote sensing for the monitoring of the stratospheric constituents such as ozone, nitrogen oxides, etc. (Ref 7, Chapter 10). Results such as those of the CIAP study illustrate the immersed role of remote sensing in the promotion of the well-being of human settlements; i.e., the instantaneous monitoring of physical variables in a large range of space scales. The CIAP study also reveals the essential components leading to the identification of actions for the control of the nitrogen oxide emissions in the aircraft wakes; i.e., the development of combustion chambers with low emissions of nitrogen oxide for future aircraft engines. These essential components may be identified as follows:

1. Data gathering on physical phenomena of interest in the identification of potential problems that would have an adverse effect on the well-being of human settlements. Reference 5 is a compilation of data necessary for the understanding of the composition (Chapter 3), radiation (Chapter 4), chemistry (Chapter 5), and air motions (Chapters 6 and 7) in the stratosphere. Both remote and in situ sensing have played a role in the gathering of data for the stratospheric composition.*

2. Physical modeling of the effect of aircraft emissions of nitrogen oxides on the ozone decrease (Ref 7, Chapters 4 and 5), and the ultraviolet increase from the ozone decrease (Ref 8, Chapter 5); i.e., the modeling of the ultimate physical effects with an impact on the well-being of human settlements.

---

*In contrast with remote sensing, in situ measurements utilize sensors placed on platforms (e.g., aircraft, balloons, etc.) that are in direct contact with the variables being measured.

3. Understanding of both the effects on man, animals, and plants
(Ref 9) as well as the implied economical consequences of such
effects on society (Ref 10).

4. Interpretation of the results from the physical and socio-
economical models to provide inputs for the development of
national and international regulations of aircraft engine emissions and/or aircraft fleet sizes as well as aircraft flight altitudes (Ref 11).

Subsequent steps that remain to be taken in the future may be
identified as follows:

5. Actual decisions by national governments, as sponsored perhaps
by the United Nations, to control in the future the aircraft engine emissions and/or the fleet sizes and flight altitudes.

6. Feedbacks or interactions between scientist and policy makers
to ensure the following: (a) accurate determination of the results from uncontrolled or controlled aircraft operations in the
stratosphere, so as to improve the modeling of physical phenomena
with an impact on the well-being of human settlements, and (b) to
educate the nonscientist regulators so that they may be better
equipped to deal effectively with the risks involved of particular
activities dealing with habitat.

APPLICATIONS OF REMOTE SENSING IN THE MESOSCALE

The mesoscale is a term used in meteorology to denote space scales
corresponding to the dimensions of provinces, states, or small
countries. A number of examples have been documented where remote
sensing in the mesoscale has been used to assist in planning for
developments, monitoring effects of man's activities, and improving the management of the material and human systems involved (Ref
12). These examples are summarized in Table 1, which is discussed
below.

TABLE 1   Sample Impacts of Remote Sensing

1. Land-use planning (e.g., Green Swamp, Florida)

2. New-land accretion (e.g., Bangladesh)

3. Oil-spill detection (e.g., coastal waters)

4. Urban lands vs agricultural lands (e.g., Phoenix,
    Arizona)

5. Flood mapping and disaster assistance (e.g.,
    Mississippi River, Indus and Chenab Rivers,
    Pakistan)

6. Water management and ecological models (e.g.,
    Florida Everglades)

7. Geologic hazards (e.g., faults and landslides)

8. Agriculture (e.g., crop inventory)

Data from remote sensing was used to identify and locate land classes, such as wetlands, pine flatwoods, and uplands, in the Green Swamp area of Florida for land-use planning (Ref 13). The wetlands are important to the preservation of wildlife and conservation of water resources. The pine flatwoods, which are used for pastures, are essential for preserving the hydrologic balance. The uplands are appropriate for agricultural, residential, and transportation purposes. These uses of uplands do not seriously affect the conservation of wildlife and hydrologic balance. An agreement between the developer of this area and the State Attorney General for land-use planning was based on data gathered by remote sensors.

Scientists in Bangladesh have conducted a study of land accretion on the islands in the Bay of Bengal. The problem addressed is that new land tends to be used immediately for agricultural purposes before it becomes stable, and as a result the new land is washed away during the next flood. The objective of the Government of Bangladesh is to identify and stabilize the new land rapidly by planting trees on it and eventually open the land for agricultural uses. To achieve this objective, a map has been prepared from LANDSAT data which shows stable land, new land, and areas of water containing large amounts of turbidity where new land will be forming (Ref 12).

Regular monitoring of portions of coastal waters are conducted by aircraft to search for oil spills. More recently, oil spills have been identified from LANDSAT data (Ref 12). Easy identification from the satellite data requires special processing. This capability is important for enforcement and offers additional potential for prospecting for oil by locating natural oil seeps on the continental shelf.

Data from remote sensors is also important for drawing public attention to problems that may be well known to scientists and planners, e.g., the uncontrolled urban growth into important agricultural lands. A graphic example of this situation is illustrated by satellite data for Phoenix, Arizona (Ref 12).

A study of 1200 miles of the Mississippi flood of 1973 was conducted using LANDSAT data (e.g., Ref 14). This study demonstrated important engineering, economic, disaster relief, and planning applications of remote sensing to flood studies. Data obtained before and during the flood were essential in conducting these studies. In April 1975, the lower Mississippi and its tributaries flooded again. By comparing land-use maps derived from remote sensing and the areas flooded, the Louisiana Office of State Planning was able to determine that the flood covered 8,000 acres of urban and other highly developed regions, 300,000 acres of farmland, 109,000 acres of upland forest, 698,000 acres of wetland forest, and 2,800 acres of sand and silt areas. The maps showing the affected areas were used by the State for rapid analysis of flood damage to establish needs for disaster relief.

Studies of a flood on the Indus and Chenab Rivers in Pakistan identified the total extent of the flooded areas, the changes in

the river channels, the ponded water in the flood plain as the
flood water receded, the leakage under a dam, the location of
canal breaks and leaks, and the location of potential sources of
ground water along mountain flanks (Ref 15).

Data from remote sensing has been used to develop water management
and ecological models in the Florida Everglades (Ref 16). Water
storage areas are very flat. Vegetation in these storage areas
makes it difficult to map the bottom topography. In situ measurements, combined with repetitive remote sensor data has made it
possible to estimate volume of water in these storage areas.
Identification of vegetation types and distributions combined with
knowledge of faunal and floral associations has been a major element in developing an ecological model that can be used to determine water requirements. These studies have provided major steps
forward in addressing the problems of water availability, demand,
and alternatives.

Linear geological features are relatively easy to identify on
images from remote sensing. In some cases these linear features
represent critical faults. Even in a well mapped area such as
California, new active faults have been identified on satellite
data from LANDSAT and Skylab (Ref 17). Identification of the
location of faults and determination of their relative degree of
activity is of importance in locating power plants, construction
of dams, etc.

Other hazardous geological features such as potential landslide
areas can often be identified by remote sensing methods. These
are identified by their geomorphic features and/or thermal inertia that gives an indication of the degree of water saturation.

Remote sensing is being used to determine the distribution and
yield of crops in the United States by means of a Large Area Crop
Inventory Experiment (LACIE) as described in Ref 18. The area
estimates are made from classifications of LANDSAT data and the
yield estimates are determined from regression models relating
precipitation and temperature to grain yield. For additional
applications of remote sensing to earth's resources, the reader
is referred to Ref 19.

THE POTENTIAL ROLE OF REMOTE SENSING IN HABITAT

The ultimate objective of remote sensing in habitat is to provide
information from which could be derived an accurate identification
of options for the control of basic characteristics of human settlements. These characteristics include the environment, utilization of available resources, hazard to life, etc. The identification of alternative options would be a result of the steps
identified in Fig. 1, which are as follows:

1. Data acquisition, which is the gathering of observable data
for the description of physical phenomena.

2. Data processing, which involves the reduction, corrections,
or calibration of the new data.

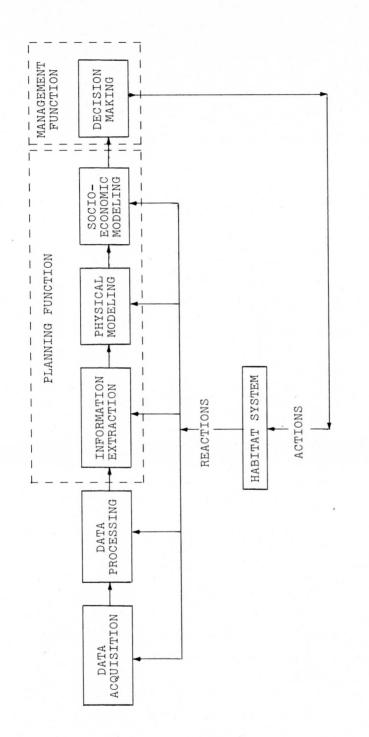

FIG. 1. Role of remote sensing in decision making.

3. Information extraction, which involves the conversion of the processed data into useable, meaningful information.

4. Physical modeling, which represents the theoretical description of the measurements. This step becomes important for predictions of the magnitude of the variables outside the range of their measurements; and, in addition, allows for the prediction of effects into the future.

5. Social-economical modeling, which project the social (quality of life) and economic (cost benefit) effects on the human settlement for the various alternatives, based upon the predictions from the physical models. Socio-economic models must consider the impact on community projects of factors such as water resources, alluvial land, energy requirements and availability, population trends, etc.

6. Decision making, which involves the accurate identification and evaluation of options for the optimization of the socio-economic variables affecting the well-being of the human settlements. An important factor to be considered by policy makers has to do with agreements on standards for allowable effects.

7. Feedbacks, which involve the actual physical and socio-economical reactions of the habitat system to the actions that are taken based on the previous steps. A number of habitat variables may serve as feedbacks, which are important for adjustments, corrections, or improvements in each of the foregoing steps. This feedback mechanism would identify the direction for further developments of sensors, data processing, models, and user's needs.

Table 2 is a summary of the foregoing basic steps. The operation of the above factors in a closed loop mode (i.e., Fig. 1) would, therefore, be a basic requirement for the achievement of successful human settlements from the remote sensing point of view.

TABLE 2   Information Needed for Effective Planning

Physical Models
    Modeling of involved physical phenomena
    Suitability of input and output parameters

Socio-Economic Models
    Use of environmental outputs from physical models
    Energy requirements
    Land values
    Population trends
    Identification of options for decision making

Decision Making
    Selection of options from socio-economic models
    Establish standards

Feedback
    Sensor development
    Data processing development
    Model development
    User education

PHYSICAL MODELS

Physical measurements must be obtained and processed to generate data needed for the development of valid physical models. Some of the major categories of physical phenomena of interest are identified in Table 3, where each category shows some physical characteristics that must be measured. Clearly, climatology and weather, water supply, and water and geological hazards have had strong influences in habitat selection and location. Air and water pollution, noise and radiation are generally effects of settlement or industrialization.

TABLE 3   Acquirable Data for Physical Models

Air Pollution
   Oxides of nitrogen, sulfur dioxide, carbon monoxide, suspended particles, hydrocarbons, ozone

Climatology and Weather
   Storms, seasonal temperature, precipitation

Water Supply
   Surface water, ground water, snow, ice, rain

Water Pollution
   Chemical, pesticide/insect, toxic, thermal, waste

Water Hazards
   Tsunami, floods, glacier, dam

Geology
   Faults, resource availability

Bio-Mass
   Infrared reflection and distribution

Noise
   Intensity and frequency duration

Radiation
   Ionizing, nonionizing

Land Use
   Urban and rural mapping

Most of the measurements of physical characteristics can be obtained from remote sensors; some, such as air pollution parameters can best be obtained from in situ or sampling sensors. Some of the measurements require extensive interpretation as, for example, the location and mapping of geological faults. Others require only direct measurements, such as noise pollution. After suitable human or machine processing, the measured characteristics can be used for model development and monitoring purposes to assess impact. The model then interpolates between data points, extrapolates outside the range of the measurements, and predicts future effects. A recent study (Ref 20) on the use of satellite data for disaster assessment indicates that such data is most suitable for the monitoring of floods, fire, glacier movement, and drought areas.

Samples of physical modeling have already been identified in the
protection of the ozone shield. Other examples are given by the
computer simulations of air pollution (e.g., Ref 21), weather
(e.g., Ref 22), hurricanes (e.g., Ref 23), the present climate
(e.g., Ref 24), noise (e.g., Ref 25), radiation phenomena (e.g.,
Refs 5, 7), etc. The scope, nature, and validation of the phy-
ical models depend strongly on the availability of relevant experimental data.

SOCIO-ECONOMIC MODELS

As indicated in Table 2, the development of socio-economical
models must start with use of inputs from the simulated phenomena
by the physical models. The nature and scope of the socio-
economical models may be illustrated by the Arizona trade-off
model (Ref 26). This model is an operational environmental management tool that analyzes economic growth versus natural environmental issues. The model is designed to assess the impact of
specific policy or program alternatives on the economy and environment of Arizona. Two of the more important aspects in this
model are land-use and resources analyses. Land use is analyzed
for each six-by-ten-mile grid cell for the State. Each grid receives a general classification of its surface resources such as
water, urban land, cultivated and pasture land, etc.

The major objective of this Arizona trade-off model is to serve
as a tool for use by decision makers in evaluating trade offs and
relationships between potential economic development, environmental quality programs, and trends in the State of Arizona. It
was recognized that not all questions concerning these relationships could be completely answered during the initial development
of the model. Therefore, the model is constructed in a modular
framework so that critical elements can be modified and updated
as the state-of-the-art improves. Although the primary objective
of this model is to relate economic growth to environmental quality, the model yields information on items such as (a) analysis
of environmental impact of specific industries and households,
(b) specification of means for implementing objectives, etc. A
simplified flow diagram of the Arizona trade-off model is shown
in Fig. 2.

The trade-off evaluation loop in the model evaluates the total
environment subject to the environmental constraints as set by
the output of the physical models. This step uses an iterative
procedure involving either modifications within an industry or
the selection of new industries until the environmental constraints are satisfied. Thereafter, the model continues to a
projection submodel and the determination of any changes from the
inputs to the model.

DECISION MAKING AND FEEDBACKS

The basic concept suggested in Fig. 1 by the remote sensing panel
has not yet been applied in practice. However, the basic elements
in Fig. 1 had been identified, for example, by Russell E. Train,
first chairman of the Council on Environmental Quality (Ref 27),

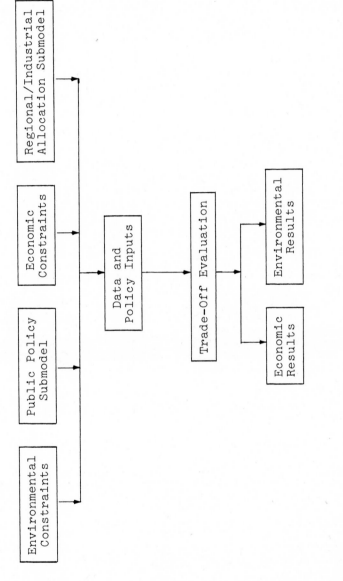

FIG. 2. Sample of socio-economical model.

who recognized two key elements in the effective management of
urban settlements: (1) the need for the best information and
feedback for decision making, and (2) the follow-up of decisions
and tasks. He also recognized the need for accurate and timely
information on the status of the environment in the formulation
of sound public policy and in the effective implementation of
environmental quality programs. He already pointed out that very
detailed data are necessary for certain types of planning and enforcement; i.e., in our increasingly complex technocratic society,
there is a need for a constant improvement of the research base
for the identification of both environmental problems and environmental standards. The effects of pollutants on human health,
for example, must be determined as accurately as possible. The
economic and social impacts of alternative regulatory systems
must then be analyzed in order to help provide a basis for the
most effective control strategies (Ref 27).

CONCLUDING REMARKS

Remote sensing can play a limited but important role in providing
inputs to habitat in space scales that range from the mesoscale
to the global scale. In the mesoscale, remote sensing techniques
can assist in the optimization of urban developments by supplementing conventional information. In the global scale, remote
sensing can provide instantaneous measurements of physical variables in a global scale. This capability may acquire increased
importance in the future in the preservation of the ozone shield
to solar ultraviolet radiation, a shield that may be degraded by
uncontrolled activities from modern civilization.

It is important to recognize that the effective management of
habitat requires the operation of a closed loop system, as the one
identified in Fig. 1. The physical data must be processed through
the controlling ecological and socio-economical factors, so as to
provide meaningful inputs for action in regard to the preservation
and promotion of the well-being of habitat. Conversely, there is
a need for feedback mechanisms that (1) would continue to improve
the modeling of physical and socio-economical variables in
habitat, and (2) would adequately educate the nonscientist policy
makers on the controlling variables for the well-being of habitat.

ACKNOWLEDGMENT

The authors wish to thank R. Bernstein, P. Castruccio, J. DeNoyer,
H. Kritikos, and S. Verner for their contributions during the de-
liberations of the remote sensing panel in the USERC Workshop.

REFERENCES

(1) USERC Environment, Resources, and Urban Development Workshop,
     Greenbelt, Maryland, 12-14 November 1975 (Proceedings to be
     published).

(2) Hidalgo, H., "Assessment of the Potential Impact of Strato-
     spheric Flight on the Ultraviolet Radiation at the Earth's
     Surface," AIAA Journal (to be published, 1976).

(3) McElroy, M.B., "Chemical Processes in the Solar System: A Kinetic Perspective, MTP International Review of Science (1975).

(4) Molina, M.J., and F.S. Rowland, "Stratospheric Sink for Chlorofluoromethanes--Chlorine Atom-Catalysed Destruction for Ozone," Nature, 249, 810-812 (1974).

(5) The Natural Stratosphere of 1974, CIAP Monograph 1, Climatic Impact Assessment Program, DOT-TST-75-51, U.S. Department of Transportation, Washington, D.C., September 1975.

(6) Propulsion Effluents in the Stratosphere, CIAP Monograph 2, Climatic Impact Assessment Program, DOT-TST-75-52, U.S. Department of Transportation, Washington, D.C., September 1975.

(7) The Stratosphere Perturbed by Propulsion Effluents, CIAP Monograph 3, Climatic Impact Assessment Program, DOT-TST-75-53, U.S. Department of Transportation, Washington, D.C., September 1975.

(8) The Natural and Radiatively Perturbed Troposphere, CIAP Monograph 4, Climatic Impact Assessment Program, DOT-TST-75-54, U.S. Department of Transportation, Washington, D.C., September 1975.

(9) Impacts of Climatic Change on the Biosphere, CIAP Monograph 5, Climatic Impact Assessment Program, DOT-TST-75-55, U.S. Department of Transportation, Washington, D.C., September 1975.

(10) Economic and Social Measures of Biologic and Climatic Change, CIAP Monograph 6, Climatic Impact Assessment Program, DOT-TST-75-56, U.S. Department of Transportation, Washington, D.C., September 1975.

(11) Grobecker, A.J., S.C. Coroniti, R.H. Cannon, Jr., The Effects of Stratospheric Pollution by Aircraft, CIAP Report of Findings, Final Report, Climatic Impact Assessment Program, DOT-TST-75-50, U.S. Department of Transportation, Washington, D.C., December 1974.

(12) Status and Plans of the Department of the Interior EOS Program, U.S. Geological Survey, Open File Report 75-376, July 1975.

(13) Coker, A.E., A.L. Higer et al., "Automatic Categorization of Land-Water Cover Types of the Green Swamp, Florida, Using Skylab Multispectral Scanner (S-192) Data," Earth Resources Survey Symposium, NASA L.B. Johnson Space Center, Houston, Texas, 1975.

(14) Deutsch, M., and F. Ruggles, "Optical Data Processing and Projected Applications of the ERTS-1 Imagery Covering the 1973 Mississippi Valley Floods," Water Resources Bull., 10, 5 (1974).

(15)   Deutsch, M., F. Ruggles, and G. Rabchevsky, "Flood Applica-
       tion of Earth Resources Technology Satellite," Earth Envi-
       ronment and Resources Conference, Philadelphia, Pa., 1974.

(16)   Higer, A.L., E.H. Cordes, and A.E. Coker, "Water Management
       Model of the Florida Everglades," in ERTS-1, A New Window
       on Our Planet (R.S. Williams and W.D. Carter, Editors), 159-
       161, U.S. Geological Survey, Reston, Virginia, 1976.

(17)   Lamar, D.L., and P.M. Merifield, "Application of Skylab and
       ERTS Imagery to Fault Tectonics and Earthquake Hazards of
       Peninsular Ranges Southwestern California," California Earth
       Sciences Corporation, Technical Report 75-2, July 1975.

(18)   MacDonald, R.B., R.B. Erb, and F.G. Hall, "The Use of LAND-
       SAT Data in a Large Area Crop Inventory Experiment (LACIE),"
       Proc. Symp. on Machine Processing of Remotely Sensed Data,
       Purdue University (1975).

(19)   Bauer, M.E., "Technological Basis and Applications of Remote
       Sensing of the Earth's Resources," IEEE Trans. on Geoscience
       Electronics, 14, 1 (January 1976).

(20)   Robinove, C.J., "Disaster Assessment and Warning With LAND-
       SATS," International Symposium in Remote Sensing of Envi-
       ronment, 10th, Ann Arbor, Michigan, 1975.

(21)   Belanger, W., "Computer Modeling of Air Pollution Using AIR
       MOD," Earth Environment and Resources Conference, Phila-
       delphia, Pa., 1974.

(22)   Thompson, Philip D., Numerical Weather Analysis and Predic-
       tion, MacMillan, New York, 1961.

(23)   Carrier, G.F., "The Intensification of Hurricanes," J. Fluid
       Mech., 49, 1, 145-158 (1971).

(24)   Manabe, S., "Climate and the Ocean Circulation, 2, The At-
       mospheric Circulation and the Effect of Heat Transfer by
       Ocean Currents," Mon. Weather Rev., 97, 775-805 (1969).

(25)   Freeze, T.W., Indoor Noise Prediction Using Digital Computer
       Techniques, Proc. of the 1974 International Conference on
       Noise Control Engineering, Washington, D.C.

(26)   Myers, C.W., "Arizona Trade-Off Model: A Tool for State
       Growth and Land-Use Policy," EPA-600/5-73-010, Managing the
       Environment, Washington Environmental Research Center,
       Office of Research and Development, U.S. Environmental Pro-
       tection Agency, Washington, D.C., 276-287, November 1973.

(27)   Train, Russell E., "Management for the Future," EPA-600/5-
       73-010, Managing the Environment, Washington Environmental
       Research Center, Office of Research and Development, U.S.
       Environmental Protection Agency, Washington, D.C., 8-11,
       November 1973.

LEGISLATION AND HUMAN SETTLEMENT

John Swan
Faculty of Law, University of Toronto
Toronto, Ontario

The focus of this paper will be on two features of law. The first is that all law (and this, of course, includes legislation) is a means to an end. This end will be determined by political institutions in each society and will reflect that society's values. The second is that once an end has been determined, the law will offer a variety of legal methods to achieve this end. Any society can determine how its members will live together, what the environment will be like and what values will be acknowledged as determining that environment. The role played by the law in these decisions is essentially the same whether the society is democratic or not, whether the political structure is unitary or federal, or whether there is a capitalist or socialist economic system. This is not to say that the characteristics of the way in which the law will operate will not depend on the particular society, but only that there are a finite number of ways in which law can operate and every human society is limited to these in dealing with the problems raised by human settlement.

The starting point for any analysis of law in regard to human settlement is the realization that unless the scarce resources required by all human settlement are allocated or controlled in some way, the inexorable logic of the "Tragedy of the Commons" will ultimately render the conditions of life intolerable. Garrett Hardin, in developing the logic of the common and its eventual destruction suggested that the solution lay in changing ideas of morality. But if we consider the hard facts of human nature, a change in morality is unlikely to be satisfactory. It is hard to induce people to accept a set of moral values when to do so is, from an economic point of view, irrational. The only alternative is the imposed morality of the law. As Hardin points out, the law has for a very long time helped to avert the tragedy. The institution of private property has ensured that the land is not overused. For

some people, but not, of course, for all, life in organized settlements has
been tolerable and even pleasant because the exclusive possession conferred
by the institution of private property has ensured a method of allocation of
one scarce resource, land. The problem which human society faces now is that
the allocative function performed by private property is either unsatisfact-
ory in resolving the problems facing human settlements, or is rejected as a
basis for social organization on the ground that it is an inappropriate way
for social decisions to be made. The right of property, after all, can be
regarded as the right to make decisions about the allocation of economic
resources.

No society can tolerate an unrestricted power based on private property.
Every society has the idea of certain common property. The most obvious
examples are the roads and streets of any town. A concern for an existence
that is not just functional, may add parks, public gardens and other amenities
to the list of common property. Modern developments in regard to limitations
on private property have increased the scope of social control over the use
to which property, acknowledged to be private, can be put. This has led to
the existence of comprehensive plans for urban and rural development, to
standards of building construction, to the preservation of open spaces and
green belts. It has also led to the control of air, water and noise pollution. Apart from these negative or restrictive developments, societies have
organized themselves so that sewage treatment and water works are provided,
so that roads are maintained and built, so that public transit systems are
provided (or encouraged by the grant of monopoly rights).

One feature of this organization has been the creation of sub-units of the
society. We may take the present division of the world into sovereign
countries as a given fact, but the creation of units within these countries
is the result of conscious decisions on the part of each country and the
society it represents. Canada, the United States, the U.S.S.R. are federal
jurisdictions in which the power exercised by the governmental organizations
is divided between a national and provincial or state legislatures. But
within these subdivisions there are smaller units, cities, towns and rural
districts. The same subdivisions exist in unitary states. It is trite to
say that these subdivisions exist through the law. It is not so obvious that
the way in which these subdivisions are organized and function will say a

great deal about the way in which decisions are made. Legally it may not
matter much whether a particular planning decision is made by a central government official or a local government official. The acceptability of the decision may, however, depend on the extent of the participation of local residents
in the decision-making process. On the other hand, it may not be possible
for local institutions to deal with large-scale problems and decisions in
regard to those may have to be made by a central government. At one extreme,
of course, problems are global and no one government can hope to have anything
but an insignificant influence.

There is a tension between those who believe that decisions in any society
should be made by the central government for that country and those who believe that decision-making should take place at the lowest possible level.
The choice in many respects may be largely a matter of political opinion.
But in others the choice of what decision-making level should have the power
to decide must be related to the problem that has to be solved. River basins,
for example, have a tendency to ignore political boundaries. On the other
hand, national standards of air and water quality may not be desirable as
they may be either too strict in the case of industrialized areas or not
strict enough in wilderness areas.

The principle ways in which the law can operate in controlling human conduct
are:

1. By making certain conduct criminal and hence subject to punishment.
2. By providing that a civil remedy in damages or by injunction is available
    to anyone who may be injured by another's actions.
3. By requiring that a licence be obtained before a certain activity is
    carried on.
4. Through state ownership of resources so that the state may exercise all
    the rights of an owner.
5. Indirectly, through taxes and subsidies, and by such devices as the pub-
    lication of studies of environmental consequences of development.

Any attempt to control human conduct in any area has to use one of these types.
Of course, the method chosen may involve more than one of these. A licensing
scheme may be supplemented by the criminal law or by tax concessions.

1. The criminal sanction. The criminal sanction is the most direct way of

controlling social conduct. It is the way most people have in mind when they
think that some activity should be stopped. The purpose of the criminal law
is to set limits to permissible conduct. It operates by punishing those who
overstep the limits. Therefore, the criminal law must be certain: it must
set limits that can be known in advance. In addition, it must acknowledge
that man is a rational creature and is punished because punishment will deter
him from doing the act again. It is implicit in this that the person who
committed the criminal act could have avoided the act if he had wanted to.

These features operate to limit the effective scope of the criminal law.
First, the specification of the crime must be relatively concise. This means
that more complex forms of regulation cannot be directly the subject of control by the criminal law. Thus it is not proper to make the construction of
a building that does not comply with a building code criminal. Instead, the
failure to obtain a licence or to allow an inspector to see if the building
code has been complied with could be the basis for a criminal prosecution.
The difference is not technical; it reflects the fact that the use of the
criminal law is a crude instrument of control.

Second, the specification of the offense should leave some room for the defence that the person charged did not intend to commit an offence. There has
been an increasing tendency in recent years on the part of many legislatures
to make liability strict. This removes the defence based on intention. Such
a rule can be brutally absurd. A person may be convicted and branded as a
criminal for doing something which he may not have had any effective power to
control. The reason for excusing a person who did not intend to commit a
crime from liability for it, is the same as that for excusing a person who is
not of sound mind.

Third, the specification of the offence must not be vague. The command,
"Thou shalt not pollute!", cannot be made into a criminal offence without
doing much the same damage to the legal process as the failure to observe the
previous points will do. Again, the justification for such a law is often
based on the need to spread the net to catch polluters widely. The safeguard
against everyone's being convicted is said to be the responsible way in which
charges will be laid and the prosecution conducted. The objection to this is
that it gives the power to the government to harass individuals for whatever

reason is thought good. This can only lead to a loss of respect for the law.

The criminal law will always be a necessary feature of any legal system.
However, this does not mean that it should always be used for every case where
conduct has to be controlled. It helps to provide that people living together observe minimum standards of conduct. Any response to the present
concerns about the environment in which we live will take us far beyond the
minimum standards.

2. The Civil Remedy. Every legal system will offer its members redress
against those who do them harm. There is no reason why the harm caused
through pollution of whatever kind may not be redressed in this way. Like
the criminal law, the civil remedy has its place and its limitations. Its
place is principally to provide compensation to one who has been directly
and particularly injured by the acts of another, when those acts involve a
risk of harm or injury beyond that which the law allows. Many things we do
harm someone else, but the law only provides a remedy for a limited range of
harms. For example, generally speaking no remedy will be given for the loss
of a pleasant aspect from one's house. On the other hand the omission of
foul smells or excessive noise may make one liable to a neighbour. Most
legal systems provide not only for the award of money damages but also for
the granting of an injunction, i.e., the order of a court that the defendant
stop doing something.

This is a very effective remedy and, from the point of view of the complain-
ing party, may be exactly what he wants. There are two difficulties with
this remedy, however. The first is that pollution in urban areas affects a
great many people to an extent which would not justify any one individual
incurring the expense and trouble of a law suit. Class actions may alleviate
this problem, but they do not remove it. Very often the polluters may be
very numerous, e.g., the operators of motor vehicles. It is simply not
practicable to seek a civil remedy in such a case.

The second difficulty is once again that the remedy may be too crude. There
is no guarantee that the polluting industry will be effectively controlled by
this method. The amount of compensation awarded may either be too small to
discourage harmful activity or it may be crippling and prevent a necessary

industry from operating. The granting of an injunction may force the complete closure of a plant even though this may lead to widespread unemployment. Such decisions may be necessary, but they should not be made by courts that are not (and cannot be) responsive to political pressure or control. These decisions are political ones.

3. Licensing schemes. This is the principal method used in legislative devices for controlling conduct in human settlement. It has the advantages of extreme flexibility and sophistication. Typical planning legislation operates by requiring that development be licensed. Under such a scheme, the authority responsible for the implementation of the plan can closely control the development of any area. A licensing scheme can, for example, control the number (and competence) of doctors and taxi-drivers. It could also be used to control the use of insecticides and pesticides by licensing those competent to use or buy them and prohibiting their widespread use.

The licensing scheme can only work if there is a sufficient administrative structure to support it. No scheme of development, no matter how well conceived, can work if there is no plan to which the development should conform. Many planning problems have arisen simply because there has been no idea on the part of the administrators of what should be done and how it should be done. One consequence of a licensing scheme and the administrative structure it entails is that the administrators are more or less subject to supervision of the courts. The courts take the view that the owner of property can do what he likes with his own, and if he cannot do so, the onus is on the government to show why he should not do so.

Part of the problem with any licensing scheme is that the grant of a licence involves the allocation of a very valuable right. Conversely, the taking away of the right to develop land can be regarded as the expropriation of the property of the owner. Planning schemes have run into trouble in many countries because the courts have treated such expropriation as unconstitutional. Since the grant of a licence to develop confers a financial benefit on the owner, there is a tremendous pressure to grant licences. Various proposals have been made for resolving the problem caused by this feature of any licensing schemes. Among them have been attempts to expropriate the development value of all land and to pay the owners for it. Thus, when the land is

developed, the increase in value belongs to the state and not to the owner.
By restricting the development of land, the state is making an already scarce
resource scarcer and, hence, more valuable.

The consequences of this for the law are important. Any scheme will present
competing pressures: the need for orderly and carefully planned development;
the owner's desire to maximize his profit from his land; the need for fair
procedures for decision-making so that those who are harmed by being denied
the chance to develop their land cannot upset the plan in court. All these
pressures have to be resolved in each society in a way which reflects that
society's views of the appropriate ways to make decisions. This, in turn,
must be responsive to the concerns mentioned earlier about the level at which
decisions are made. The decision of a central government as to how development should be controlled may be less subject to local political pressure which
might undermine the plan. But, at the same time, the decision of a local
authority may be more responsive to the wishes of the residents of the area
and hence more acceptable to them. It is only clear that whatever decision
is made, it will have to be made carefully and with a complete awareness of
all the problems that the attempt to control development will have to face.

4. State ownership. The legal problems of implementing any control over land
development or any other activity are far simpler if this method is chosen
than under any system where the law has to influence the actions of individual
owners. No licensing scheme can approach the comprehensiveness of the controls
possible if the state owns all the land. In every society this method of control has been used. The planning of new towns or the renewal of slum areas
has often been achieved by the expropriation of the property of the owners in
those areas and by the assertion then by the state (in whatever form) of its
powers as owner.

5. Indirect Methods. There are a variety of indirect methods of control.
Tax laws can encourage some kinds of activity and discourage others. Subsidies
can have the same effects. These may have to be used in conjunction with other
methods. Used on their own they are unlikely to have any significant effect.

Among the indirect methods of control can be included provisions requiring full
public disclosure of proposed development. The environmental impact statement

can be used to provide the opponents of any proposed scheme with as much
material as they need to mount an effective criticism or opposition. Full
disclosure of all the facts can only help to make decisions more sensible.

Human life will go on with or without legislation and law. The role of law
is, however, to make it more pleasant, to prevent its becoming, in the words
of Thomas Hobbes, "solitary, poor, nasty, brutish and short." From one point
of view the law can be seen as simply the organized force of society brought
to bear on the individual who does not conform. From this point of view law
shares much of the sordidness of mankind. From another point of view, however,
law can be seen as making possible much that is good. It can provide a framework for human co-operation and living together, it can provide for the allocation of scarce resources, and it can help social decisions to be made in ways
that are both fair and efficient. Like all that is human, it can be debased
and abused. It can (and must) represent the values of the society in which
it exists. If these are evil, the law will share them. But equally, if
these are good, the law will share them as well. The topic of legislation or
law and human settlement is simply the topic of law and how it will impinge
on men.

FINANCIAL AND TECHNICAL MANAGEMENT FOR HUMAN SETTLEMENTS

D. N. Dewees
Institute for Environmental Studies, University of
Toronto, Toronto, Ontario M5S 1A4, Canada

THE PROBLEM

The problems of urban areas in the modern industrial age are numerous and seem to be multiplying rapidly. Foremost among these problems are two that have received increasing attention over the last decade, and that, although seemingly unrelated, may have a common solution. These problems are finding sources of municipal revenue to finance the ever-increasing demand for public services in urban settlements, and controlling the multiplying environmental problems that arise from growing urban conglomerations of human and economic activities.

The financial or fiscal problems of urban areas arise from the convergence of increasing demands and expectations for public services in urban areas that must be financed out of a limited set of fiscal measures. The property tax, the sales tax, and in some cases even an income tax are primary sources of revenue for most municipalities. When the rates at which these taxes were levied were minimal, the opposition to them was no more than the usual grumbling of taxpayers who feel somehow that tax money is wasted money. As tax levels have increased, however, there has arisen greater and greater resistance to any further expansion of these revenue sources. While few cities have reached maximum limits at which these taxes can be levied, it is clear that above some level there are great political repercussions from higher taxes.

In addition to the practical problems of public acceptance of higher tax levels, there are serious economic inefficiencies caused by high rates of such taxes. These harmful side effects arise because taxes have two consequences: they raise money and they affect individual behaviour. A sales tax on specific commodities, for example, introduces a divergence between the value of that commodity to the consumer and the cost of supplying the commodity. If a tax rate is high enough, some consumers will reduce their consumption or do without. Even though their value for the commodity is greater than the cost of production and distribution, it may not be great enough to include the magnitude of the tax. Thus, any tax on specific commodities will have distorting effects in the economy, reducing overall consumer satisfaction from the bundle of goods and services that is purchased.

The property tax has even more serious side effects. In the first place, it acts like any sales tax in raising the price of a commodity and therefore lowering the amount that people on the whole consume. When tax rates reach ten cents on every dollar of assessed evaluation, as they have in some cities such as Boston, Massachusetts, then the cost of owning or renting housing is tremendously increased. The tax becomes almost confiscatory. In addition, because property taxes apply to land and improvements, they impose high costs upon those who would renovate or improve urban properties. The owner

of a property in a deteriorating urban area must face first the cost of
renovating the property and second the increased taxes payable every year
because of that renovation. Thus there is a strong disincentive adequately
to maintain buildings that are exposed to high rates of taxation. Thus, a
measure designed purely to raise money has the actual effect of reducing the
quality of urban structures.

Finally, even the income tax has serious incentive problems. A local or
municipal income tax will fall most heavily upon high income workers, and
tend to drive them to other jurisdictions where tax rates are not so high.
This can have a snowballing effect in which the income base of the city
shrinks, necessitating continual increases in the tax rates. In addition to
this mobility effect, a high rate of income taxation reduces the incentive
for further work by an individual. A number of persons, including
professionals and hourly wage earners, have some choice about the number of
hours per week that they work. The higher the income tax rate, the less
money the worker receives for his overtime or additional work, therefore the
less he is inclined to contribute to his job and therefore to the national
and local economy. In many areas, income tax rates have risen to a level
that clearly discourages further work effort.

We can see from the above that most of the currently popular tax sources
have a variety of undesirable side effects. As taxes increase, these side
effects can only become more serious.

While urban fiscal problems become more serious, urban environmental problems are still a major urban priority. As the size of human settlements
grows geographically, it becomes more and more difficult to work in the
city and escape its environmental problems in one's residence. As national
production grows and the total amount of economic activity increases, the
potential for pollution emissions also rises. Higher standards of living
are associated with more automobiles, more electricity consumption and more
consumer-oriented activities with environmental side effects. Thus even
aside from major industrial projects such as steel mills or oil refineries,
growing urban areas will experience continued environmental problems from
consumer activities. There is some fear that the expanding environmental
control legislation cannot keep pace with our increasing ability to
generate harmful wastes.

A DESIRABLE OUTCOME

It would be desirable to find sources of municipal revenue that would avoid
the serious distorting effects common to most current sources. This would
allow public representatives to set tax rates based upon the demand for
public services, without excessive concern that serious inefficiencies will
thereby be introduced to the economy, possibly leading to stagnation or
wastes of economic resources.

In addition, it would be desirable to have some legislation that could
assure that total pollution of a particular type in a particular area would
not increase beyond current levels or would decrease at some predictable
rate. It would be particularly desirable if the pollution control program
could insure that environmental improvements could occur despite increases
in economic activity or the appearance of new products with substantial
environmental side effects. There would be real advantages to pollution
control programs whereby products that involve particularly undesirable

environmental effects either in production or in consumption were substantially higher priced than similar products without those side effects.

SOME FEASIBLE SOLUTIONS

The fiscal and the environmental problems can be attacked simultaneously by
levying taxes precisely upon the emission of harmful pollutants into the
environment. The ability of the environment to carry off wastes or to
provide a satisfactory living condition is a valuable resource. Currently
we distribute that resource free of charge to those who would use it for
their own enjoyment or to carry off wastes. While we frequently impose
regulations upon the quantity of waste that may be discharged by a particular
source, within those regulations the discharge is entirely free. There is
currently no cost to using the environment for waste disposal purposes, and
there is no barrier to new sources being added to those that already exist
causing increases in total emissions.

All this would change if in addition to some maximum limit on pollution
emissions, charges were imposed for all emissions within that maximum. Under
such a system, the value of the environmental resource would be specifically
recognized by the price imposed upon those who would use the resource. The
firm that met existing environmental standards would have a continuous
incentive, as a result of the effluent charge, to reduce its emissions
still further, or eliminate them completely. Any reduction in pollution
emissions, because it would reduce the effluent charge, would become just
like any cost reduction in the production process. There is a continuing
financial incentive to look for ways to reduce this aspect of the firm's
cost. Thus, effluent charges combined with maximum regulations on emission
limits can provide powerful incentives for continuing improvements in environmental quality over time.

In addition to improving the environment, effluent charges are a source of
revenue. Every dollar of effluent charge that the consumer or manufacturer
pays is also a dollar of revenue to the jurisdiction that imposed the charge.
Thus a municipality could substitute charges on environmental degradation
for conventional tax sources. The property tax or the sales tax could at
least in part be replaced by charges upon individuals and firms for discharging particulates or sulphur dioxide from furnaces and factories, for
discharging organic or other harmful wastes into the sewer system or local
water courses, and a variety of other charges could be imposed for other
pollution emissions.

The automobile in urban areas causes air pollution, noise, and serious congestion problems. Since there are limits to the extent to which noise and
air pollution per vehicle-mile can be reduced, it would be desirable to have
an independent charge based upon the number of vehicle-miles driven for the
remaining noise, pollution, and congestion effects. Thus manufacturers
would have incentives to build lower pollution cars, and motorists would
have powerful incentives to drive less. A tax levied at the rate of five
cents per mile would probably be adequate to compensate for the remaining
pollution noise and congestion effects in an average city, and might reduce
motoring by 20% or more. Furthermore, the revenues from a five cent per
mile automobile tax would be approximately equal to those from a five per
cent sales tax in some jurisdictions.

It is sometimes complained that effluent charges are not a certain means of
reducing pollution emissions. It is suggested that some polluters will
choose to pay the charge rather than clean up their emissions. In fact, any
sensible polluter would respond to some extent to an effluent charge, and
rates could probably be ascertained that would ensure any given reduction
in pollution emissions. However, for those who do not place confidence in
such fiscal devices, there is another alternative that would provide certain
pollution reductions, and the same fiscal advantages. This is the effluent
rights scheme as proposed by Professor Dales of the University of Toronto.
Under such a scheme, the jurisdiction would specify the total amount of
pollution that could be discharged over a given time. For example, it
might specify that no more than 100 tons a day of particulates could be
emitted within the city. All polluters who discharge particulates would
be required to purchase permits or rights that entitle them to discharge
the amount they anticipated using during the upcoming year. However, only
100 tons per day of rights would be issued. The rights would be sold in
an auction whereby the price would rise until the demand for rights was
just equal to the amount to be issued. Thus the jurisdiction would be
certain that no more pollution could be discharged than the specified
quantity of rights. If the restriction were severe, the price would be
high, with consequent large revenues for the municipal authority. Thus the
income for the municipality would be similar to that of an effluent charge,
but the environmental consequences would be certain, since they are specified
by the program itself.

PROBABLE IMPROVEMENT IN HUMAN SETTLEMENTS

The proposal here is that we reduce taxation of things that are generally
regarded as desirable and impose taxes instead upon things that are
generally regarded as undesirable. In this way, necessary municipal revenues
can be gathered for undertaking worthwhile public services, and at the same
time serious urban problems can be attacked through the incentive effects
of the taxes themselves. Imposition of taxes on environmental pollution
could be expected to reduce the amount of pollution discharged by firms
and individuals in urban areas. Imposition of a congestion charge on
motoring would reduce automobile noise and air pollution, as well as
levels of urban highway congestion. All air and water pollution in urban
areas could be similarly reduced. In addition, the harmful side effects
of current taxes could be reduced as these taxes were replaced by environmental charges. The current disincentives for urban property owners to
renovate or improve their properties would be reduced or eliminated by the
attendant reductions in the property tax.

CONCLUSIONS

Many of our current tax instruments were originally adopted when the tax
rates themselves were negligible, less than one per cent of income or sales
or far less than one per cent of the assessed value of the property. Over
time tax rates have grown to the point where they are far from trivial; in
fact they are often substantial and punitive. As a result, the harmful side
effects of these taxes are now beginning to be felt in many sectors of
many countries' economies.

It is proposed that when substantial revenues are to be raised, taxes should
be imposed not upon universally desired commodities such as housing and
consumer goods and work effort, but upon undesirable commodities such as

air pollution, highway congestion and water pollution. By shifting at least part of our tax base from the sales, property and income taxes to environmental taxes we can solve two problems at once. First, we open up new sources of revenue for hard-pressed municipal coffers. Second, we provide economically efficient means for encouraging the reduction of environmental degradation in urban areas. While a complete replacement of existing with proposed taxes is not recommended nor desirable, a substantial replacement could increase the efficiency of the economy, and solve one of our major urban problems.

References

For an analysis of the distortions of a variety of taxes, see George F. Break, "The Incidence and Economic Effects of Taxation" in A.S. Blinder & R.M. Solow, et. al. eds, The Economics of Public Finance, Brookings, Washington, 1974.

Effluent charges are discussed in D.N. Dewees, "The Economics of Pollution" in L. Officer and L.B. Smith eds, Issues in Canadian Economics, McGraw-Hill, Toronto, 1974.

The pollution rights scheme is presented in J. Dales, Pollution, Property and Prices, University of Toronto Press, Toronto, 1968.

HUMAN SETTLEMENTS AS SOCIOTECHNICAL-ECONOMIC PROCESSES

Harold Chestnut
General Electric Corporate Research and Development
Schenectady, New York, USA

ABSTRACT

In recent times, increasing numbers of people in the world
have migrated to the cities. There they have become a part
of a sociotechnical-economic system from which they must obtain
goods and services with which to live, and to which they should
contribute their skills and efforts. Many of the goods and
services require much money and time to be made available and
require joint funding and public approval to be initiated.

A city can be viewed as a feedback system in which continued
guidance and adaptation is required to meet the changing needs.
In order to compare different cities, it is desirable that some
common basis be agreed upon for identifying the different major
sectors that make up the needs of the people of a city. Major
sectors such as Personal Goods, Personal Services, Sales and
Trade, Government, Industry, and Utilities are set forth, and
subsectors under each are described.

It is proposed that a joint effort be undertaken to get meaningful data on a number of human settlements so that different
cities can be compared on a similar basis, for example, those
of the major sectors and subsectors. The modest effort of this
sort currently under way should be stepped up on a national and
international scale. In this way it should be possible to understand better and more quickly the increasingly critical sociotechnical-economic processes that take place in the world's
cities.

NATURE OF PROBLEM

Years ago there were many fewer people in the world, and each
family or small group lived in such a way as to be responsible
for the major factors which influenced their life and liveli-
hood. Today, when a billion more people are being added to the
world in a 10-15 year period, and when approximately 1/4 of the
world's people live in human settlements of over 20,000 people,
i.e., cities, it is essential for life that cooperative ways or

systems be developed and maintained which will make it possible
for the growing number of people on earth, currently about 4
billion, to continue to exist. These human settlements or
cities are growing in size and number and form the environment
for an increasing percent of the world's population. It is
necessary that they be studied and understood in a detailed
and quantitative way so that those responsible for their
decision-making and leadership will have the necessary information in adequate time for them to make wise judgments.

In order for individuals and organizations to act intelligently
in planning their current and future activities, it is advantageous for them to have a clearer picture of their environment;
what is happening now and what activities currently under way
will probably mean for the future. Although each person has
his or her individual needs and concerns, there are many fundamental physical and cultural needs that provide the general
goals that all persons in the society are seeking.

Included in these goals are individual needs such as for food,
shelter, clothing, health, and education; group needs such as
those for transportation, communication, defense, and environmental quality; and individual desires such as for recreation
religion, safety, and self-respect. It is important that individually and collectively we try to understand better the nature
of these goals, and the processes whereby they can be achieved
in our society. Our efforts will be directed to trying to understand the processes better rather than to insist that we know
them perfectly.

A CITY AS A FEEDBACK SYSTEM WITH ADAPTATION

A starting point for describing the city is its population,age-
distribution profile for the males and females. This population
information for the city, coupled with income, education,
cultural, and other socioeconomic data can provide a basis for
an understanding of the needs and desires of the community. As
shown in Fig. 1, the actual values and present plans for the
needs of the society provide inputs for decision-making and
plans for future activity.

The other parts of the human settlement process shown on Fig. 1
include the implementation of decisions and the city itself
which is represented by its present capabilities and projected
values for the society. It is these present capabilities and
present plans which represent the city and are fed back as information to provide the inputs for the process. Viewed in this
light the city appears to be a feedback system in which the pro-

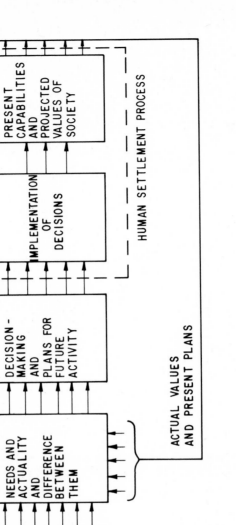

FIGURE 1: THE CITY AS A FEEDBACK SYSTEM

cesses of establishing the estimates of needs, of decision-making and plans for the future, and of implementing the decisions provide the means for adaptation of the system to the changing environment. Inputs from outside and exports to outside are important parts of this external environment.

In order for one to be able to understand what is taking place in the city in time for the necessary actions to achieve a desirable future, perhaps 5 to 20 years in advance of critical need, it is important that information be obtained from the city on an on-going basis. What should be the nature of that necessary information? The following section presents one way of organizing this information.

MAJOR SECTORS OF A CITY

The social needs of a city's people are being met today with the aid of technical utilities and industry all operating under the direction of an economic set of decision rules. It will be advantageous for the various physical, social, economic, technical, and other needs of society to be grouped into a small number of major sectors for purposes of subdivision and more detailed analysis. It is appreciated that there are many different ways in which such major sectors could be selected, and it is recognized that different sectors, no matter how chosen, will interact with one another with some degree of closeness of coupling.

The six major sectors listed in Table 1 are presented as a useful way of thinking about some of the primary needs for the inhabitants for a city. These sectors--personal goods,personal services, sales and trade, government, industry, and utilities-- can serve as a basis for a more detailed study of the activities which take place in a city. Thus, for example, the personal goods are represented by such subsectors as food, housing, clothing, and equipment; and utilities include subsectors of energy, communications, transportation, and water and sanitation. It may be of help for one to think of these sectors as having been derived in a historical sense. Each person over the years has had to be concerned with such personal goods as food, clothing, etc. as necessities. Personal services were required or found even in primitive tribes where health, recreation, and religion were present. Sales and trade also took place in the early times of history at the barter level of trade. Of course, the current finance, banking, insurance subsectors are a more

TABLE I

MAJOR SECTORS OF A CITY

A. Personal Goods

    1. Food

    2. Housing

    3. Clothing

    4. Equipment

B. Personal Services

    1. Health

    2. Recreation and Entertainment

    3. Religion

    4. Legal

C. Sales and Trade

    1. Retail Sales

    2. Wholesale Sales

    3. Finance and Banking

    4. Insurance

    5. Real Estate

D. Government

    1. Protection (Defense)

    2. Education

    3. Administration

    4. State and National Government

    5. Environment

    6. Welfare

E. Industry

    1. Agriculture, Forestry, Fisheries

    2. Mining

    3. Contract Construction

    4. Manufacturing

F. Utilities

    1. Energy

    2. Communications

    3. Transportation

    4. Water and Sanitation

modern facet of city activities.

The government sector is an increasingly important part of the
city as protection, education, administration, and other
activities are needed and provided as services to the inhabitants.   Increasingly a role for government is developing in
environment and welfare.   Industry is another sector of the
city which has changed with time as agricultural emphases have
decreased and manufacturing activities have developed and grown.
Mining and construction have changed significantly over the
years.   The utility sector represents in some respects the most
recent, in a historical sense, of the city's activities; it
includes energy, communications, as relative newcomers as well
as transportation and water which have been of concern from
olden times.

In order to obtain the necessary information about a city and
its sectors and subsectors, one should take advantage of the
considerable data which are available on people, trained man-
power, businesses, money, and other resources and needs under
the present systems of data gathering.   It may be necessary
however to obtain these data more frequently in time, or more
specifically in detail, than has heretofore been reported.
Further, for other sectors such as personal service, or subsectors such as religion, legal, and environment there may be
considerably less information known about the relationship of
the effort expended to the effectiveness of the results.

The initial efforts with regard to the sectors and subsectors
of the city are to obtain information on the inputs and outputs
from each to the others.   These inputs and outputs should be
expressed in terms of materials and energy flows, money, man-
power, equipment, information, and other pertinent terms.
Figure 2 illustrates in input/output terms some of the inter-
connections and flows among the major sectors.   In reality,
for each goods or service which moves from a sector there is a
reverse flow of money or credit to serve as payment.   The flows
shown on Fig. 2 are representative rather than complete.   In
addition to the various sectors of a city providing other sectors with inputs, there will be imports and exports from other
geographic areas that may provide significant materials, equipment, money, and other goods and services that enable a city to
meet its needs.

The operations that have been outlined above provide the basis
for understanding in terms of men, money, materials, equipment,
etc. what is taking place in a city.   From the study of such
data, it should be possible to identify what appear to be the

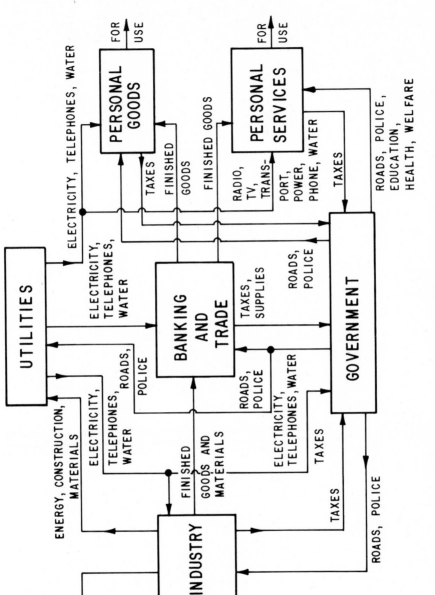

FIGURE 2: SECTOR INPUTS/OUTPUTS OF A CITY

critical areas where too much or too little of the various city
resources presently exist, and to suggest ways in which in the
future a better match between needs and capabilities can be
achieved. The organized information about the city can provide
individuals and organizations the necessary data for business,
government, industries, and educational institutions to improve
their decision-making capability in planning and operations for
both the short-time and longer-time needs of the city.

Figure 3 shows that the city and its sectors can have data
gathered from them. The data can be organized and made
available for display. They are then ready for use by the many
decision-makers--governmental, industrial, business, education
and others who have need of such data for planning and operating
the city and its sectors. Data from other sources provide
information about opportunities, other cities' experiences,
and future changes that are likely to take place. Some of these
changes may be favorable, others unfavorable; the main thing
is to have sufficient warning about possible situations which
require action in sufficient time to take the appropriate steps.

The important thing that is being presented here is the idea
that a city as a human settlement requires that many different
areas of activity be operated simultaneously with different
objectives and interacting processes producing results that are
not always understood at the time of the actions. It appears
that if cities in the future are going to be able to meet these
various objectives in a satisfactory fashion, better information
must be made available to decision-makers in sufficient time
and with sufficient data to enable them to take appropriate
and timely action.

COMPARISONS BETWEEN CITIES--A STUDY OF EXPERIMENTS

Having prepared such a set of input/output balances for one
city, it would be of interest to see how this information
compares with such data for other cities in other parts of the
country or of the world. If one considers each city to be
running an experiment on how best to operate a city, it would
be useful to be able to compare the results of these experiments from several different cities having significant
similarities. Since it takes considerable time and money
and inconvenience to make major changes in a city, it is
desirable for the people responsible for making such major
changes to have some prior information about the likely outcome
from similar changes that were already made elsewhere, hopefully
under comparable conditions.

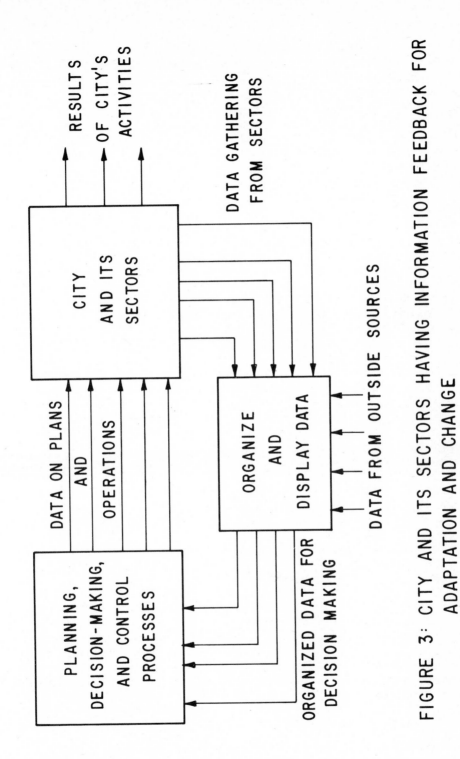

FIGURE 3: CITY AND ITS SECTORS HAVING INFORMATION FEEDBACK FOR ADAPTATION AND CHANGE

To the extent that common ways of understanding the operation of
cities can be developed and used for comparable cities, this
would make it possible for such information to be used more
readily and be more effective for purposes of data exchange.
Although it is clear that different social, political, and
economic bases for operation are to be found in different cities
throughout the world, there are certain physical, material, and
human phenomena which are relatively less affected by the obvious differences. Hopefully, in time it will be possible to
identify what transformations or changes are applicable to the
data among the comparable cities.

Already in some instances such as in the case of traffic lights,
air traffic control, electric power distribution, telephone
exchanges, radio, supermarkets, and hotel chains, some efforts
are taking place to use experience gained in one part of the
world to be applied elsewhere. Hopefully, more of this can
be considered in the future to help our rapidly growing cities
to be more comfortable and more enjoyable places in which to
live.

CONCLUSIONS

It is more and more a man-made world in which more and more
people are living in cities. There must be found better ways
of understanding what is taking place in the cities and what can
be done about continually modifying the cities to make them
more livable and enjoyable for their inhabitants.

In order for this understanding of cities to take place more
effectively, data are needed from the many experiences which are
currently taking place in parallel in the many cities of the
world. It is proposed here that the city be considered as a
feedback system made up of major sectors and subsectors, and
that data be gathered in an ongoing fashion for these sectors
and subsectors as well as for the various material, men, money,
and equipment variables which interconnect them.

Interested and capable people should be charged with the task
of describing the city in a reasonably common format, getting
the data for this format, and making it available for use by
the interested parties. Combinations of representatives from
business, industry, government and education should analyze the
data and suggest ways in which individual cities can be improved
for the future.

A proper social balance must be sought between freedom for the
individual to live what he or she considers to be a worthwhile

life, and regulation or control based upon the overall group
needs and the requirement that the society can exist and
flourish.   To accomplish this worthwhile objective is a necessary and challenging task.

A stepped-up and ongoing effort is needed on both a national
and international basis for determining what sort of data
are needed, how they will be used, and how they should be
gathered.   After such data have been obtained, it should be
possible to understand better and more quickly the rapidly
changing sociotechnical-economic system of which cities are
an important part.

PLANNING FOR UNCERTAINTY
AN APPROACH FOR DECISION MAKERS[1]

Mahlon Apgar, IV
Principal, McKinsey & Company, Inc.

RISK is becoming a vital term in the lexicon of urban decision makers. As economic uncertainties loom large, and stringent spending restraints are imposed, they will have to look more critically at current and future proposals for new developments than in the boom years of the early 1970s. Indeed, of all the choices they must make, none will be more challenging than deciding among alternative development strategies and individual investment possibilities. What makes these decisions so demanding in an era of rapid and fundamental change is not the task of projecting alternative futures under a given set of assumptions, but the difficulty of arriving at the right assumption and weighing their probable impact. Each assumption involves some uncertainty. Taken together, the combined uncertainties of many assumptions - each different in its effects - can multiply into a total uncertainty of critical proportions. This is where the element of risk enters; and it is in the evaluation and containment of risk that neither decision makers nor their advisers are well-served by conventional planning approaches and techniques.

In an attempt to fill this gap, a process called commitment planning has been developed for identifying and reducing the formidable risks of urban development. Commitment planning helps decision makers in both the public and private sectors to limit their exposure, contain capital and operating costs, and preserve future flexibility by highlighting the critical conditions and contingencies that should be evaluated before new or expanded commitments to a project, area, or form of development are made. It also provides a basis for reviewing the key assumptions and concepts guiding ongoing projects when unexpected events require changes in public investment and development strategy.

As important as the process itself, however, is the understanding among decision makers and planners alike that a new approach is needed to cope with change. Thus, the first section of this paper summarizes the main limitations of conventional planning practice in recognizing risk. Then, the basic structure of the commitment planning process is outlined. Finally, a concluding note raises the questions a decision maker can ask to assess whether commitment planning would be useful in his situation.

LIMITATIONS OF CURRENT
PLANNING PRACTICE

Despite considerable lip service to the idea of flexible development
strategies and advanced simulation techniques to test the effects of change,
little has been done to implement responsive planning processes that are
geared to achieving results. As MacMurray puts it (with specific reference
to the British planning system):

> "Structure plans, town centre maps, district plans, are
> said to be flexible and responsive to uncertainty, but
> are used as rigid prescriptions where it is comfortable
> or politically necessary to promote certainty. At the
> same time, planners decide on applications in an ad
> hoc and incremental way, responding to uncertainty
> implicitly by making 'best judgements' on a day-to-day
> basis, but still bemoaning the lack of a structure plan
> context that offers certainty." [2]

This paradox stems partly from the nature of development risks themselves. Important new schemes always present alluring ultimate prospects in
the form of grand designs and massive construction projects. Yet the long
time span all too frequently confounds the originators' hopes and intentions:
early assumptions about costs, absorption rates and development pace can
become a drain on available funds, time and energy.

Moreover, the high visibility of development programmes subjects them
to the scrutiny of environmentalists and other interest groups, and their complexity forces the development agency to rely on the cooperation, support or
approval of an ever-widening array of other bodies. Hence, the inherent
uncertainties of long-term planning assumptions are multiplied by the vulner-
ability of these programmes to external events.

Likewise, critical planning assumptions may be invalidated long after
commitments have been made by changes in demand for specific project
features. A persistent challenge for urban planners is to recognize the
mundane reality that people measure successful development by the workability
of minute details - not by the conceptual elegance of grand strategies. Is the
bus stop conveniently located? Are there enough shops of the right type to
meet local needs viably? Is the street furniture comfortable and durable? Is
the TV reception good? These and hundreds of other criteria determine
overall performance yet are curiously overlooked when planning assumptions
are adopted that may curtail future opportunities for effective response.

Thus, the problem in urban development, more than in most human
enterprise, is that once initial commitments have been made it is hard to
change direction to meet new conditions. Beyond market-related demand
fluctuations - in land-use mix, housing types, commercial facilities - existing
political commitments, infrastructure and community facilities further limit the
alternatives.

The 'commitment effect' - that initial plans and occasional investment decisions to extend a development programme influence its entire direction and determine prospective viability - is reflected in several ways. Though the direct financial commitment may appear small, substantial subsequent commitments are thus implied. The local commitment, made with the choice and purchase of a site, is determined by specific environmental conditions that may be largely unexplored. A political commitment is also involved, because to renege on intentions expressed at the time of purchase would result in serious loss of local credibility and reduce the possibility of exploiting other opportunities. Finally, a managerial commitment is made in terms of a declaration of growth intentions and of an implied promise to staff that the project will be going ahead.

A realistic assessment of key project commitments, of course, would be based on a detailed evaluation of all the elements of the project that affect costs and revenues - i.e., markets, buildings, services, and their phasing over time - as well as on an assessment of how the various uncertainties (e.g., environmental delays) would affect it. But when a purchase or expansion decision seems urgent, as it usually will, most of the risks in these commitments go unrecognized until it is too late to turn back.

While many analytic tools and methods are available to help the planner and developer overcome the inherent risks, current planning practice has three major shortcomings. First, technical details, important as they are to the specialists, may easily obscure key issues for the decision-maker. Analyses are often too narrow to highlight overriding policy issues, yet without some overall idea about the criteria for success, the essential elements of a project, and the relative importance of various issues that might be raised, much planning effort can be wasted on detailed plans for project components - e.g., sophisticated communications or transportation systems, ecological control techniques, recreational facilities - that are ultimately excluded from the final development plan.

Second, financial and market analyses often are weak. Despite the amount and level of technical detail usually provided, planning processes are dominated by the tasks and techniques of land use planning, engineering, architectural design, and construction. Relatively less attention is paid to thorough evaluation of market and financial results covering year-by-year outcomes, life-of-project cash flows, break-even analyses, sensitivity testing, competitive strengths and weaknesses, and the product/market mix. While these concerns are typically associated with private sector sponsors, there is just as much need to approach public investment decisions on a rigorous, business-like basis. The mix of objectives may differ, but the need for analytic depth to underpin commitment decisions is pronounced.

Finally, risk analysis and contingency planning are seldom used. The desire to create momentum in a new project may encourage an extensive commitment to facilities, programmes and products without considering the constraints these commitments may place on future flexibility. Moreover, with effort concentrated on solving the physical problems of site planning and construction, relatively little attention is paid to the evaluation of risk and planning for predictable contingencies. Market, financial and physical plans are typically based on single-value assumptions of prices, sales rates, costs, etc., rather than on probable ranges. The development plan is laid out for the whole site, rather than being staged to accommodate future changes. Land uses and infrastructure are determined for the total life of the project - even if it has a 10- to 15-year programme well beyond existing capabilities to make prudent forecasts with any degree of confidence. Project image is defined and targets are set by the amenities, product types, and prices chosen at that stage in planning.

Obvious as they may seem, these inadequacies can reach absurd proportions. In one major project reviewed recently, the loan covenants prescribed the types of use in extreme detail - e.g., '4,200 sq. ft. of shoe store space' - projected to 1995. Yet no estimates had been built in to accommodate unexpected changes, nor had the key sensitivities of overall project economics been determined as a basis for financing arrangements. Hence, it should have been no surprise that the development was in technical default almost from the day construction began, and radical restructuring was eventually required. Moreover, the value of early analysis as a basis for more prudent commitments was completely diluted.

Containing and overcoming the limitations of current practice is possible with a different approach to the planning process. Plans should be focused on defining the key issues and contingencies before major financial, political and organizational commitments are made. The development concept and approach should be derived from thorough local product/market and site analysis, avoiding overreliance on untested assumptions and behavioural theories. Commitments should be based on full life-of-project cash and contingency planning to ensure that the project can withstand potential delays, uncertainties and liquidity constraints now being faced in many major projects. And, finally, future development options must be preserved by carefully staging project commitments and the development activities that ensue.

COMMITMENT PLANNING:
A STRATEGIC APPROACH

Commitment planning is designed to implement these principles by helping the decision maker to avoid overexposure, retain his flexibility, and maintain control over numerous activities, despite mounting pressures on his time and resources. It comprises four main stages, each quite simple in concept: (1) quick, economical definition of needs and opportunities before project planning starts; (2) evaluation of alternative 'project concepts' before making the key decision to go ahead; (3) development of a 'commitment plan' to define both the decision routes open and the risks involved in taking them before any major investment is made in the project; and (4) establishment of effective implementation controls before undertaking detailed planning or construction. Such a strategy is designed to build progressively on success

while preserving the flexibility to withdraw or redefine the plans at each
phase of development.

Stage 1:   Defining
Development Needs

Before committing themselves to a site proposed for acquisition or development, both the development organization and the associated bodies obviously
need considerable information on the area and the site itself.   But the data
must be geared to the needs of the decision maker – not, as is customary, to
those of planners, researchers, statisticians and other specialists.   Each aspect
of the local product/service mix, site features and political conditions may of
course need to be extensively analysed.   But the decision maker needs only
those key facts that will enable him quickly and economically to identify the
most promising priority areas in terms of needs, compare sites within those
areas, spotlight the significant risks associated with each, and set up sound
policy criteria to guide site selection and project planning.

To obtain a broad overview of existing needs and constraints, yet
avoid an information overload, data will be needed on (1) general economic
conditions – e.g., population and employment base size and growth – bearing
specifically on the relative strengths and weaknesses of the site under consideration; (2) demand levels and patterns; (3) product characteristics,
including site size and features, existing services, etc.; and (4) environmental factors, such as building, planning and pollution control regulations.

Having assessed the site's opportunities and limitations, the decision
makers involved, usually drawn from a variety of organizations with different
and often competing interests, must agree on their common goals, criteria and
resources, which can constrain project feasibility just as significantly as can
physical or economic factors.   Rough planning guidelines should be drawn up
specifying (1) financial, social, political and environmental criteria; (2) relevant experience in designs, layouts, facilities and equipment from previous
successful projects; and (3) overall assumptions – e.g., cost and availability
of capital, waiting list allocation procedures, etc.   These guidelines can later
be challenged and further refined if necessary.

Stage 2:   Evaluating
Project Concepts

Once the development opportunity has been identified and defined in
outline, it is possible to formulate a complete, quantified description of target
groups, land uses, buildings and community facilities, and the respective
roles envisaged for those organizations to be involved in the development.
The decisions that must now be made on each of these points will collectively
set the overall level of managerial and financial commitment and establish the
framework for all the thousands of activities in the development process.

Drawing on the data gathered in Stage 1, a set of alternative development concepts for the site area is first sketched out in a few weeks.   Next,
the target markets are specified for each concept.   The key elements here are

total size, patterns of growth and mobility over the project life, and expected
user requirements.   Only the main demographic characteristics of the target
groups used should be included - e.g., age and income ranges, occupations,
family size - as well as data on the retail, office and/or industrial base that
will be needed to support the projected concept.

From all this structured information it is relatively ease to derive the
mix of 'products' (houses, shops, offices) required to serve these target
groups. The variety of possible product and price ranges for most large
projects is obviously immense and, of course, new breakthroughs in building
technology are making it possible to build structures that can be readily
adapted to different uses over time. As density increases, mixed-use projects
are becoming more acceptable, so that shops, flats, restaurants, and a host of
support services are brought together in a single building. Hence, it is well
worth brainstorming the possibilities of various product/user options with a
knowledgeable group of experts from various disciplines (i.e., design, social
services), laced with the ideas of housewives, shopkeepers and others who
represent the users' viewpoints. A few days invested at the front end in
creative analysis, spliced with the fact base from Stage 1, will pay rich
dividends in better decisions and more acceptable products.

The wise decision maker will also seek, through negotiation with the
other participants in the development process, to structure their respective
contributions to reduce his risks and leverage his resources. Since most projects will lend themselves to a variety of such arrangements, it is advisable,
when projecting construction time, throughput and cash flow, to quantify
ranges rather than single values.

To avoid unnecessary work later on, a product specification should be
drawn up summarizing for each concept the type and number of units, price
range, pace and density assumptions thus far. Comparisons can then be made,
using consistent figures, and detailed changes can be evaluated without having
to re-examine the entire range of assumptions.

The completed project concept, then, lays out quantified working
assumptions on target groups, products, developer roles and development pace,
which can now be weighed against the criteria set out in Stage 1. The most
significant determinants of cash flow will also need to be assessed to see how
potential strikes, delays in planning approval and other such contingencies
could affect the project's viability.

During this stage, important issues that might otherwise be overlooked
may come to light. For example, one project concept for a 50-acre site would
have required twice as much space and three times as much investment in
leisure, community facilities and support programmes to break even as either
of two viable alternatives. This concept had originally been favoured by the
project team because of its higher projected sales, but once the support
requirements were spelled out they saw that it came nowhere near meeting
the established development criteria.

Conceptually, the procedure just described is simple enough, but it can prove troublesome in practice, since many decision makers would rather rely on intuitive judgement and on 'feel' than grapple with needlessly complicated analyses that are produced by their staff specialists. But it is vitally important for establishing a coherent, consistent basis for development and investment decisions. Also, of course, the project concept will be indispensable as a summary of working assumptions and forecasts, should unforeseen changes demand that the chosen concept be modified later on.

Stage 3: Developing A Commitment Plan

Unrealistic forecasts of cost structure and the timing of site services and planning approval, or random delays resulting from labour or technical problems, can play havoc with a project's viability. The commitment plan helps the decision makers to minimize these risks and preserve future flexibility by highlighting his options at each stage of development and phasing all commitments - financial, physical, managerial, political - in the light of the project's risk profile. By dividing the project life cycle into phases and specifying contingency plans for the key uncertainties of each phase, it compels all concerned to take the effects of uncertainty explicitly into account.

There are two main steps in developing a commitment plan: (1) pinpointing the key uncertainties; and (2) structuring the plan to provide a framework for action in light of both upside and downside potential.

1. __Pinpointing uncertainties__. Possible variations in assumptions can, of course, easily affect the very feasibility of a project concept. If the local government is 2 years behind in provision of planned roads or sewers, the costs of delay can easily double. The impact of such variations on relative performance (unit volumes, costs, subsidies, prices) can be just as drastic. For example, if a typical residential project was only 80 per cent complete on its Year 1 target, peak debt would far exceed the expected limit, eliminating the next 3 years' cash flow. Assumptions relating to feasibility should be discussed at the time when financing is negotiated, since it may turn out that the project is doomed unless the concept is changed. Variances from performance assumptions are more likely to affect the amount and structure of early financing, or to alter the detailed phasing of implementation.

The most volatile elements of revenue, cost and timing can often be discerned intuitively, but careful analysis will be required to get a precise idea of their respective financial and political impacts and pinpoint those relatively few combinations of circumstances that could destroy the project's feasibility or undermine its attractiveness.

2. __Structuring the commitment plan__. Once the key uncertainties in the project concept have been identified, the developer and his financial sources can turn to the task of laying out and staging the elements of the overall commitment plan: __products__ (e.g., buildings, facilities, sewers) and

programmes (e.g., letting, construction, financing). By agreeing to base future commitments on the attainment of specified results at specified future decision points, they will avoid premature investment.

The first step is to define the strategic options for each element of the project concept. Typically, several possibilities can be identified at each critical point in the development process - for example:

-    Advance - the strategy to be pursued to achieve the
     expected results, assuming that all goes according to
     plan

-    Hold - a 'wait and see' strategy to be adopted if the
     project is in trouble, where pulling out would be
     premature in view of progress already achieved and
     commitments made but not yet implemented

-    Withdraw - the strategy to be used if the original
     prospects for success have evaporated, or the pro-
     ject has run into such serious trouble that no
     satisfactory holding strategy is available.

The decision maker will usually pursue an 'advance' strategy, repre-senting a commitment great enough to ensure initial acceptance without swamp-ing the project with financing and overhead costs should later expectations fail to materialize on schedule. In order to be able to exploit unforeseen opportunities, 'advance' strategies will need to be structured carefully at each stage of the process.

Obviously, each strategic option will have to be worked out in some detail, specifying facilities, site uses, and the key financial, spatial and political factors. These options, built up on a piecemeal basis for each major element, such as residential, retail, office, etc., are then aggregated in an overall commitment plan. Figure 1 summarizes the range of strategies for these elements in a large, mixed-use project.

Based on the benchmarks set out in Stage 1, criteria for the choice of the appropriate strategy (advance, hold or withdraw) are established at each checkpoint as illustrated at the bottom of Exhibit 1. These criteria simply specify what results should have been achieved at the checkpoint to justify the selection of a particular route. The checkpoints do not merely mark the phases of development; rather, they signal decision points where feasibility, assumptions about the future, risks, and strategic direction are formally reassessed against overall criteria, in the light of results achieved and new conditions prevailing at that time.

Though he will have a fairly firm idea of where he wants to end up, the decision maker cannot know at the start of his journey the exact route he will take or what detours he may encounter. At A, B, C, etc., therefore, detailed criteria can be established for a reasonable planning horizon - say,

Physical Financial Control

EXHIBIT 1

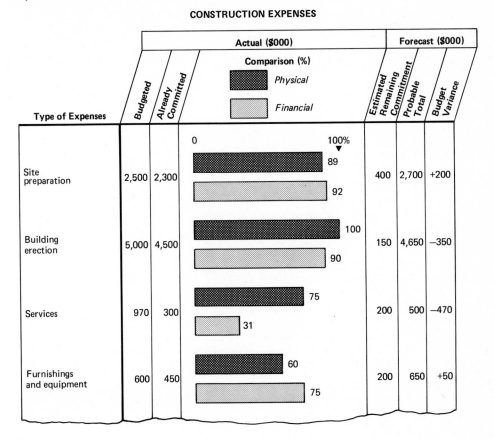

CONSTRUCTION EXPENSES

18-24 months - and the commitment plan refined, given the economics of the decision at that point. These detailed criteria, too, are subject to major uncertainties even over that short period, so the aim here is not to target specific results but rather to establish ranges of performance and investment levels. The presentation format illustrated has proved helpful in visualizing the main strategies - i.e., the alternative directions for action at each stage - and highlighting the implications of each.

Unlike a critical path network, the commitment plan is selective rather than comprehensive, focusing on a handful of key performance indicators and 'make-or-break' activities. By highlighting those elements in the project that will critically change the risk, return and cash-flow profiles if events do not go according to plan, it provides a basis for setting overall business and investment priorities.

Stage 4:   Setting Up Effective Controls

Control of implementation is an integral part of effective commitment planning. In today's environment, however, the comprehensive information and reporting systems of the 1960s have proved cumbersome, costly and ineffective. Simpler, more flexible measures are needed to keep a day-to-day watch over large funds flows and volatile requirements and to move quickly when corrective action is needed. Controls must answer the key questions at each commitment planning checkpoint: Are project elements proceeding according to plan? Are costs under control, both against budget and against physical progress on site? Are revenues and planned surpluses for quality investments being maximized? Should the cash plan be revised to accommodate a possible shortfall in the next period?

Traditional financial controls, geared mainly to tracking progress, are unable to meet this need directly. Comparing financial results with financial forecasts will not show how sources and uses of funds are linked to physical results. Fundamental questions thus go unanswered. Have we paid what we planned for actual construction thus far? Have budget targets been achieved by building less or building to a lower quality, thus risking the market? Cash slippage can, of course, be detected in any good cash management system. But correct diagnosis of overruns or surpluses requires comparison of physical and financial results.

The basic technique is to match construction and lettings progress against actual cash flows, in light of the forecasts at each checkpoint. This means comparing committed funds with their corresponding construction targets. The 'commitment value', expressed as a percentage of budget, is compared with physical measures - e.g., square feet of building space, road miles - expressed as a percentage of the total called for in the plan. For example, in Exhibit 2, building erection has required commitments of only 90 per cent of the budget for 100 per cent of planned construction. Since additional work costing $150,000 remains, the probable total forecast is

EXHIBIT 2

Commitment Plan

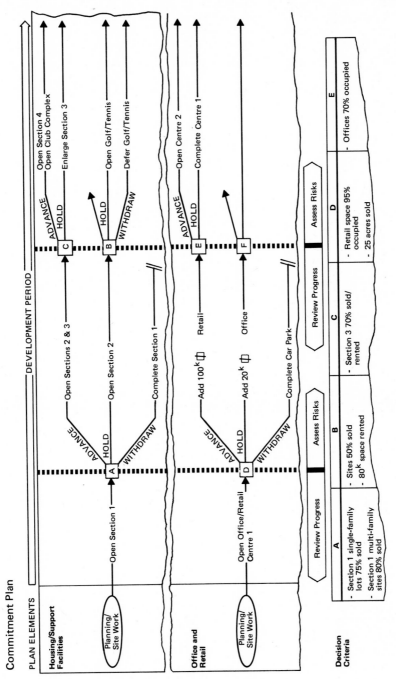

$4.6 million compared with $5 million budgeted - a possible surplus of $400,000. On the other hand, expenditure on furnishings and equipment is already running 15 percentage points ahead of actual procurement and installation and is headed for an overrun of $50,000.

To express commitments in physical terms is not difficult, given thorough preparation of the forecasts. For example, when plans and contracts for each project element are drawn up, the approximate percentage that each section of a site, building, etc., represents in physical terms, can be calculated with little extra effort. Both construction expenses and operating cash flow - i.e., comparing the percentage square feet of office space leased with the percentage of total income expected - can be included.

Coupled with the usual measures of project status and conventional cash accounting, simple data such as these can help the investor or lender to track performance and progress during the crucial preliminary stages of development. They enable the developer to evaluate his remaining commitments - i.e., what activities and expenditure remain, what revenues can be expected - forecast further slippages, and take timely defensive action.

CONCLUDING NOTE

Like any management tool, commitment planning must be tailored to the purposes and style of the development organization and the characteristics of its projects. But the need for close, continuing audits of basic assumptions and past results before commitments are initiated or extended is well-nigh universal. Any decision maker would be well advised to ask four questions:

-   Do our current project plans identify all the key
    issues and contingencies before we negotiate major
    financial and political commitments?

-   Has our development concept been explicitly derived
    from thorough site analysis and consistently linked
    to the specific conclusions drawn from the analysis?

-   Have we identified our key assumptions? Do we
    know the potential impact on project feasibility and
    performance if any one of them should prove to
    have been over-optimistic?

-   Can the agreed commitments and current cash
    structure withstand these potential uncertainties?

If the answer to any of these questions is 'no', the investment in question is probably carrying a higher risk than necessary, and its viability is threatened. Both problems can be resolved through consistent application of the principles of comprehensive, rigorous review that are the core of the commitment planning process.

REFERENCES

1. This paper is adapted from Apgar (ed.), <u>New</u>
    <u>Perspectives on Community Development</u>,
    McGraw-Hill, 1976, Chapters 5-7.

2. MacMurray T., 'Planning for Market Uncertainties',
    <u>The Planner</u>, Vol. 60, No. 8, September-October
    1974.

ENVIRONMENTAL QUALITY, PUBLIC GOOD AMENITIES AND LOCAL GOVERNMENT POLICY: AN OPERATIONAL POLICY

Albert M. Church
The University of New Mexico

Urban sprawl, the degredation of environmental quality and the high public and social costs of local government supplied public services have all engendered demands for tax and expenditure policy and direct land use controls to mollify these undesirable effects of contemporary urban life. However, these direct and indirect policy tools have been formulated on an ad hoc, piecemeal and largely uncoordinated basis. The result is often an inconsistent hodge podge of policy tools. One reason for this failure is the inability to specify and measure precisely how each individual tax, subsidy, or regulation affects a desired target and how effects interrelate when multiple targets achieved through multiple policies are desired. However, the crux of the problem is the specification and measurement of social goals. Land use planners heretofore have relied on received theory, intuition, and "political realities" in formulating goals and plans to achieve them.

Economists have devoted a good deal of energy to the problem of environmental management by primarily relying on the theory of externalities. This body of knowledge demonstrates how the private marketplace may be inefficient or break down when an action by one individual directly affects the well being of one or more other individuals where voluntary compensation might not be forthcoming. The voluntary exchange of one individual's hourly services for a wage normally engenders no externalities, whereas coerced criminal exchanges or a power generating plant polluting the air and affecting the health and aesthetics of nearby property owners are examples of externalities. Efficient resource use requires that criminal coercion be dissuaded and that air pollution be regulated and its damaging effects be compensated for. A major problem with externality theory as applied to environmental quality is measuring the publics' willingness to pay for this amenity.

Some argue that the market place internalizes externalities either by the receptor bribing the creator to modify his activity or the courts assigning the receptor the right to sue for damages. However, an optimal voluntary solution may fail for two reasons. The first is that the cost of organizing a large number of receptors without the use of government coercion may be larger than the potential gains from modifying an externality. Take air pollution resulting from private automobile emissions. The cost of organizing those affected to negotiate with the large number of automobile owners and drivers is obviously enormous. A second problem is that if an activity is modified, the beneficial effects may not be able to be excluded from non participants e.g. air pollution. This "free rider" problem is a primary characteristic of "public goods" - those goods which cannot be divided among members of society e.g. national defense and air quality.

The free rider problem implies that government bureauracies must indirectly measure the "demand" for public goods since individuals have an incentive not to reveal their true preferences when they can consume the public good without being "charged" for it. However, public goods which are either technologically linked or associated in consumption activities with private goods can have their demand estimated indirectly through the linked private good. The environmental quality amenity varies among and within regions by location. It has been shown both theoretically (Mäler[2], Polinsky[4], Strotz[7])and empirically (Church[1], Oates[3], Ridker[6]) that the marketplace capitalizes the consumers evaluation of public good amenities and environmental quality into land prices. It should then be asked does this relationship then provide the "proper" signals for local governments in formulating land use policies? If land prices are the appropriate targets for policy, a simultaneous empirical estimate of how policy tools and their indirect effects on environmental quality affect land prices will provide an operational guide. Portney and Sonstelie [5] have shown that if amenities are purely private goods, then property value maximization is an appropriate target for local governments. Here we analyze the effects of public goods and externalities.

In order to investigate the relationship of individual consumer choice, maximization of social welfare and the validity of property value maximization as the objective of local government policy it is necessary to specify models of economic behavior. We investigate a simplified model of h consumers whose preferences are summarized by utility functions (U^h) and who consume land in two zones. Utility is assumed to be a function of a private good (X^h), land in each zone (L_1^h, L_2^h) and the public good of site amenities or environmental quality where all residents in a zone experience identical environmental conditions. L_1^h represents the proportion of land in zone 1 consumed by individual h. This public good is expressed as a function of the relative amenities or environmental quality in each zone ($Z = Z (Z_1,Z_2)$:

$$U^h = U^h (X^h, L_1^h, L_2^h, Z) \qquad \sum_h L_1^h = 1 \quad ; \quad \sum_h L_2^h = 1$$

It is further assumed for simplicity that the public good is the only distinguishing feature between the zones and it follows that the marginal rate of substitution between the zones (partial derivatives are denoted with subscripts) is solely a function of their relative environmental quality (see Mäler [2], pp 192-195):

$$\frac{U_1^h}{U_2^h} = MRS_{12}^h = B^h (Z) \tag{1}$$

Rearranging (1) gives:

$$\frac{U_1^h}{B^h} = U_2^h \tag{2}$$

which is a partial differential equation the solution of which is:

$$C = B^h L_1^h + L_2^h \tag{3}$$

Substituting (3) in the utility function gives:

$$U^h = U^h \, (B^h \, L_1^h + L_2^h, \ X^h, \ Z)$$

We assume that if the demand for the public good is zero, then the demand for complementary private goods is zero. This assumption of weak complementarity is weaker than strict complementarity (see Mäler[2], pp 183–185) and allows the utility function to be expressed by

$$U^h = U^h \, [B^h \, (Z) \, L_1^h + L_2^h, \ X^h] \tag{4}$$

Given the normalized price (P_1, P_2) and the property tax (T_1, T_2) in each zone, the normalized price of the private good (P_x) and consumer income (Y^h) allows us to write the budget constraint as:

$$Y^h - [\ (P_1 + T_1) \ L_1^h + (P_2 + T_2) \ L_2^h + P_x \ X^h \ ] \geq 0 \tag{5}$$

Consumer choice can be described as maximizing (4) subject to (5) where λ^h is the Lagrangean multiplier. The corresponding first order conditions are:

$$U_1^h \, B^h - \lambda^h \, (P_1 + T_1) \leq 0$$

$$U_1^h - \lambda^h \, (P_2 + T_2) \leq 0$$

$$U_2^h - \lambda^h \, P_x \leq 0$$

Solving for the multiplier and assuming an interior solution gives:

$$\lambda^h = \frac{U_2^h}{P_X} = \frac{U_1^h}{(P_2 + T_2)} = \frac{U_1^h \, B^h}{(P_1 + T_1)} \tag{6}$$

Since B^h is soley a function of Z, (6) implies the following conditions:

$$B^h > (P_1 + T_1) \ / \ (P_2 + T_2) \ X_1^h > 0; \ X_2^h = 0$$

$$B^h < (P_1 + T_1) \ / \ (P_2 + T_2) \ X_1^h = 0; \ X_2^h > 0$$

If we make the stringent assumption that B^h is the same for all consumers, then in market equilibrium we have:

$$B = (P_1 + T_1) \ / \ (P_2 + T_2) \tag{7}$$

Relationship (7) implies that market prices adjusted for taxes reflect differences in public good amenities and environmental quality.

Societal optimization requires that the social welfare function be optimized subject to a fixed supply of the private good $(\bar{X})$ and land in zone 1 $(\bar{L}_1)$ and zone 2 $(\bar{L}_2)$. Furthermore, the availability of public good site amenities (access, utilities, zoning controls etc.) as well as regulation which affect environmental quality requires resource inputs. We assume that tax revenues from each zone equal the cost of supplying the public good (a balanced budget in each zone). For simplicity the public good (Z_1, Z_2) is assumed to be measured in dollars and to be supplied at constant marginal costs. Maximizing a weighted sum (the weights (α^h) are arbitrary welfare weights, or the partials of the Bergson social welfare function) of individual utilities (a proxy for the social welfare function) yields Pareto optimality (economic efficiency). The problem becomes [Lagrangean multipliers are expressed to the left of each constraint and recalling that $Z = Z(Z_1, Z_2)$]:

$$\max \ \sum_h \alpha^h \ U^h \ [B^h \ (Z) \ L_1^h + L_2^h, \ X^h]$$

$$\text{s.t.} \ P_X \ [1 - \sum_h X^h \geq 0]$$

$$P_1 \ [1 - \sum_h L_1^h \geq 0]$$

$$P_2 \ [1 - \sum_h L_2^h \geq 0]$$

$$\delta_1 \ [\sum_h L_1^h \ T_1 - Z_1 \geq 0]$$

$$\delta_2 \ [\sum_h L_2^h \ T_2 - Z_2 \geq 0]$$

The first order conditions are:

$$\alpha^h \ B^h \ U_1^h - P_1 + \delta_1 \ T_1 \leq 0 \tag{8}$$

$$\alpha^h \ U_1^h - P_2 + \delta_2 \ T_2 \leq 0 \tag{9}$$

$$\alpha^h \ U_2^h - P_X \leq 0$$

$$\sum_h \alpha^h \ U_{Bh}^h \ B_1^h \ L_1^h - \delta_1 \leq 0 \tag{10}$$

$$\sum_h \alpha^h \ U_{Bh}^h \ B_2^h \ L_2^h - \delta_2 \leq 0 \tag{11}$$

The first order conditions differ from those found for individual utility maximization (6) in that the public good is a policy instrument which government must optimize. Conditions (8) and (9) diverge from (6) by the factor that taxes (T_1 and T_2) direct resources into supplying the public good and thus individual preferences ($\alpha^h \ B^h \ U_1^h$; $\alpha^h \ U_1^h$) plus societal evaluation of the public good [the first term in (10) and (11)] weighted by the tax rate must equal the shadow price of scarce land (P_1, P_2). Conditions (10) and (11) are those for the optimal supply of a public good in that the <u>sum</u> of individual marginal utilities equal the marginal cost (in terms of <u>taxes</u>) of supplying the good.

Problems of revealing preferences for public goods, in measuring and aggregating utility functions, and in specifing welfare weights means that maximizing a social welfare function is a non-operational concept. However, market equilibrium expressed by individual choice (7) implies that property taxes and public goods are capitalized into the price of land. A policy of maximizing aggregate land rents in each zone wherein the indirect effects of the property tax and the locational effect of public good amenities are the public policy tools yield some beneficial insights. The objective is to maximize total land value:

$$\text{max.} \quad P_1 (T_1, Z_1) + P_2 (T_2, Z_2)$$

subject to the constraint that the government budget in each zone is balanced (the multipliers are λ_1, λ_2);

$$\text{s.t.} \quad \lambda_2[T_1 - Z_1 \geq 0]$$

$$\lambda_2 [T_2 - Z_z \geq 0].$$

The first order conditions are:

$$\frac{\partial P_1}{\partial T_1} + \lambda_1 \leq 0$$

$$\frac{\partial P_2}{\partial T_2} + \lambda_2 \leq 0$$

$$\frac{\partial P_1}{\partial Z_1} - \lambda_1 \leq 0$$

$$\frac{\partial P_1}{\partial Z_2} - \lambda_2 \leq 0$$

Assuming an interior solution and solving for the multipliers gives:

$$\frac{\partial P_1}{\partial T_1} + \frac{\partial P_1}{\partial Z_1} = 0 \qquad\qquad (12)$$

$$\frac{\partial P_2}{\partial T_2} + \frac{\partial P_2}{\partial Z_2} = 0 \qquad\qquad (13)$$

Expressions (12) and (13) state that public good amenities and environmental

quality should be enhanced in each zone until the point that the marginal cost
of supplying it in terms of taxes diminishing market price is equal to the
positive marginal effect of the amenity on site valve. Conditions (12) and
(13) are the result of land rent maximization assuming that taxes and the
effects of the zone specific public good are capitalized into price as implied
by equilibrium aggregate market value (7). It follows that since the multipliers in the maximization of the social welfare function for the zonal balanced budget constraints (δ_1, δ_2) are equal [from (10) and (11)] to aggregate
utility engendered by the public good,

$$\delta_1 = \sum_h \alpha^h U_{Bh}^h B_1^h L_1^h$$

these multipliers also equal the effect of the public good (Z_1, Z_2) on land
rents (P_1, P_2). The market equilibrium condition (7) and individual utility
maximization (6) guarantees this correspondence if we continue to assume that
all utility functions are identical. The effect of a local government per-
suing property valve maximization further ensures Pareto optimality since the
amenity is adjusted until its marginal effect on price just equals the marginal
tax effect on price [(12) and (13)]:

$$\delta_1 = \frac{\partial P_1}{\partial Z_1} = \frac{\partial P_1}{\partial T_2}$$

$$\delta_2 = \frac{\partial P_2}{\partial Z_2} = \frac{\partial P_2}{\partial T_2}$$

Thus property valve maximization ensures that the Pareto optimal level of the
public good is supplied. Substituting the above, and combining (8) and (9)
derived from social welfare maximization gives:

$$\frac{U_1^h}{B^h U_1^h} = \frac{P_2 + T_2 \frac{\partial P_2}{\partial T_2}}{P_1 + T_1 \frac{\partial P_1}{\partial T_1}} \tag{14}$$

Since we assume that individuals do not realize that their preferences for
public good amenities are revealed through land rents, they act as if taxes
and land rents are parameters. It follows that (14) is equivalent to individual consumer utility maximization (6). The apparent difference between
(6) and (14) is a reflection of the free rider problem. However, what the
above demonstrates is that market equilibrium and local government maximizing
zonal land values ensures that the public good is supplied optimally and all
conditions sufficient for Pareto optimality are met.

The advantage of the property valve maximization objective is that it is
operational. However, the assumptions leading to this result must be kept
in mind. The most critical of these is that all individuals possess identical
utility functions. Without this assumption the correspondence between property

valve maximization and Pareto optimality may no longer hold. In any case, since efforts relating tax effects, environmental quality and public services with land valve support the capitalization hypothesis and demonstrate that empirical estimation problems can be overcome, property valve maximization is a workable signal. Further empirical work is necessary so that the relevance of this policy to land use, transportation planning, the timing and location of publicly supplied amenities such as utility systems, and tax and user charges can be tested.

FOOTNOTES

[1]   Church, Albert M., "Capitalization of the Effective Property Tax Rate on Single Family Residences", National Tax Journal, 27 (March 1974) 133-122.

[2]   Maler, Karl Goran, Environmental Economics - A Theoretical Inquiry, The Johns Hopkins University Press, London/Baltimore 1974.

[3]   Oates, Wallace E., "The Effects of Property Taxes and Local Public Spending on Property Values: An Empirical Study of Tax Capitalization and the Tiebout Hypothesis", Journal of Political Economics, 77 (November/December 1969), 957-971.

[4]   Polinsky, Mitchell A. and Steven Shavell, "Amenities and Property Valves in A General Equilibrium Model of an Urban Area" working paper 1207-5 the Urban Institute (1973).

[5]   Portney, Paul R. and Jon C. Sonstelie, "Property Valve Maximization as a Decision Criterion for Local Governments", Resources for the Future unpublished paper, 1975.

[6]   Ridker, Ronald G., and John A. Henning, "The Determinants of Residential Property Valves with Special Reference to Air Pollution", Review of Economics and Statistics, 49 (May 1967), 240-256.

[7]   Strotz, Robert H., "The Use of Land Rent Changes to Measure the Welfare Benefits of Land Improvement", in Joseph E. Haring (Ed.), The New Economics of Regulated Industries in Rate Making in a Dynamic Economy (Los Angeles: Economic Research Center, Occidental College, 1968).

GUARDING FOR CLEAN URBAN ENVIRONMENT

Ora Patoharju
Secretary, Environment Protecting Commission,
City of Helsinki

The capital area of Finland is composed of an urban conglomerate, the original heart of which is the City of Helsinki, founded 1550. The population of this area, 800 000 at present is soaring towards 1 million people due to the rapid growth of the satellite towns Espoo (119 000 inhabitants), Vantaa (114 000) and Kauniainen (7 000), while the population of Helsinki itself (500 000) is continuously diminishing. Within this region we already have substantion of growing social pressure due to urbanization. However, taken as a whole, the state of our technical and social environment is rather healthy.

The Townscape

Humaneness and attractiveness of the townscape are cultivated by preserving the most valuable parts of the old buildings in Helsinki urban area. The Museum of Finnish Architecture has on the city's request prepared a list of the most valuable buildings, numbering some 300 houses that should be preserved. 'Empire-Helsinki' in the centre of the City has already been almost completely restored, and the city's face towards the sea preserves its traditional look. Last year (1975) we got an alteration in the Building Act, that forbids unnecessary demolition of old houses. The city's buildings programme also contains the conservationist redevelopment of a large number of houses all over town, apart from those contained in the list mentioned. This redevelopment has become a practical possibility since the Government approved the granting of housing-loans also for this group of buildings. The number of small houses of 1-2 families that Finns favour has also been augmented in the city's housing construction programme, which, in turn, adds to the attractiveness and diversity of our city.

However, as urban building technique has become more efficient, the environment has become increasingly monotonous. We have started to use colours on apartment blocks, whereas before we prided ourselves on our clean, white housing areas. At the same time more attention has also been given to the part played by greenery for the attractiveness of living areas. The growing season in Finland is short, only one third of the year, we would need plenty of coniferous evergreens to maintain this attractiveness. Unfortunately, coniferous trees are particularly vulnerable to contaminated air and disturbances caused by building and traffic and efforts are made to substitute hardier varieties from other areas for indigenous pine trees.

Energy conservation

28 % of the energy consumption in Finland goes to heating, and of this
amount 71 % is obtained from imported fuel. Now that the cost of fuel has
become such a vital factor, it is natural that special attention is paid to
heating economy. Our climate gives us an excellent opportunity to use the
waste heat produced in generating electric energy for district heating.
If electricity and heat for the city were produced separately, 60 % more
fuel would be used. At the moment, all the region's power plants are
connected to the district heating network and by 1985 district heating can
be used for at least by 80 % of the inhabitants of the region and over 90 %
of the room volume in the city area of Helsinki, i.e. all the apartment
blocks. From the point of view of environment protection, this is an excellent thing, as air pollution can be controlled and oil leakage into soil
minimized.

In order to improve the heating economy also at local level, outside walls
and attics are being equipped with thicker insulation than ever. In houses
built with government grants windows must be triple, and at least the
largest radiator in an apartment must have a thermostat. This small investment keeps the room air comfortably warm and in particular it prevents ex-
cessively hot rooms on the sunny side of the building – something that may
be uncomfortable in the early spring. To save energy, builders have also
been ordered to abandon oversize windows. The recommended room temperature
in all residential apartments has been reduced from 22 ^{o}C to 20 ^{o}C.
We have found that people have reacted favourably to the change.

The region intends to change over to nuclear power in the coming decade.
The location of the power plant proved a difficult problem, as for safety
reasons it ought to be far away, but it should also be absolutely possible
to use the waste heat for district heating. Nuclear power would reduce air
pollution appreciably, compared with energy from fossil fuels.

Air pollution control

Traffic, heating power plants, industry and local heating and waste in-
cineration are the worst air polluters in Helsinki. There has been an
increase in complaints about the air because of damage to vegetation and
because of corrosion. We, too, have proofs of the influence of air pollution
on respiratory diseases. As heating plays a large role in energy consumption,
its pollutive effects are greatest in winter. The large-scale change-over
to district heating in Helsinki has improved the situation a great deal, but
the increase in energy consumption has reduced the benefits gained from this.
The greatest air pollution in Helsinki is caused by sulphur dioxide derived
from the energy production. But not even the percentage of sulphur dioxide
has yet reached a dangerous level, as most of the city's imported fuel is
Polish coal of moderate sulphur content, and in the summer, we have got some
lots of eastern oil with extremely low sulphur.

We have started checking and controlling air pollution in the city last year
in the area affected by the largest power plant, and our aim is to extend
this later to the whole region.

The measuring system will be based on automatic analyzing equipment for sulphur dioxide (SO_2) and carbon monoxide (CO) as well as dust measuring equipment. Information is transmitted along telephone lines to a central station where data is handled automatically and compared with meteorological parameters. According to the results the city's energy consumption policy may be modified.

Our financial recources gave us only a very limited physical air pollution control system; in order to increase our knowledge of our environment we have used some biological means of control. Already years ago a survey of the conifers in the town was begun by a private research-worker and this study has been continued, Erkamo 1944 (1) & 1974 (2); the propagation and withdrawal of <u>Picea abies</u>, <u>Pinus silvestris</u> and <u>Juniperus communis</u> have been charted over these years and the results show that the air pollution situation in the city area has uniformly got worse during these years.

The same art of lichens (<u>Hypogymnia physodes</u>) in pure and polluted environment. Photo: Kari Laaksovirta.

More sensitive study consentrates on lichens which are affected by air pollution and are commonly not found in Helsinki. The spreading boundaries of lichens in Helsinki were preliminary chaterted in 1934 (Ref. 3); a present-day investigation reveals, that the boundaries of lichens are only found in Espoo and Vantaa, no more in Helsinki. In 1975, frequencies of melanic forms of <u>Oligia</u>-moths were examined at 28 reference points inside and around the city area in order to find out the local effects of air pollution on these moths (Ref. 4).

In order to study the possibilities of the presence of the photochemical smog in city areas, a special sort of tabac (<u>Nicotiana tabacum BEL W3</u>) was chosen as an indicator. Plants carefully raised in greenhouses were placed in parks near the main traffic areas, but after two years experience no serious signs of smog were found (Ref. 5).

The sources of lead in the city air were investigated utilizing naturally occuring variations in stable lead isotope abundance $^{206}Pb/^{204}Pb$ and radio-lead ^{210}Pb activities to determine the sources of lead, as traffic, smelteries and background in special environments (Ref. 6). This study will

further help us to reduce the lead pollution when the sources will be
identified. We have been specially concerned about the high lead values in
vegetables cultured along roadsides. The state-owned refinery has already
smoothly dropped the lead content in gasoline.

These various types of biological indicators and physical monitoring used
in the Helsinki region give us clear warning signals also before the human
health is concerned. It then only depends on the political will to make
improvements on the air pollution control.

Water supply and sewerage

There is no longer enough good raw water in densely populated southern
Finland, though there are plenty of clean water recources in central and
nothern Finland. Blasting began last year on what we believe will be the
world's longest tunnel, from Helsinki to Lake Päijänne 120 km to the north,
where the water so far is rather good. To protect Päijänne from pollution
Helsinki has made the investment of granting a sulphite pulp mill on the
lake a long-term loan for treatment of its waste water. Consequently, our
future raw water supply source is one of those very rare lakes on the earth
where the quality of the water since the 1960ies is getting steadily better.

Today, about 87 % of the region's and almost 95 % of the city of Helsinki's
households are connected to the public sewer network. In the oldest part of
Helsinki, the city proper, the combined sewers take both rainwater and household sewage. In all the new housing areas, rainwater and sewage go in
separate sewers. Sewage is treated at 10 biological and at one mechanical
treatment plants. Though the winter is sometimes very cold, biological treatment works well under the open skies. Sewage water is warm enough to be used
for melting snow after it has been cleared, and thus we are spared from
enormous heaps of dirty snow, which would otherwise take all summer to melt
away.

There are two goals for water pollution control in Helsinki. We want to get
the coastal water off Helsinki so clean that we can swim in it and go fishing for pleasure. The other goal is to play our own part in fighting the
risk of Baltic pollution. As none of the coastal states can unilaterally
decide on the problems of the Baltic, Helsinki is particularly proud to have
been instrumental in calling together all the coastal states of the Baltic
to a conference in March 1974, which decided mutual protection of the sea.

A mistake was made in times past in that the treatment plants were located
at the end of shallow bays. As a result the shallow water eutrophied and
the inshore waters became polluted. A few years ago new principles were
adopted for sewage treatment in the region. They include piping all sewage
water to treatment plants, supplementing the treatment by removing the
phosphorus chemically, and then leading the treated water out to the edge
of the open sea through tunnels. The method of purification is the so-called
"Helsinki-Method", developed by us, in which both biological and chemical
purification take place in one single operation. This is much more economical
than purification in separate stages.

Sewage sludge is digested and will be mechanically dried. We are so far
a little anxious about using the sludge on the fields due to its rather
high heavy metals content. The parks department of the city is very keen
for getting all treated sludge for greenery building.

Large trees

The amount of verdure and particularly the large trees have an important
effect on the comfort of living and working environment. Greens planned on
paper for new housing developments and saplings no thicker than a fishing
pole are no good; people need large, spreading trees, a traditional 'home'
spruce or birch. This has been emphasized by the City's Environment Protecting Commission in its 'Directions for the Protection of Trees' aiming
towards the preservation of fullgrown trees withstanding the pressure of the
city's building activity. We have not yet been able to forbid all tree fell-
ing without permission, but we have distributed several thousand copies of
our 'Directions' to the city builders etc. and we trust that the opinion is
slowly changing into favoring big trees.

In some places another traditional factor is in evidence: the Forest-Finn's
tree-felling instinct. In times past forest was cleared to make fields and
was regarded as an adversary. This tendency should be erased from the
present-day city builders.

Social environment

The social environment can't actually be distinguished from the technological
environment, they are penetrated by each other in to-day's industrial
society. Competition, haste and stress are not included in man's natural
environment, but are products of urban milieu and reveal multiple damage of
the social environment.

One obvious reason why the city-dweller feels ill at ease, with attendant
stress, is the twofold lack of perspective:

- *his projection in time has been cut off on moving to the city, his
  previous traditional environment had created a feeling of security,
  ancestors followed and protected the activities of the household and
  traces of the work of previous generations could be seen everywhere in
  his living environment.*

Having to move from an underdeveloped area to the city for work is in itself a tragic occurence. All ties with the past are cut off. Comfortable
living is the main object, but attitudes toward the city environment may
even be hostile - in any case there is no interest towards cultural values.

- *his connection with the physical scale of his environment has also been
  severed, many-storeyed buildings and hulking concrete monsters, motorways
  and factory halls are out of proportion to his own size and so are
  experienced as strange and hostile. A dwelling-house should be 5 storeys*

at the most, in order to suit the scale of a citydweller of several generat-
ions, and a healthy person should be able to walk up the stairs without
having to use the lift: these would be factors of a proper physical scale.

A special problem posed by fast urbanization is strangers having to become
close neighbours without a free choice or change to group voluntarily.
A feeling of solidarity and security are values that can be promoted by
physical planning.

In order to predict how a person will function in an environment of many-
storeyd buildings we ought to know much more than we do about our behaviour
patterns. It is quite possible that he will try to adjust himself to this
new environment in accordance with his inherited genetical code, and this
attempt at adjustment is expressed as the social stress and asocial behaviour typical of present-day city-diseases. One typical expression of this
disease is the claustrophobia caused by crowding: frequent references to rat
experiments attest to the consequences. Another context is violence: Behind
the waves of violence hides a socio-economic change, causing a conflict
between expectations inherited from a previous time, and circumstances developing as a result of this change. In order to relieve the pressure caused
by this conflict the individual seeks escape in activity giving a maximum
of emotional experience. Violence is an alternative easily chosen.

One of the prophets of environment planning, the late architect Doxiades
points out the worst thing about our cities: "The main factor is the loss of
scale which has two basic expressions. The first time humans tell their
children not to move out of their home because of the very great dangers.
Thus, very early in life, we transmit the message that our home is surrounded by enemies and killers. The second expression is the creation of inhuman
buildings" (Ref. 7).

One fundamental part of the city-dweller's cosiness, often forgotten, is the
fact that he will not be treated as a machine by machines, but as an individual served by other living individuals. Let's take an example:

  - Lack of personal services can be referred to the city collective
    traffic: The trams and buses leave end-stations and bus-stops
    according to a tight time schedule; the inhabitants of the city
    dependant of this means of conveyance are forced to run to the
    end-stations only to find out that the tram leaves only after a
    quarter of an hour, or to run to a bus stop to sorely afflict that
    the bus just left 'off his nose'. In both cases they feel them-
    selves deeply humiliated of being at technology´s mercy. However,
    the bus loses its exact time schedule after the first traffic
    lights and a humanly treatment of an individual wouldn't have cost
    it any minutes of time. But as long as the present 'inhuman'
    collective traffic is a generally accepted rule, people don't
    trust this method of conveyance and use private cars, which leads
    to "auto-sclerosis".

    My proposition in this case is a clearly visible light signal at
    the end-stations, when the time for bus leave approaches, and the

bus personnel to be obliged to give a thorough look at stops to
calmly collect all people wanting to join the bus ride.
Comparison: Private car drivers are to a great extent served by
road traffic authorities by a beforehand information of traffic
light changing speed; that kind of service, without question of
its costs, is commonly accepted for the main roads. Why not give
the same service to collective traffic passengers?

From ecology we have learned that diversity is important for eco-systems,
and the monocultures created by man are not fit to live. This must be adapted to community planning - no urban monocultures, specialized centers for
industry, business or living. A city should contain a harmonious proportion
of places of work, living accommodation, business areas and greens, forming
a pleasant and functional community.

Selective bibliography

1. Erkamo, V.: Ueber die ursprüngliche Vegetation im Stadtgebiet von
    Helsinki, Ann.Bot.Soc. 'Vanamo', 19, 27-33 (1944)

2. Erkamo, V.: Occurrence and thriving of the native conifers in the city
    area of Helsinki, Memoranda soc. Fauna Flora Fennica, 50, 15-30 (1974)
    (Finnish original, German review)

3. Vaarna, V.: Ueber die epiphytische Flechtenflora der Stadt Helsinki,
    Ann.Bot.Soc. 'Vanamo', 5; 6, 1-32 (1934)
    (Finnish original, German review)

4. Mikkola, K.: Frequencies of Melanic Forms of Oligia-Moths as Measure
    of Atmospheric Pollution in Finland, Ann.Zool.Fennici, 12,197-204 (1975)

5. U.S.Dept of Health, Education, and Welfare/NAPCA Publication No.AP-55:
    Tobacco, a Sensitive Monitor for Photochemical Air Pollution,
    Cincinnati 1969

6. Kauranen, P. & Miettinen, J.K.: Specific Activity of ^{210}Pb in the
    Environment, Intern J. Environm.Anal.Chem., 3, 307-316 (1974)

7. Cohen, D.: Diagnostician for cities, New Scientist, 65,934:262-4 (1975).

THE PROGRAMME FOR NOISE CONTROL
IN THE CITY OF TORONTO

R. M. Bremner, P. Eng., F.I.C.E.
Commissioner of Public Works and City Engineer
City of Toronto, Canada

As Commissioner of Public Works for the City of Toronto, I am concerned that our citizens are afforded the protection of an effective, practical and enforceable programme for the control of noise. The City of Toronto now has such a programme underway as a result of the "City of Toronto Noise Control Study", done as a joint effort by the firms of James F. MacLaren Ltd., Valcoustics Ltd. and City Works Department staff and comprising two years of investigation and analysis of Toronto's sound environment and public opinion regarding noise. To my knowledge, no more intensive study has been done in any city in North America.

The Noise Control Study had two main components: a Physical Survey to provide data on the sound levels pertaining throughout the City and Social Perception Surveys to find out the reaction of citizens to these levels and to noise in general.

The physical survey was based on recording 40 second samplings of sound every 20 minutes for 24 hours at some 600 locations in Toronto. These points were determined by superimposing a grid of lines spaced at $\frac{1}{4}$ mile intervals on a map of the City. (Fig. 1) Wherever the lines intersected, a monitoring station was established. The grid technique was devised to ensure that monitoring stations were located randomly with no bias towards particular noise generating sources, in order to ensure that the final results would be credible as a general survey of the City's noise climate. Each monitoring station was classified according to the type of land use there and the kind of thoroughfare it was near.

To sample the sound a portable instrumentation package was developed. (Fig. 2) It contained a two-channel tape recorder, microphone, amplifier and control system. Toronto Works Department staff mounted these devices on utility poles and trees throughout the City. Each unit was operated for a 24-hour period and then was moved to a new location.

All the sound recordings were converted to punch tape in a laboratory where a digital computer provided a detailed statistical analysis of ambient sound levels during the day, at night, and over the full 24-hour period, as well as a breakdown of the minimum and maximum levels reached. (Fig. 3)

The Social Perception Study consisted of two opinion surveys. The first survey involved interviews with 7,500 citizens in the streets of Toronto. The second social survey was aimed at pin-pointing the individual's degree of concern with noise around his home or his place of work. Two thousand, five hundred people took part in the questionnaire-type interviews.

A number of important findings resulted from the physical and social studies. First, it is evident that transportation in all its various forms is the

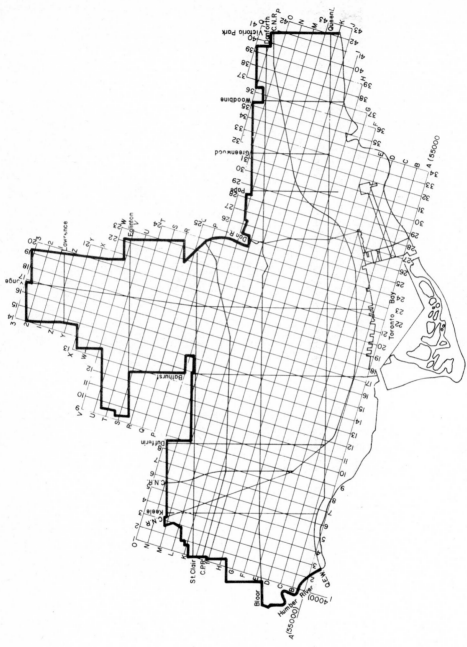

Fig. 1 City of Toronto Monitoring Grid Point Locations

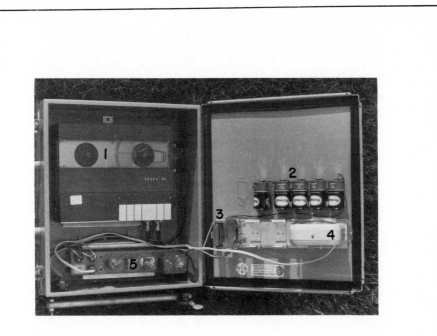

1. Tape Recorder
2. Power Supply
3. Power Supply (Microphone)
4. Clock Timer
5. Modular Circuitry

Fig. 2

Noise Monitoring Package

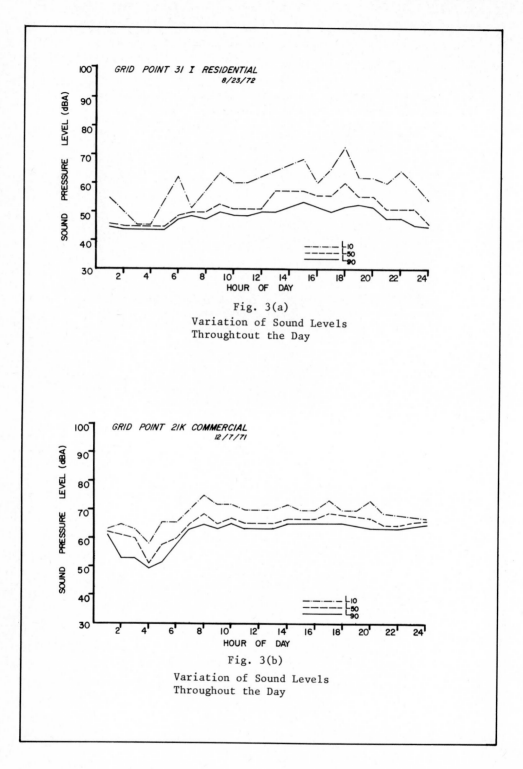

Fig. 3(a)
Variation of Sound Levels
Throughtout the Day

Fig. 3(b)
Variation of Sound Levels
Throughout the Day

predominant sound source in Toronto. Sound levels in residential areas tend
to vary inversely with the distance from major traffic arteries.

Average background sound levels (L90) were 47 dB(A) for residential areas,
56 dB(A) for commercial areas and 58 dB(A) for industrial areas. Twenty-four
hour sound energy equivalent levels (LEQ) ranged between 50 and 70 dB(A) in
residential areas and below 80 dB(A) in commercial and industrial areas.
(Fig. 4) Indeed, only six of the points monitored showed an LEQ value over
80 dB(A); in each case a major road, main rail line, or both, were involved.
Comparison of these results with available data for some major American and
European cities seem to indicate that Toronto is a relatively quiet place.

The results of the social perception surveys supported this conclusion.
While 65% of the people interviewed on the streets considered noise a problem
in Toronto, as a priority they placed it well behind air and water pollution.
The most annoying noises to these people were, in descending order, trucks,
radios, cars, motorcycles, people shouting and construction equipment.
Although 72% of respondents felt that noise was increasing and thought we
should have legislation to control it, a large number of people did not react
unfavourably to the higher sound levels. Most of the respondents interviewed at home rated their neighbourhoods quiet to fairly quiet and most
people working in commercial and industrial zones rated these areas as
average. (Fig. 5) Nevertheless, they did register a definite concern that
noise was increasing and that we should do something to keep it under control.

Given this finding, that noise levels in Toronto were generally acceptable,
the City's Noise Control Programme rejected the conventional approach of
zoning the City into areas of permissible lot-line levels. With the low
levels already extant in many areas, such a method might simply have
constituted a license to pollute. Instead, the strategy adopted sought to
maintain present levels, where they were good, by controlling future activity
which might increase these levels. In addition, various specific problems
would be attacked directly at source. Finally, complex "objective" criteria
were to be avoided where possible, since feedback from other cities indicated
problems with enforcing such regulations.

The Study identified six areas where action was needed. These form the basis
for the Noise Control Programme now in effect.

First - land use. We are making sure that developments which propose changes
in the nature or intensity of existing land uses are evaluated in the light
of their potential impact on our sound environment. Before a rezoning is
granted the applicant must submit a noise impact statement showing that his
proposal will best fit the sound climate of that particular area. Factors
to be considered are the potential impact of the area on the development, the
development on the surrounding area and impacts internal to the development
itself.

For example, a certain developer has a proposal to build an apartment tower
with windows and balconies overlooking a main rail line. However, before he
can submit an acceptable noise impact statement, he will either have to
redesign the project to reorient windows and balconies away from the tracks
or demonstrate that the construction materials used will yield an acceptable
living environment inside the units.

Second - transportation. While the Study showed this to be a key area for

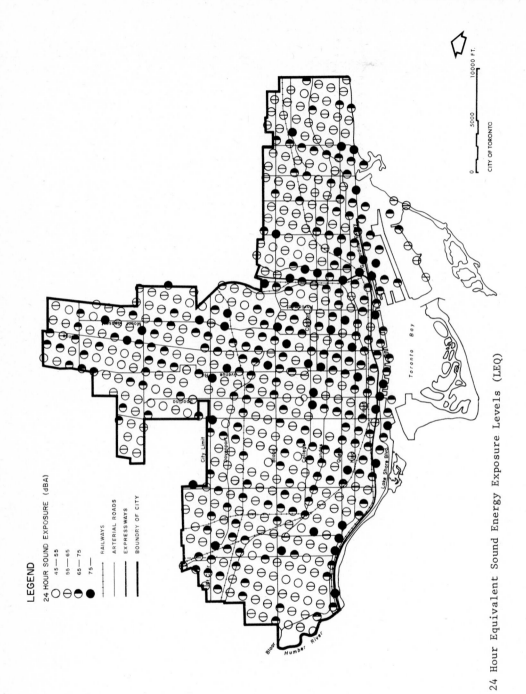

Fig. 4 24 Hour Equivalent Sound Energy Exposure Levels (LEQ)

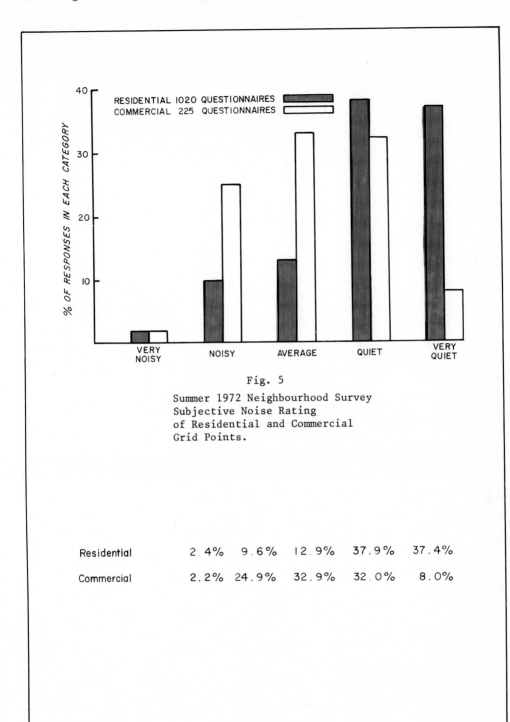

Fig. 5

Summer 1972 Neighbourhood Survey
Subjective Noise Rating
of Residential and Commercial
Grid Points.

Residential	2.4%	9.6%	12.9%	37.9%	37.4%
Commercial	2.2%	24.9%	32.9%	32.0%	8.0%

noise control, in Toronto's case the responsibility all lies with senior
levels of government, namely the Province of Ontario and the Federal Government of Canada. We have recommended to the Federal Government that it
establish or upgrade minimum limits of sound generation for air and rail
systems, for interprovincial bus and truck carriers, and for all motor
vehicles to be sold in Canada, including related equipment, like tires. To
the Province of Ontario we have suggested that a series of stations be
established where motor vehicles can be checked to see that they comply with
the noise limits. (Incidentally, air emission and safety requirements could
be checked at the same time.) Indications are that the Province is now
giving this approach serious consideration.

Third - we must look to noise attenuation in buildings. Instead of simply
laying down sound transmission specifications for various building components,
we intend to take the more practical and effective approach of establishing
"as built" sound attenuation standards. Occupancy of a building, be it for
dwelling, work, recreation or shopping, will not be allowed until the builder
has shown that these standards have been met. Terms of reference for a study
to develop these standards are now being set up.

Fourth - Toronto has a new noise control by-law. This by-law does not follow
the pattern of many recent ordinances that attempt to set lot-line limits for
sound levels. Experience has shown such legislation to be cumbersome, costly
and impractical to enforce. Consider, for example, that the City of Toronto
was almost totally built-up prior to World War II and, thus, is dominated by
housing on lots 25 feet or less in width. As a result, many normal types of
outside household activity such as children playing, hammering and sawing,
etc. would violate the lot line sound level limits typically imposed
(generally 55-65 dB(A) during the daytime). In another example, samples
taken over 24 hours of noise levels in a large cemetery showed that these
standards might be exceeded for up to half the time. Thus, even in the
absence of any local activity, background noise levels (due to traffic on
nearby arteries) may make such standards unrealistic. Nor is it a practical
solution to simply make the limits higher. To do so would permit certain
sounds to occur at levels that were clearly unacceptable, for example, air
conditioners and fans. So instead, Toronto has restricted the use of
objective standards to laying down acceptable levels for specific pieces of
equipment, thus attacking noise at its source. Beyond that what is basically
required is that Torontonians show consideration for their neighbours. To
ensure this, the new noise by-law relies on outright prohibitions of certain
types of noise during certain hours, (e.g. no noise from model airplanes
between 2100 hours of one day and 0730 hours of the next) or on a subjective
evaluation of the noise as to whether it is excessive, disturbing or likely
to disturb.

For enforcement, a Noise Control Group has been established whose inspectors
investigate noise complaints. These officers seek to resolve problems by
mediation at first, but if necessary their testimony can be called upon to
verify that, from the viewpoint of the reasonable man, an offence took place.
This approach has already been successfully tested in the courts. Some
operators of pornographic establishments on one of our main streets were
convicted and fined for assaulting the ears of passers-by on the sidewalks
with tape recorded blandishments blared from loudspeakers over their doorways.
Since then, the practice has effectively ceased. In another case an
injunction was granted prohibiting a so-called "church" from conducting its
"services" in a semi-detached dwelling; the noise had made sleeping, studying

and relaxing impossible for the next door neighbours.

However, it should be emphasized that only a very few complaints ultimately result in prosecutions; most are resolved satisfactorily through the mediation efforts of the Noise Control Inspectors. A dust collector on a factory roof which made life unbearable was found to have faulty bearings. A domestic air conditioning compressor was moved to a location more distant from the neighbouring patio. Probably the most permanent solution was the crowing cock which was eaten by its owner to the delight of his previously sleepless neighbour. A few enquiries have resulted in referrals to the Public Health Department of people in need of psychiatric help and, of course, there have been a few crank or baseless complaints. Table 1 shows a breakdown of more than 1,000 complaints received to date and how they have been resolved.

TABLE 1   Analysis of Noise Complaints Received
by Noise Control Group

Noise Sources

Dogs	20%
Construction	15%
Air Conditioners	13%
Music, Loudspeakers	13%
Garbage Collection/Delivery Vehicles	5%
Industrial	4%
Traffic	3%
Public Transportation	1%
Voices	1%
Miscellaneous	25%
	100%

Resolution of Complaints

1.	Repair, replacement or improved operation	19%
2.	Limitation of hours of operation	12%
3.	Complaint withdrawn after explanation	12%
4.	Removal of source of noise	9%
5.	Reduction in amount of noise emanated (music, etc.)	9%

6. Short-term noise: completed before investigation   7%

7. Referred to Provincial Ministry of the Environment   6%

8. Relocation of machine   4%

9. Referred to Police   3%
    (N.B. incomplete figure – some enquiries referred without
    record being made)

10. Agreement between neighbours   3%

11. Referred to Buildings Department (zoning)   3%

12. Referred to Public Health   1%

13. No violation found or complaint unconfirmed   12%
                                                                          ―――――
                                                                          100%
                                                                          ―――――

N.B. An insignificant number of complaints have resulted in prosecutions

Fifth – construction and service equipment. The City of Toronto is a big
user of this equipment. It can provide the "shop window" in which others can
see the technical and economic feasibility of reducing noise at the source
and of the standards incorporated in the Noise Control By-law.

At our own initiative we experimented with silencing portable air compressors
until we were satisfied that we had developed the quietest that was practically
possible. We now specify these standards in our purchases of new compressors
and in construction contracts. We are continuing experimental work on
silencing present equipment. As practical, enforceable standards are
developed these will be incorporated into the Noise Control By-law and into our
specifications for contracts and new equipment purchases. A programme of
annual analysis of noise produced by various types of machines will, in a few
years, result in enforceable standards being set for all construction equipment being operated in the City.

At the same time, it is vital that the City of Toronto maintains a close
dialogue with equipment manufacturers, construction associations, refuse
haulers and others, so that everyone concerned can make a cohesive effort to
develop practical noise control. Rigorous inspection of machinery used by
private contractors in the City has resulted in increased vigilance on the
part of contractors to ensure that construction machinery is properly
maintained and operated. Suppliers of rental equipment are sending their
best machines into the City. Many contractors now regularly request noise
inspection of their machines before starting work in the City.

Sixth – is the administration of the Programme. This is largely vested in
the Noise Control Group, mentioned earlier, whose role goes beyond simply
receiving and investigating complaints. It includes:

1. Maintaining a centre of technical expertise and research on sound in order
    to assist various City Departments in their responsibilities in the Noise
    Control Programme.

2. Continuing to monitor sound levels and test citizens' reaction at grid point locations, maintaining and updating the basic sound inventory and exploring possible statistical relationships.

3. Directing the noise reduction programme on City equipment in co-operation with manufacturers.

4. Developing and directing a public information programme to inform Torontonians of the need for noise control and the techniques that will accomplish it.

The latter role is particularly important. Two slide presentations with co-ordinated tape commentary have been prepared and are being presented by the Noise Control staff in high schools, universities, ratepayers meetings, etc. These presentations have been most effective in stirring up interest in noise control. A third presentation is being drafted for groups of construction workers and supervisors. This presentation will be completely different from the previous two, in that it will be technically-oriented and designed to show the people working in the field what can be done to reduce noise from construction sites.

The Noise Control staff have prepared a pamphlet to advise people on the proper mounting and placement of air conditioners. Material is being researched to develop a further pamphlet dealing with what has emerged as the prime single cause of complaint to the Noise Control Group - barking dogs!

The experience of the Noise Control Group in handling complaints has vindicated the emphasis placed on the educational programmes. As stated previously, most problems have proved amenable to solution, usually by simply educating offenders on how their activity affects others and how it can be modified to reduce or remove the annoyance created.

I am aware that the approach taken by Toronto's Noise Control Programme contrasts sharply with what is currently in vogue. Typically, discussions of urban noise control centre on selecting appropriate sets of numbers to describe the desired ambient conditions for a variety of land uses at different times of day. This approach may have a certain academic appeal given its apparent objectivity, but, as a practical man, I have found it advisable to reject it. In my experience, to adopt the "objective" approach would make noise control a futile exercise. I say futile, because noise is fundamentally a subjective phenomenon. It is unwanted sound, a condition that is the result of evaluations by individuals operating in a highly personal manner.

My experience in Toronto has shown that the vast majority of complaints result from activities that are simply people acting thoughtlessly. In one sense, what people are really objecting to is the alienation of modern society, the seeming inability of neighbours to discuss and resolve a matter of mutual concern without the intervention of some official third party. The Noise Control Officers fulfil this latter role, and the success of our programme is a good measure of the soundness of our approach.

Of course, there is a role for objective measurement. Much of our efforts are directed at making machinery, cars, trucks and other mechanical sources of noise as quiet as is technically possible at a reasonable cost. I firmly believe that by attacking noise at the source, in this way, we can make a real impact on ambient urban sound levels.

In adopting the Noise Control Programme described above, we have sought to take a measured, reasoned approach to noise control, one that is practical and effective while extending maximum respect for individual rights and freedoms. Toronto is fortunate in that it is still a relatively quiet City. I intend to keep it that way.

THE GROWTH OF BRADFORD, ENGLAND WITH SPECIFIC REFERENCE TO THE PROBLEMS OF HUMAN SETTLEMENT AND THE SOLUTIONS SO FAR PUT FORWARD

Charles Reginald Atkinson
Director of Development Services,
City of Bradford Metropolitan Council, England

If you carefully study any city, you can usually find and understand a reason for its being. In the case of Bradford you note
that the sheep rearing areas in the Yorkshire Dales, linked to
the nearby abundance of coal, the presence of iron, the soft water
supply so essential for cleaning the wool and the invention of
machinery at the time of the Industrial Revolution, led to the
boom type growth of Bradford from a rural village community to a
densely populated industrial city, which was quickly established
on a world basis as the centre of the wool trade. Many cities
have grown evenly in population and area over a long period of
time and this gave an opportunity to shape and control the
ultimate form of the urban settlement. A city that has grown
gradually is likely to be faced with urban renewal problems on a
more manageable scale. Figure 1, illustrates a typical even
growth situation.

In the case of Bradford, however, there was tremendous growth
over a relatively short period of years, and this undoubtedly
caused problems at the time it was happening. Figure 2,
illustrates the unique rate of growth situation for Bradford. It
is still causing problems in that the City Council are now faced
with urban renewal on a vast scale. A very large proportion of
the sewage system, the housing stock, the schools and industrial
buildings are suddenly out of date all at once and inadequate for
present day use. The sheer magnitude of the renewal programme
needed, therefore, is a problem in itself particularly as life in
the city has to continue in the midst of demolition and reconstruction projects.

A very old map of the Bradford area shows a series of village
communities well separated from each other, and these human
settlements at that time would be very similar in many ways to
those that still exist in the area of the Yorkshire Dales National
Park. The Bradford area has always had the advantage of hills
and vistas and in the pre-industrial revolution era it is easy to
visualise the village of Bradford nestling in the hollow at the
point where the Bradford Beck joined the Bowling Beck on its
journey downstream to the River Aire at Shipley. At this time
there would be an abundance of grass and trees, clear streams and
the wonderful views to the hills surrounding Bradford. For a long
period of time the rate of change will have been minimal and this
will have in turn provided a measure of stability that is so

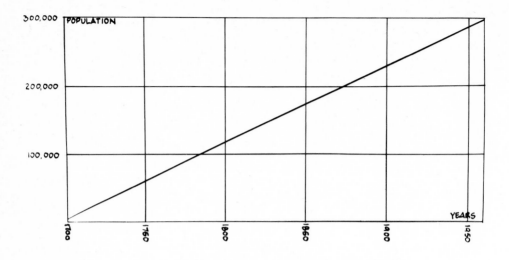

Fig. 1. The gradual growth of a City

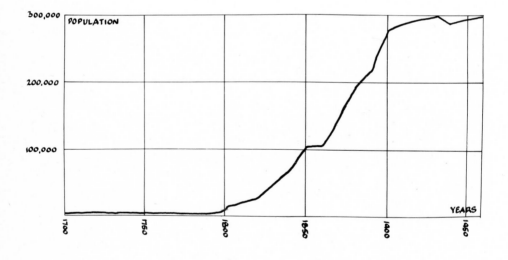

Fig. 2. The boom type growth of Bradford at the
time of the Industrial Revolution.

lacking today. The contours served to dictate to some extent the
siting of the village settlements. Life at Queensbury, which is
sited at a level of 1,200 feet above sea level, would be very
much different to life even in those days at Manningham (400 feet
above sea level) which lies in the valley midway between Bradford
and Shipley. It is a feature of Bradford that many of the
differing characteristics of these village communities have
survived even to the present day, and Fig. 3 is a present day
photograph of the village of Esholt which lies wholly inside the
city boundary.

It has been said that the world changed for Bradford as the
century turned into 1800 and the village or township by the
troutstream changed into the smokey city. It was a period of
rapid and uncontrolled expansion and a young reporter on the
staff of the London Morning Post toured the area in the year 1849
and reported back that Bradford may be described as "an accumula-
tion of mean streets, steep lanes and huge mills, interspersed
here and there by odious patches of black muddy, vast ground
rooted up by pigs and strewn with oyster shells, cabbage stalks
and such garbage".

The pace of development was far too hectic as events and
inventions toppled over one another in apparently endless
progress. For the great mass of the inhabitants it must have
been a life of real misery and there is a super-abundance of
historical material which adequately describes the conditions
that existed at that time. Figure 4, which is a general
picture of the centre of Bradford taken many years ago clearly
illustrates the drabness of this period.

When things are so bad there is usually an increasing demand for
improvement and Bradford and its people pioneered many changes in
the years which followed the Industrial Revolution. The part
played by Richard Oastler in his crusade for factory children,
the achievements of W. E. Forster in the cause of education, are
two examples which spring to mind. Of greater relevance to the
theme of this Conference was the appreciation of the importance
of cared for open space and a number of urban parks were established in the city all of which have survived to the present day.
Any study of human settlement is likely to include a reference to
Sir Titus Salt and his pioneer new town of Saltaire which was a
major step forward and a positive attempt to improve the quality
of life for the people working in his mill. The original village
survives to this day and Fig. 5 illustrates the excellence of the
work initiated by Sir Titus Salt.

So far in this paper I have attempted to describe the extent of
change from village and troutstream to smoky, industrial city. I
have stressed the sheer pace of the change and indicated the
appalling misery that was created. Out of adversity can come
benefit, however, and the years following on from the Industrial
Revolution saw the character of the Bradford people moulded and
turned to the extent that is so clearly apparent today in many
aspects. Think of stubborness, independence, determination and
thrift and you are thinking of Bradford and its people. Think

Fig. 3. Esholt Village.

Fig. 4. City centre of long ago.

Fig. 5. Saltaire Village.

of music, brass bands, competitiveness in sport, home-ownership and the Building Society movement and you are thinking of Bradford. The strong community spirit which is essential for successful human settlements was forged during the hard times in Bradford and has remained a characteristic of the area. Over the years people from overseas have come to Bradford and been success- fully integrated into the community and it is possible to list the Germans, Irish, Ukranians, Hungarians, Poles, and more recently the Indians and the people from Pakistan. Apart from such obvious elements as housing, schools and jobs we see that a successful human settlement needs culture in the form of concert halls, theatres, art galleries and museums; it needs facilities for recreation and leisure; it needs adequate provision of open space; it needs the basic services such as water and gas and it needs communications. Tracing the history of Bradford from 1850 to 1950 one can see from the provisions made what were the basic community needs which were so lacking at the time the reporter, quoted earlier, wrote of his visit in 1849.

It is interesting now to move to the more recent past and in particular to the post-war years since 1945. To start with there were major housing development programmes, and large housing estates were built on virgin land sited on the periphery of the built-up areas. As part of this development there was a full programme of school building to serve the new housing areas and real attempts were made to refurbish the worn out areas of the city. The clearance of sub-standard housing was tackled, programmes to convert the gas street lighting to electricity were initiated and vigorously pursued, as were projects to make up the miles of un-made streets. It was a period of real activity but even so it was possible in 1965 to clearly detect trends which if not checked and reversed could lead to a most serious situation.

So much of the city had grown old together that the size of the urban renewal task was quite staggering. The general appearance of the built-up areas was so reminiscent of the "dark satanic mills" image that it not only discouraged those who might think of a move into the city but more important it encouraged those already here to seek pastures new. The industrial structure in the city was too narrowly based and the young economically active members of the community were migrating to seek better job opportunities and a more attractive environment in which to live. If this trend had been allowed to continue Bradford would have been left with an ageing population and a very much reduced capacity to tackle the many urgent problems facing the City.

The review of the situation which was undertaken at that time gave a number of reasons for optimism in the future. The national motorway network had been extending north for many years and was soon to make its impact on the Bradford area. The siting of Bradford in relation to the new motorways could not have been bettered; the M.62 from Liverpool to Hull was immediately to the south of the city and the extension of the M.1 northwards would place Bradford at the crossroad of two of the most important

motorways in the country. A study of the major ports and
industrial centres showed Bradford in the "centre of gravity"
position. No effort was spared to grasp the opportunities
presented by this circumstance and real progress was made in
diversifying the industrial structure and widening the type and
range of job opportunities in the area. Major roadwork contracts
were agreed in order to provide first class linkage with the new
motorways and industry and commerce were not slow to spot the
tremendous potential for investment in the area. As the job
opportunities increased, so did the wage rates and this gave an
increasing ability to solve the many problems still to be tackled.

By 1970 the real benefits of the smoke control orders were
apparent to all and the once smoke blotched city was completely
transformed. For well over 100 years the city had been
completely covered by thick smoke which cut out the sunshine,and
which blackened the buildings to give an overall picture of dark-
ness and gloom. In a relatively short period of years all this
had gone and the beneficial effect cannot be over exaggerated.
From all over the city there were vantage points which only hills
can provide. The success of the smoke control programme led on
to an ambitious clean-up campaign on the smoke blackened
buildings themselves. The dirt and the grime was washed away and
the overall effect on a stone-built city such as Bradford was
quite dramatic. Most of the buildings were of local stone which
has a warm colour and an international reputation for its quality
as a building stone. A major transformation took place in the
city centre itself and many of the renewal projects were purpose-
ly planned to bring lawns and trees and flower beds right into
the centre. The present day photograph shown in Fig. 6, of the
centre of Bradford emphasises the change that has taken place.
In 1965 there had been a noticeable shortage of service industry
in Bradford, by 1975, real progress had been made in this
direction and commerce now accepted Bradford as a regional type
centre for office development. The post-war Broadway shopping
area has been most attractively pedestrianised and a further four
acre development at Kirkgate, right in the centre of the city,
has been recently completed and provides one of the finest new
shopping developments in the north of England.

The above activity on smoke control, clean-up of buildings, the
emphasis on trees and flowers in the city centre was a part of
the attack on the environment which was seen to be so essential
if the City Council were going to fully succeed in their efforts
to reverse the trends of 1965. Further important work to improve
the environment and thereby the quality of life for the people in
the area was taking place simultaneously in other parts of the
city. In particular I would refer to the General Improvement
Area projects. These schemes were concerned with residential
areas which were badly in need of a facelift and which were
showing clear signs of deterioration. Past experience had shown
that when deterioration started in residential areas, it soon
escalated and in time a lack of confidence developed and from
that stage it was a relatively short time before one was forced
to think in terms of wholesale clearance. Once a General Improvement Area had been designated the Council embarked on environ-

Fig. 6.   City centre present day.

Fig. 7. Barkerend area before improvement works.

Fig. 8. Barkerend area after improvement works.

mental improvement schemes and made grants available for the
improvement of dwellings. The immediate effect of this was to
restore confidence in the area and in most cases give a possible
extra 30 years life to the dwellings. The response from the
occupiers has been all that could be hoped for and the people
living in the houses have not only taken full advantage of the
house improvement grants available, but have clearly gone ahead
with new curtains and furnishings. In brief they have been
reassured so far as the future is concerned and the before and
after photographs prepared for the General Improvement Area
reports indicate a most remarkable transformation. Figure 7, is
a photograph in the Barkerend Area taken before work was undertaken on the improvement scheme and Fig. 8 is the equivalent
photograph taken on completion of the work. Properties have been
given a new lease of life, the quality of the environment in
which these dwellings are sited has been most markedly improved
and perhaps more important the people involved have not faced the
need to move and lose contact with people they have known for a
long time.

So many of the earlier major slum clearance programmes broke up
communities and in many cases forced people to move against their
wishes.

I wrote earlier in this paper of the character of the people and
the strength of their community involvement and the experiences
in Bradford have served to highlight the importance of these
aspects. The successful General Improvement Area schemes have
depended on a real response by the people themselves, to
compliment the works undertaken by the local authority.

Consideration has been given at one time and another to all the
elements that lead to a successful human settlement and I think
you start first with a need to secure a sound and broadly based
industrial structure which can in turn provide the means whereby
the other essential elements can be achieved. Given a wide and
stable job opportunity and add to it an increasing wage rate
situation for the area, one has then got the firm foundation on
which to build for the future. Housing is obviously an important
element and I would emphasise the added importance of choice of
housing. Our past experiences in Bradford with smoke control and
the cleaning of buildings spotlight the impact of the environment
on the quality of life, and finally I would comment on the need
for culture and a sense of belonging which play such a prominent
role in enhancing the character of the people.

We have had successes in Bradford and I have referred to them
earlier. We have also had some failures. For instance the major
slum clearance programme broke up communities, we have experienced
the social problems associated with tall blocks of flats, and the
building of large housing estates on the outskirts of the city
has played some part in reducing the amount of activity in the
city centre during the evenings.

Looking to the future I would like to see further study into the role and importance of the family as a unit and I would also like to see some study into the importance of roots into a community. In my experience the material aspects of good housing, open space, recreational facilities etc. are all important elements but a successful human settlement is dependent above all else on the character of the people themselves.

DEVELOPMENT WITH A COMPATIBLE MINIMUM OF POLLUTION

Armindo Beux
President of the National Federation of Engineers
Rua Andrade Neves 14/301 - Porto Alegre, RS, Brazil

ABSTRACT

This paper supports the theory that industrial development is possible with
a minimum of environmental pollution by making full use of modern technological
resources and the natural physical resources of particular areas, and by the
appropriate siting of industry, preferably downstream of urban centers or,
where possible, in seaboard areas.

GENERALITIES

Many countries are pursuing extensive industrial development without regard
to contamination, whereas others are sacrificing industrial progress in order
to enjoy contamination-free environmental conditions.

We personally are in favor of industrial development with a compatible
minimum of contamination, through the use of technoligical resources where
necessary, and the proper location, with regard to urban centers, in the
case of those industries producing an unacceptable level of pollution. Some
industries, of course, cause little or no pollution, so the problem does not
arise.

Maximum advantage of natural conditions offered by freshwater lakes or rivers
which flow into the sea is obtained by locating contamination-producing
industries downstream of urban centers. The freshwaters can be extracted,
utilized, and purified before being returned to flow into the sea, and
similarly industrial wastes can be treated before being released directly
into the sea.

A CONCRETE CASE

In the State of Rio Grande do Sul (Brazil) we enjoy such natural conditions
for locating contamination-producing industries without deleteriously
affecting the environment. (Other countries do, of course, possess similar
advantages.) This is the sparsely populated region of our deaboard located
between the Lagoa dos Patos (Duck Lake) and the Atlantic Ocean, a flat area
15 - 20 km. wide at its narrowest point. The Lagoa dos Patos is freshwater
and tideless except in the channel where it connects with the Atlantic Ocean.
The appended map clearly shows this area.

Since these freshwaters are used for various industrial purposes they have
to be recycled and disinfected before being returned to the lake and finally
discharged into the sea. One method of achieving this is that used by our
rice-planters, of simply treating the waste irrigation water before returning
it to the lake. Alternatively, as in our case, where we have numerous small
lagoons in the above mentioned seaboard, the wastewaters can be directed into
these lagoons and the impurities removed by a process of decantation and

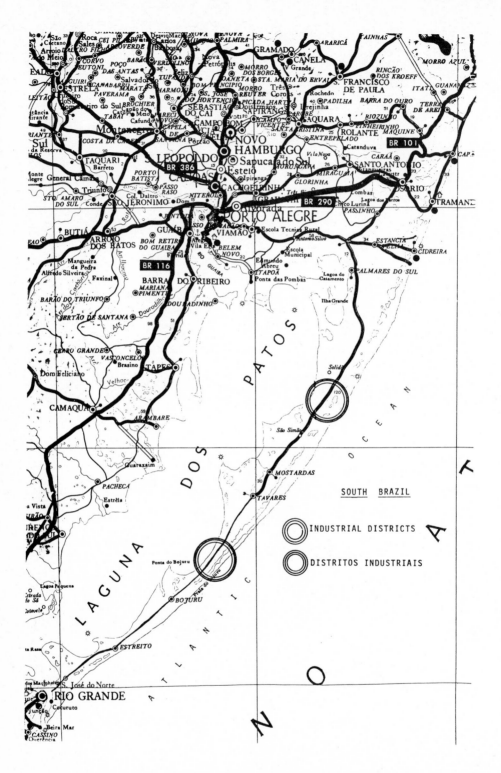

SOUTH BRAZIL

INDUSTRIAL DISTRICTS

DISTRITOS INDUSTRIAIS

filtration. Where these facilities are not available, artificial lakes can be constructed by simple excavation. Using either of these systems, organic wastes can be dealt with by normal bacteriological processes.

This deals with water pollution, but what of atmospheric pollution?

Our industrial area in question suffers minimally in this respect. Owing to its geographical position, east or west winds disperse pollution over the lake or the sea, respectively, without any harmful effect to anyone. Again, owing to its narrowness geologically, north or south winds deal effectively with any pollution produced industrially.

GENERAL CONCLUSIONS

This paper illustrates that industrial development can be achieved, even in these days of increasing pollution, without deleterious effect on mankind or the environment by adhering to the following guidelines:

1. Industry should be located away from urban centers - where geographically possible, downstream in areas irrigated by or between rivers, lakes and the sea, or on seaboards where winds can disperse atmospheric pollution.

2. Full use should be made of technological resources to reduce pollution of the atmosphere by smoke, gases, etc., and of waters by solid wastes, etc., and to recycle used waters.

3. Where available or applicable, natural or artificial lakes or lagoons should be utilized to effect decantation and filtration of wastewaters, the resulting wastes to be deposited in the sea.

PLANNING FORMS FOR 20TH - CENTURY CITIES

The Centre-City concept providing proximity to
the centre, economical public transport and
balanced city growth.

Gabriel Epstein, AA Dipl (Hons) Hon D Litt FRIBA
Shepheard Epstein & Hunter, Architects Town
Planners and Landscape Architects, London.

INTRODUCTION

This paper describes the need for new cities due to the vast scale of
present and future urbanization. It argues that enough is known of the
functions and needs of 20th century cities to allow us to make proposals
for their overall form and organization and that of their extensions. We
shall describe what these needs and functions are and shall outline the
Centre-City concept, setting it in its regional context. We shall touch on
questions of practical implementation and conclude by referring to some
of the wider implications of these proposals. We shall not discuss the
case for or against cities: we shall accept that they are needed.

Many new cities and city extensions have been planned or have grown in
these last 3 decades but very little consistent experience has been gained.
Basically different solutions are proposed each time, as if each case was
completely unique which is only partly true. Cities in the past, such as
the medieval ones, followed similar patterns although their actual forms
varied greatly due to particular conditions. What most of the new city
developments have in common is an overall organization based on
reasonable social or technical considerations; what they lack is that most
people do not like to live in them. The diagrams have not maintained their
promise at the level of human life.

THE NEED FOR NEW CITIES

In the next 30 years a vast additional number of people will live in cities.
Enormous population increase produces the steep graphs we are familiar
with, yet the graphs showing urbanization (the number of people in cities
of over 100,000) is even steeper due to the migrations from country to city.

The figures show that the main problem is the new city because additional
millions of people will either live in entirely new cities or in extensions
of existing ones, extensions so large as to virtually constitute new cities.
In the last few decades many cities of the third world have grown so much
that the original town is by now just a small nucleus in the middle of a vast
concentric growth. This is a pattern which industrialised countries have
seen develop over 2 centuries, with the familiar handicaps of choked
centres, long journeys, lack of contact with the countryside or the centre,
expensive servicing, etc.

And yet, the new cities will grow. Can we make them grow intelligently and economically? Can they become pleasant and human cities?

THE FUNCTIONS OF CITIES

The needs of today's cities are well known by now; they have changed little over the last few decades. Our aim is to develop a structure which can fulfil these needs. There are obvious differences between the needs in industrialised and developing countries, as well as differences in climate, social systems, topography and tradition. But the basic functions a city has to fulfil are similar everywhere.

We shall now describe some guidelines based on these functions. They are made up of the needs and desires of city people and also of the requirements of the planners and administrators who guide the city's development. There is no conflict between these two; they are inter-woven.

1. The city must be economical to build and to run.
2. It must grow without upsetting the completed parts. Therefore construction work should only take place contiguous to the already existing areas.
3. The eventual size of a city or a city-extension should not be written into a programme since it cannot be foreseen. While growing, the city must maintain a balance between the number of dwellings, central areas, shops, schools, industry, green areas, etc. It must be a finished entity at all stages of its growth.
4. At the various stages of development there should be virtually no need for 'advance investment' which might prove abortive if the city fails to grow further.
5. Everyone should be able to walk from their home to the city centre, public transport, schools and green areas. Walks within the city should generally be sheltered by arcades and shaded by trees.
6. There must be economical and convenient public transport which can expand simply as the city grows. The plan should also enable the use of cars and the possibility of parking near the home and at the centre. There should be reasonable separation of pedestrians from traffic.
7. The central areas must be so planned as to leave flexible (i. e. for future decision as construction proceeds) the intensity and form of building, without reference to a rigid grid or infra-structure. There must be freedom to choose, as the city grows, what form of homes should be built, whether areas should be developed by public or by private agencies, etc.
8. The principles of planning should be clear and few in number so that architects and engineers can fit their work into the general context with a minimum of directives, and so that the inhabitants can understand what goes on and why. The total layout should enable the easy and economical distribution of services like electricity, water, gas, telephone, etc.
9. Open space and large sports facilities should be on the edge of the city but within walking distance from homes. Larger industry should also be on the periphery of the city, with ample expansion areas.
10. Residential areas should be fairly quiet while the centre must be lively and animated. The city should bring to life again the street and the square as places for people. The whole city should have a pattern and a form of sub-division which people can understand and relate to.

CENTRE-CITY

<u>General</u>   (Figs. 1 and 2)

The fulfilment of the needs and functions mentioned above is the basis of the
Centre-City concept, so named because it refers to a city which closely
relates to its centre.   It was applied in the plan for the southern extension
of Vienna (1971), the plan for the extension of Bratislava (1968), several
University campuses such as Lancaster in England and a number of large
housing areas.   It is an extensible city of limited width, enabling all
inhabitants to reach the city centre in 5-7 minutes' walk.   Public transport
runs along the line of the pedestrian Main Centre which contains the major
central facilities.   Each quarter has its own pedestrian local centre.   Public
transport stations are located where local centres run into the Main Centre,
approximately every 600 metres.

The city grows quarter by quarter, getting longer in either one or both
directions. Roads, services and the public transport line grow similarly.
The total organism is always in balance, is always complete, whether it
stops growing or not.

Fig. 1.   <u>Plan for the Extension Southwards
of the City of Vienna.</u>
Received Honourable Mention in the
International Competition, 1971.

Discussed in <u>Stadt fuer Menschen</u> by
Dr. P. Peters (Callwey, Munich, 1973):
"The way in which pedestrians and necessary
traffic can both be accommodated, and the
way in which out of all this can grow a
city-form, is shown in an exemplary manner
in the detailed solutions".

<u>Roads</u> (Fig. 2.)

The primary roads run on either side of the city.   They are connected to
each other by local roads running at right angles to them and dipping under
the Main Centre in an underpass.   Off the local roads run access roads
leading to the residential areas and serving the rears of the local centres.
The Main Centre is also served from the back via cul-de-sacs branching
off local roads, as are the car parks located behind the Main Centre.

These roads give complete access by car, van and emergency vehicles to
all parts of the city without crossing main lines of pedestrian movement and
without any 2-level system except of the underpass of the local road under
the Main Centre.   They should all be lined with trees.

<u>The Quarters</u> (Fig. 2.)

The residential area of each quarter or neighbourhood is a maximum of
approximately 22 ha. to give reasonable walking distances to the local and
the Main Centre and to public transport.   At an average density of about
350 people per ha. this gives a population of about 8,000 per quarter, plus
about 1,500 people in flats in the local centre and the related part of the

Fig. 2. <u>Diagram of</u>
<u>Part of City Centre</u>

Main Centre running
from left to right.
Residential areas
are shaded; access
roads running into
them and to the
rear of local
centres are shown as
arrows. Pedestrian
ways continue the
line of local
centres outwards
(dotted lines) into
the neighbourhood
park and beyond the
primary road.

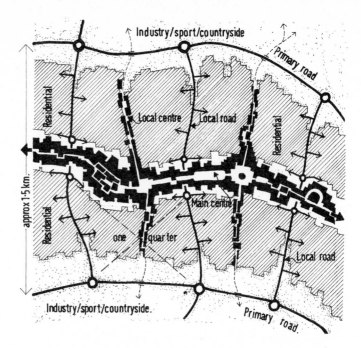

Main Centre, say a total of 9,500 people. This size is based on a maximum
distance from the back of the quarter to the Main Centre of 600 metres. In
many cases smaller distances, down to say 400 metres will be preferred
giving a population of say 5,000 per quarter. Densities will vary in different
countries and circumstances but too low a density should be prevented so
as to give people easy access to (and a choice of) different schools, shops
and other facilities.

Access roads off local roads and into the quarter are either cul-de-sacs or
loops. They will vary with housing layouts but should go to front doors for
easy servicing and parking and to the back of the local centre for supplying
it. Movement on foot will normally be from home to the local centre, and
from there either to the Main Centre or outwards to the park and beyond.
Journeys by car will normally be in the opposite direction, towards the local
road and to the Main Centre, or out to the primary road on the periphery.
Radburn-like separation between vehicles and pedestrians is possible but
probably unnecessary within the residential area.

The local centre (about 2 ha.) is a pedestrian walk flanked by shops, clinic,
workshops, nursery school, pub, library, blocks of flats, etc. The build-
up will tend to be looser towards the park and denser near the Main Centre.
There should be room for trees and benches and at least one side of the walk
should be arcaded for shelter from rain and sun. So as to facilitate direct
walks between neighbouring quarters there should be occasional pedestrian
crossings or underpasses at local roads.

<u>Outer Areas</u> (Fig. 2.)

Between the rear of each quarter and the primary road is a neighbourhood
park, smaller sports facilities as well as a primary school, thus allowing

double-use of playing fields, school assembly hall, etc., by both children
and adults. On the outside of the primary roads are large-scale sports
fields and larger industry and major green areas, with the countryside
beyond. These outer areas are reached on foot by a continuation of the
pedestrian line of the local centre outwards through the neighbourhood park
and from there either over or under the primary road. They can of course
also be reached by car or, in the case of large industries or similar concentrations, by an arrangement of mini-buses running from the nearest
public transport station.

Fig.   3.   <u>The University of Lancaster</u>

"The design successfully constitutes a
finished entity at all stages of growth
and has a flexibility which will allow
freedom of choice of development and size".
Part of citation: <u>1968 Civic Trust Award</u>
"A major asset of Lancaster is its
environmental success in human terms ...
the urban concept ... makes Lancaster a
model for University plans in the future".
Birks, T., <u>Building the New Universities</u>
David & Charles Ltd., Newton Abbot, 1972.

<u>Main Centre</u>   (Figs. 4 and 5.)

On an area of say about 6 ha. per quarter (12 ha. on both sides) will be
found all central facilities such as shops, offices, public buildings,
entertainment, secondary and higher education, hotels, flats and related
parking. They are disposed along a varied pedestrian area arcaded in part
or in whole, narrow in places, widening here and there into squares or
planted avenues. The buildings are supplied from the rear, along a cul-de-
sac branching off the local road which also leads to the carpark at the back
of the Main Centre used by those working, shopping or living in it. The walk
from this carpark to the Main Centre is via the intersection of main and
local centres next to the public transport station. This intersection is a
natural pedestrian gathering point and is likely to be a lively square.

The character of the centre, its intensity and type of use will vary along its
length; some uses like entertainment and restaurants might bring about a
widening of the centre into a network of pedestrian alleys while elsewhere
there might be quieter or more formal areas. What matters is that there
should be a balance between the number of inhabitants and the facilities in
the central areas so as to ensure their intensive use both day and evening.

The whole central area is built on natural ground; no fixed grid or concrete
infra-structure are required. The expensive pedestrian concrete "deck"
is absent and people are thus able to walk on the ground, away from traffic;
trees can be planted, changes in level can easily be accommodated, and
later alterations or renewal works are possible.

<u>Public Transport</u>

Public transport runs along the line of the Main Centre and is extended as
the city grows. The stations are at the intersections of main and local

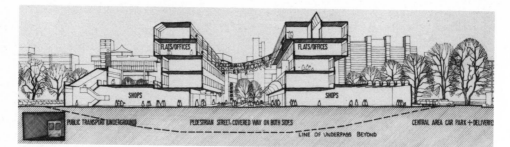

Fig. 4. Section through one possible kind of Main Centre.

Fig. 5. Sketch of Main Centre

The intersection of the Main
Centre (running from bottom
left to top right) with local
centres. The metro runs
below the far side of the
Main Centre; its station is
at the corner of the square
with a second entrance from
the parking area at the rear.

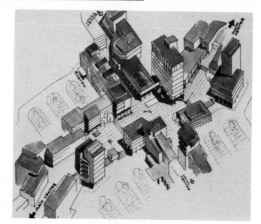

centres, i.e. approximately every 600 metres which is similar to the
distance between metro stations in central Paris.

The type of transport will vary from case to case. In the early stages of
growth large investments may not be justified and a bus in a sunken road at
the rear of one side of the Main Centre might serve. This road would pass
under the shallow part of the local road underpass. In other cases it might
be a tram and the road would be roofed over when it becomes economical
to transform it into a metro. Sophisticated automatic systems are available
combining high speed for long journeys with detachable stopping carriages.

It is a line-system, not a network, and as it has a potentially large
catchment area it should be economical to run and could therefore provide
a frequent service. It can be reached in a few minutes' walk from any home
and provides transport to all other parts of town without changing. Stations
are located at the natural 'desire points' and since it runs at a shallow level
it can be reached by descending a single flight of stairs. The reason for
placing the line at the rear of the Main Centre and not below it is, first, that
conflict with the foundations of buildings is avoided and, second, that an
open-cut road can be maintained for buses if desired and, third, that no
deep excavation is required to avoid the lower part of the underpass. At
the end of the built-up area the line would loop and after further growth of
the city the loop would be shifted along.

The nearness of stations to homes and shops suggests the possibility of
using public transport for deliveries of goods to depots at stations, to be

collected on foot, by trolley or by car.

Density, Growth and Regional Context

An average residential density of 350 pph results in a maximum population
of some 10,000 per quarter including residents in the central areas, giving
a length of about 600 metres for every 20,000 inhabitants. The width
between primary roads is an average of 1.35km and the total width of the
city including European-type industrial and recreational facilities, is about
3km. For a city of 100,000 this gives a length of 3km and a similar width.
As the city grows, the width and accessibility to the centre and to public
transport remain the same. Only the length increases which underlines the
need for a fast and economical transport spine. Lower densities are of
course possible and often desirable; however, they would cause greater
city length and increased expenditure on roads, transport and services
distribution. For easy access and choice of facilities it makes sense to
keep to a reasonably high density within the city; some people might well
want to live out of pedestrian reach of the centre in 'villages' external to
the city and reached along a continuation outwards of the local roads.

Fig. 6. Extension of Existing
City

Centre-City extension of
typical radial city. Public
transport runs from the old
centre in to the new Main
Centre. Old radial roads
are connected to the two
primary roads on either side
of the extension.

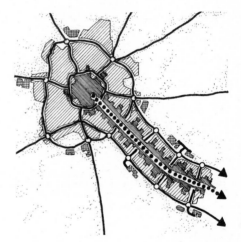

In the case of extensions of existing cities (either one or a whole star of
them) growth would be in one direction only, with public transport running
from the old centre into the new Main Centre. A new city built near a
major road or railway, however, could be connected by one or more feeder
roads and grow simultaneously in 2 directions. Smaller existing towns or
villages could be incorporated as quarters of the new town or be connected
to the prolongation outwards of local roads. In other cases 2 existing cities
would be connected by a development growing away from both.

Greater concentrations at less length can be achieved by 2 parallel Centre-
City developments, separated by open space or industry and connected by
occasional prolongations of the local roads and by public transport loops.
Sister-cities are familiar to us from towns located on both sides of a major
river, such as Buda and Pest.

Shape and overall disposition will vary in many ways, depending on
topography, regional context, traditions and many other factors; but while

the basis of the main principles is nearness to the centre, attractive public
transport and balanced growth, the broader regional implications are equally
important.   They were the subject of an article by a great architect and
planner, Heinz Rau, in 'The Guardian' on the 23 April 1963:
"....an alternative form of development to the spiderweb pattern is
proposed..... The form of development is referred to as the 'string-
settlement'.   The characteristics of this form are the disposition of various
uses of land, industries, commercial areas, residential places and
recreational areas in relation to the main lines of transport, communication
and power distribution..... The advantages of the string settlement are
many.   It enables modern rapid transport by road or rail to be exploited
to the fullest extent, free of ever-mounting congestion, with its excessive
costs, as found at the core of radial systems.   Uses of land which generate
a great deal of traffic movement are not necessarily concentrated (as in
the conurbation at a congested node) but located along a line of rapid
movement....these concentrations are all made readily possible in a string
settlement without congestion.   We have perhaps too often thought of
concentration as proximity in space rather than measuring it in terms of
travel time or cost".

It is thus that broad regional factors and the search for wellbeing in cities
point to similar solutions.

Implementation

The Centre-City concept is not a plan but a growth-diagram for a city,
large or small.   It has already brought about very varied plans and will do
so again: plans affected by hilly sites, by existing settlements or rivers,
cities of varying densities due to climatic or economic conditions, with
endless variations in residential layout or housing types and with all manner
of central areas, some like formal avenues and squares, others more like
the bazaars of Damascus.   Not only will cities of contrasting character
emerge, but within each city there will be very different quarters, both in
road pattern and in buildings, and central areas changing in function, layout
and feeling along their length.   There will be different parks, different
heights of buildings; no doubt good as well as bad architects will be
employed.   But all variations that people or circumstances will bring about
take place within a framework intended to ensure the easy working and
trouble-free growth of the whole city-body.   It is a framework of a few
rules only; to summarize them again: the width between periphery roads
to be about 1.5km; local roads at intervals of approximately 600 metres
passing below the centre; a central line of public transport; rear road
access by cul-de-sacs to shops and public buildings; pedestrian main
centre and local centres intersecting approximately every 600m and at least
partly arcaded; open space and industry outside periphery roads; a
reasonably high residential density and the rule that new construction should
only take place next to the parts already completed.

It is a growth diagram only, not a 'master plan'.   On the regional or
national level it requires the reservation of a strip of land some 3 km wide
to be laid out in accordance with general policies related to the economy,
transport, energy supply, landscape and other regional factors.   The control
of the use of city land should be vested in the city wherever possible, with
each quarter having considerable autonomy.

There is no need for detailed layouts to be planned far ahead.   Different

residential arrangements will be proposed, different buildings for the
central area will be suggested, shops or hotels will seek suitable sites;
what the planners have to do is to make reasonable choices within the
overall arrangement and consider townscape, daylight, etc. For vitality
and economy there should be a mixture of all uses that are not incompatible.
Obviously the city will gain if planners encourage a good sequence of spaces
in the centre, or give good advice about residential layout, or plan
convenient loop roads from railway station or aerodrome to the centre. But
even a planner who simply adheres to the basic principles while being
relaxed and adaptable in detailed implementation will see a city grow that
is ordered yet human, clear yet varied.

CONCLUSIONS

This scheme for the growth of town extensions and for new cities is not
presented here because of any virtue of the linear system as such, but
because of its direct relevance to human well-being in the city. The word
'linear' has been in fashion in planning jargon at certain times; in this
case the form evolved because a) it enables everyone to live near the centre
and near the open country. b) it is the only form giving easy access to
simple and economic public transport. c) it is a pattern of growth allowing
expansion while maintaining a continuous balance between the different
elements of the city.

We insist on point a) because if democracy in large communities is to be
a reality, if young and old are to belong to their city, enjoy it, feel at home
in it, and if the crisis of the isolated family cell is to be dealt with, then
the first need is easy access to the centre, and that means access on foot.
Perhaps equally important is access to parks and the countryside.

We insist on b) because life in the city can no longer run smoothly without
good public transport. It has to be economical and must clearly be more
attractive for most journeys than the car. That means frequency of
service, no change from line to line and a reasonable walking distance
from home to station. Moreover, it must be a type of transport that does
not disrupt the centre which is reserved for the use of pedestrians.

We insist on c) because our generation is perhaps more conscious than
any other of the need for balanced city growth in which the different
elements can all grow in proportion, resulting in a complete city at all
stages. We have seen too much of paralysed city centres without trees,
without room for growth and with stupid land values. Also, we have seen
too much of suburbs with plenty of green but no central animated place and
with shops and schools far from home. We must find a balance again and
keep it.

I should also refer to the importance of cost: economy in planning, building
and running a city is essential because expensive utopias do not get built
even in the richer countries, and certainly not in the poor ones who are by
far the most affected by the problems of fast urbanization. This is one
of the reasons for building the whole city including its centre on natural
ground, which has the further advantage of avoiding sordid and uncomfortable underground areas for access and parking; what is more, walking on
natural ground gives the possibility of walking under trees.

I shall not here go into the economic assessment of Centre-City compared to other forms of development beyond saying that it shows economy in land use, overall cost of construction and energy consumption. The relationship between the layout of the city and its energy and flow systems is perhaps obvious: it results in a simple and economical distribution system. Studies have shown that the city can certainly be built at the cost of any 'conventional' one, normally for less.

There are many historical precedents for this city form: indeed many of the old unfortified agricultural and commercial villages and towns developed in length, centred on the market street or broadwalk, with buildings on either side whose market gardens and outhouses stretched back to a periphery service road, on the far side of which lay the larger fields. As to the maximum distance of 600 metres from the back of the quarter to the centre, it is the maximum dimension from town hall to city walls in the large majority of medieval cities.

People in eastern or western cities, poor ones or rich ones, will all strive for a natural progression from the privacy of the home to the relationships of street or court, to the neighbourhood, and to the city as a whole. In Centre-City each quarter may well have its own character but everyone will use, and meet in, the common centre. We all want peace and quiet at night, but at other times we want to see people or mix with them, and we can only do that on foot. Walking is in any case good for us and the animation of street and square is an antidote to the impersonality of much of our work, while proximity to park and sport is equally important to many sedentary people.

It is said that our civilization dies because our cities die; also that our cities die because our civilization dies; but we know from psychosomatic medicine that the circle of mental and physical ills can be broken into at either side. Let us then break into it where we can, and start with the cities. Inevitably we shall build large cities; let us build them with the advantages of the large and those of the smaller city.

OPTIMIZING URBAN DENSITY

Robert W. Marans and John Douglas Wellman
Institute for Social Research, Ann Arbor, Michigan

ABSTRACT

Rising costs of housing and public services, increasingly expensive and scarce energy resources, and growing demands for farm-
lands and open space indicate a trend toward greater population
density in urban areas. While studies of housing preference and
responses to crowding suggest that human problems could arise
with increasing density, definitive statements about optimal
densities are presently not possible. As a guide to action in
the face of this uncertainty, this paper suggests that planners
and designers think in terms of the human needs which may arise
out of mis-matches between people's preferred and their actual
environmental situations. Three such needs are considered --
the need for temporary escape from environmental stressors, the
need for experiencing natural stimuli, and the need for privacy.
For each need state, pertinent research findings are reviewed
and examples of ameliorative planning and design measures are
presented. It is suggested that since human needs are generated
and fulfilled in all aspects of the life space, specialists in
certain of those aspects -- such as work, housing, transportation,
and recreation -- must integrate their efforts to serve the whole
person.

INTRODUCTION

Throughout the Western world, it is becoming increasingly likely
that the population density of our metropolitan areas will be
considerably higher in the future. A number of factors point in
this direction. First, there is evidence that single family
housing is becoming more costly for the political jurisdictions
within which it is located as well as for the consumer. Low
density development requires more land for housing and for the
streets, schools, recreation areas, and institutions necessary to
support it. Costs per household of such services as police and
fire protection, trash pick-up, and mail delivery tend to rise
as density of development decreases. At the same time, the costs
of providing these services are increasing at a precipitous rate
and are being passed along to area residents. Added service
charges in the form of taxes, together with rising building costs,
have reduced the ability of many consumers to purchase new
single family housing.

Second, as the availability of gasoline decreases and its price
rises, the demand for housing at great distances from employment
and shopping centers will constrict. Conversely, there will be
increases in demand for housing concentrated around major centers
of activity. In a similar vein, the introduction of high speed
public transportation will create new nodes around which urban
agglomerations will form.

Third, the growing awareness of the value of open lands, including forests and farms, will place a premium on such lands for
recreation and agricultural uses, particularly if they are within
the confines of an urban region. Should such lands be used for
these purposes or retained in their natural state, housing to
accomodate a growing metropolitan population will, by necessity,
be built at higher densities.

The inevitable increase in the population density of metropolitan
areas raises the question of its optimum level. In considering
this question, there are several dimensions worthy of discussion.
There is the economic aspect dealing with the maximization of
return on investment and the concept of "highest and best use."
There is also the technological dimension which considers engineering capabilities of both building and infrastructure including transportation networks and utility systems. Finally,
there is the sociopsychological dimension which focuses on human
responses to density-related phenomena. While acknowledging the
interrelationships between these dimensions, this brief paper
will address itself to that one which is little understood and
often ignored by planners and builders -- the human response to
density and density-related phenomena. By way of background, an
overview of empirical research covering the effects of density
on human behavior will be presented. Next, we will suggest a way
of thinking about the relationship between people and the environments in which they find themselves. The essential notion is
that of individual needs arising from mis-matches between a person's preferred and his actual environment. Third, from the
variety of density-related needs or need-states, we will consider
three which we expect will become more prevalent in the future.
For each need state we will present relevant research findings
as well as design and planning guidelines.

AN OVERVIEW OF PAST RESEARCH

During the past several decades research on human responses to
density and density-related phenomena has taken two directions --
one dealing with people's preferences for and evaluations of
residential environments, the other focusing on human pathologies
which may result from crowding. The research on residential
evaluations and preferences has empirically demonstrated that,
in general, people have strong preferences for single family
housing on large lots (7, 14, 24, 12). People cite the desire
for home ownership and indoor and outdoor private space as the
most important reasons for their preferences. These findings
are certainly germane in any discussion of optimum human density,
but they cannot be applied without awareness of the conditioning

influence of other factors. For example, one's preference for a
low density, single family residential setting or a higher density multi-family development may depend on one's stage in the
family life cycle. Studies of satisfaction with housing at different densities have shown that whereas the elderly are more
satisfied in relatively high-density developments which foster
opportunities for socializing (28, 25), families with children
are more satisfied with low density, single family neighborhoods
than with townhouse neighborhoods (16).

The second area of research on human responses to density is concerned with the hypothesis that crowded conditions produce stress
in humans, and that this stress leads to various forms of physical, psychological and social dysfunction. Much of the interest
in density and human pathology has its genesis in the so-called
animal studies. Research conducted animals by Calhoun (1),
Leyhausen (18), Southwick (32), and Christian, Flyger and Davis
(3), among others, has strongly suggested the existence of a
causal linkage between population density and pathology. Numerous popular treatments (see ref. 38) have helped raise this relationship to the level of a prevailing belief, not only with
respect to animals but to human populations as well. The implications of a density-pathology relationship for humans have a-
roused increasing interest among social scientists concerned with
the prospects for man on a shrinking planet.

There is widespread agreement among social scientists concerned
with the effects of density on humans that the animal studies
must be accepted very cautiously. These studies have been in-
valuable as warnings and spurs to research on human populations,
but simple extrapolations from caged rats to people living in
cities are probably wrong. Nor has correlational research on
human settlements as yet provided convincing evidence of a
density-pathology link. In his census tract study of Honolulu,
Schmitt (30) found evidence of a density-sociopathology linkage.
However, this finding is contradicted by his own (31) study of
Hong Kong, and by Winsborough's (37) Chicago study. Galle, Gove
and McPherson's (10) study of Chicago found no density effect
using traditional density measures (housing units per structure,
and structures per acre), but did find a strong density effect
using what they termed "interpersonal press" (persons per room
and rooms per housing unit). Freedman (8) supports this finding
with his suggestion that the number of interacting individuals,
rather than density per se, influences human behavior. Gillis
(11) found in his analysis of Edmonton census tract data that
only building type (single family vs. multiple family) showed
significant relationships with welfare payments and juvenile
delinquency when income and ethnicity controls were applied.

We noted earlier that studies of the elderly living together in
high-density developments reveal high levels of residential satisfaction. Other studies have suggested that density by itself
may not be a determining factor in residential satisfaction;
rather, the perception of the similarity of one's neighbors contributes more strongly to that satisfaction (16, 21). The point
is that the well-being of individuals in different types of

environmental settings may be a function of the interaction between the density of development, the characteristics of the
people who live together and the perceptions of those characteristics by the residents themselves.

One factor which may mediate responses to density and crowding
is accessibility to the out-of-doors. A fascinating piece of
evidence in support of this factor is provided in Mitchell's (26)
finding that, among Hong King residents living with non-kinsmen,
those people living in the upper stories of multi-story dwellings
were significantly more likely to score high on an index of
emotional illness than were those living nearer the ground level.
Mitchell's interpretation of this finding is that crowding stress
is more likely to be experienced under conditions of forced
interaction with non-relatives than with kinsmen, and that a retreat from the stressful condition is easier for those people
living closer to the ground floor.

What can we conclude from the existing evidence on the relationship between residential density and sociopathological behavior
in humans? Lawrence (17) has examined the "meager" body of data
on human response to density, and judged that "...the only certain conclusion that can be drawn at this time is that there is
no clear demonstrable linear relationship between high density
and aberrant human behaviors, or between the social crowding of
the individual and agression." Similar conclusions have been
reached by others (38, 33, 8). It appears, and not surprisingly,
that the density connection for humans is very complex, that
people are able to adapt to a wide range of conditions, and that
whatever relationship may exist is mediated by such variables as
gender (8, 34), interpersonal relationships (26), and social and
physical structuring (19).

HUMAN NEEDS RELATED TO DENSITY

The review of past research has demonstrated the limitations in
our understanding of human responses to density. Clearly we
are a long way from being able to specify the conditions of optimal human density. One of our purposes in this paper is to suggest that some improvement in our ability to define and design
for optimal human density might be realized through an improved
understanding of certain human needs related to density.

The beginning point for this discussion of density-related human
needs is in a problem-solving model of man. Numerous theorists
have described man as an inveterate problem-solver, constantly
monitoring his environment and mapping his actual situation a-
gainst his image of preferred conditions, then seeking ways of
resolving discrepancies (13, 9). The existence of a problem
state does not necessarily mean that the person's present situation is bad. The absence of good fit may simply indicate that
things are not as good as they could be. As the poet Alexander
Pope so aptly phrased it several centuries ago:
>   Hope springs eternal in the human breast;
>   Man never is, but always to be, blest.

The formation of the image or concept of a preferred condition
is a fascinating subject in its own right. Undoubtedly a multi-
tude of variables are operating, and while a substantial discussion of this subject is beyond the scope of this paper, several
illustrations are in order. Some sources of the image of preferred conditions may run very deep. Anecdotal evidence that
man has a strong preference for natural environments is convincing; witness the longstanding interest by people in urban, industrial societies in parks, zoos, trees, gardens, house plants,
and so forth. Presumably, this interest in natural stimuli derives in part from the fact that man evolved in a natural environment. Constitutional differences such as whether one is an intro-
vert or an extrovert (6) very likely condition needs, such as
needs for privacy. Childhood experiences, information received
from the media and other learning also help determine the preferred state or image against which we measure reality.

Of the many needs generated from person-environment mismatches,
we have chosen to concentrate on three that are particularly appropriate in a discussion of human density -- the need for temporary escape from stressful conditions, the need for experiencing
natural stimuli, and the need for privacy. Before discussing
each of these, several qualifying remarks are necessary. First,
the needs we will examine are by no means all-inclusive; neither
lower-order needs such as those for food, shelter and safety,
nor higher-order needs like love and self-actualization have been
considered (23, 2). Second, while interest in human needs extends far back into history, empirical research is in its infancy,
and is fraught with methodological problems. Thus, the research
findings we will report for each need state must be accepted with
circumspection. A third point to be recognized is that needs are
temporal, and are not felt by any given individual with the same
intensity at every point in time. Both of the elements that combine to produce need states fluctuate over time; we all re-define
and adjust our preferred states as our information and perceptions
change and as we mature, and our relevant actual physical and
social environments are constantly changing in time and space.

The Need for Temporary Escape
One of our basic assumptions is that in the future most people
will live in more densely developed settlements than we do today.
Assuming for the moment that no radical changes in technology or
lifestyle occur, those future settlements will not only be more
crowded, but they will also be more complex, more confusing,
noisier, and more polluted than is the norm today. In the future,
then, we may expect an increasing occurrence of person-environment mismatch. One may deal with a mismatch by modifying the
environment, or himself, or both. In the long-run, as Dubos (5)
has cautioned us, man will probably continue to adapt to poor
environmental conditions; this is a modification of the person.
On the other side of the coin, the person can modify his environment, both by direct manipulation and by physically leaving the
scene. Direct manipulations of the environment are largely confined to one's own home and property. The ability to control
environmental stressors undoubtedly is a major factor behind the
popularity of the single family home. However, retreat to the

haven of one's home is a particular form of temporary escape
which, for the reasons advanced earlier, we expect will be less
available in the future than it is now. As constraints on single
family home ownership increase, other forms of temporary escape
should grow in popularity.

Several research findings bear on the issue of temporary escape.
Mitchell's (26) finding -- that people living in multi-family
housing units on the lower floors of high rises show less emotional strain than people in similar conditions on the upper
floors -- alerts us to the importance of the ease of accessibility to temporary escape. Mandell and Marans (20) found that
people living in poor quality neighborhoods, characterized by
crowding and poor upkeep, tend to rate temporary escape as an
important reason for outdoor recreation activity. In our study
of vacationers in northern Michigan (22) we found that one of
the most important reasons for people's being there was to leave
temporarily the pressures and problems of the urban environment.

Obviously, the most significant contributions planners and other
influentials can make toward the solution of people's needs for
temporary escape lie in making cities cleaner, quieter, and more
beautiful. However, given that we cannot realistically expect
to eliminate noise, dirt, ugliness, and other physical stressors
of the urban environment, there are other lines of action possible. For example, one measure is to provide easy access to out-
lying areas such as regional parks and open lands. In this connection, special attention must be paid to assuring access to
those living in the most stressful environments; it is likely
that those who need places for temporary escape most are also
those with the most limited opportunities to use them. Another
way of meeting needs for temporary escape is to create open
spaces in the form of parks in high-density urban centers; the
presence of a Central Park, a Bois de Boulogne, or a Hyde Park
where people can find solitude and be away from the noise and
fumes of city streets can provide more than an aesthetic experience to the urban dweller.

The Need to Experience Nature
We mentioned previously that there seems to be an intrinsic need
for man to experience nature and the out-of-doors. While there
is little research to demonstrate that the survival of urban man
is dependent upon the fulfillment of that need, there is considerable evidence from the research on residential environments
that demonstrates the importance of natural settings to residential satisfaction. Wilson's study (36) of a North Carolina community reported that adult residents described their ideal neighborhood as one which was country-like and close to nature, while
Peterson (27), in attempting to identify peoples' preferences
for the visual appearance of neighborhoods, found that "harmony
with nature" was one of the most significant dimensions of choice.
Similarly, in studies of new towns in the United States, the
proximity to nature and the surrounding countryside was a principal reason given by residents in attracting them to their communities (16, 35). Still other studies have shown that preferences for single-family homes and large lots were, in part, a desire for trees, grass, and a natural landscape (15).

In the United States, these preferences have been expressed by
individuals from all socioeconomic levels. Yet many people will
never realize their desire to live "near the country" or in a
house with "a large lot." In fact, it is apparent for the reasons discussed at the beginning of this paper that an increasing
proportion of people will have to meet their needs for the experience of natural stimuli in densely settled urban environments.
What can planners and designers do to help meet their needs? At
the level of the immediate housing unit, imaginative architectural design can help through such devices as the provision of balconies which can be used for potted plants or even small gardens.
In designing multi-unit structures, more attention should be paid
to courtyards, trees, and other landscaping efforts to soften and
naturalize the residential environment. The concept of cluster
residential development, in addition to reducing development
costs, has enabled many developers in the United States to achieve
a desired density while maintaining attractive and usable open
land. This pattern was successfully demonstrated in Radburn, New
Jersey in the 1920's and has been used in contemporary new towns
in Great Britain, the Scandanavian countries, and the United
States.

There is little doubt that, given the opportunity, most people
will choose a form of living which includes a natural environment. Since people's needs are neither generated nor consummated
in the residential environment alone, we need to consider measures to introduce natural stimuli into other aspects of their
life spaces, such as their shopping and work environments. The
downtown malls in numerous American cities have demonstrated the
economic, as well as the human, wisdom of this approach. Finally,
at the neighborhood, regional and national levels, we must continue to develop parks with varying degrees of naturalness, from
the city vest-pocket park to national wilderness areas, as well
as complementary means of access to them.

The Need for Privacy

The importance of privacy in residential satisfaction has been
shown in numerous studies covering both the individual dwelling
and the larger neighborhood setting. In contemporary houses,
lack of privacy is often a source of irritation because of lack
of partitions. In the density studies of high rise buildings in
Hong Kong, a source of irritation for members of families was the
limited opportunity to get away by themselves (26). At the same
time, a major complaint of people living in high density developments with common party walls was the transmission of sounds between housing units. Concern was expressed about their neighbors hearing them as well as their hearing the neighbors. Indeed, noise is a dimension of privacy greatly affecting people's
responses to where they live. Quiet neighborhoods are viewed
much more favorably than are neighborhoods where dwellings are
exposed to noises from nearby neighbors, children playing out-of-
doors, and heavy traffic (21). As dramatized by the recent
"piano murders" in a Japanese highrise, sound transmission under
certain residential conditions is a major problem and requires
much greater attention from both building technologists and be-
havioral researchers.

CONCLUSIONS

Our beliefs on several aspects of the question of optimal human
density should be clear at this point. We believe that human
densities in urban areas will inevitably be higher in the future.
We feel that without serious planning and design efforts to miti-
gate the problems for people latent in such densely settled areas,
the long-range prospects for urban man are not encouraging.
Though we are concerned with the potential impacts of high density living on the inhabitants of such environments, we are convinced that our understanding of the ways in which density may
lead to problems is very rudimentary and in need of extensive
research. We believe that one fruitful way of considering the
impact of density on man is to think in terms of need states a-
rising from mismatches between preferred and actual environmental
conditions. In this connection, we feel that much work is required in developing our collective understanding of the ways in
which people develop and modify their images of preferred environments. While we are convinced that much more must be known about
the density-related aspects of the man-environment interface, we
believe that we cannot wait until all the necessary information
is in hand, and that improvements can be made by attuning planning and design professionals to the human needs exemplified in
this paper. Finally, we hope it is clear that we believe that
man-environment relationships must be approached systematically,
rather than piecemeal. Improvements in the livability of residential environments are important, but they may be nullified by
losses in other aspects of the urban activity system. People
move through many environments, and if we are to help the whole
person -- and nothing less is enough -- we have to consider all
those environments. It is imperative that scientists, planners,
designers and other decision-makers who now are concerned ex-
clusively with work, home, transportation, and recreation begin
to integrate their work with that of the others.

REFERENCES

(1)   Calhoun, J. B., Population density and social pathology,
        Scientific American, 206: 139-148 (1962).
(2)   Cantril, H. (1966) The Pattern of Human Concerns, New
        Brunswick, N. J., Rutgers University Press.
(3)   Christian, J., V. Flyger, and D. Davis, Factors in the mass
        mortality of a herd of sitka deer (Cervis Nippon),
        Chesapeake Science, 1: 79-95 (1960).
(4)   Cooper, C., Residential dissatisfaction in multi-family
        housing, in W. M. Smith (ed.), Behavior, Design, and
        Policy Aspects of Human Habitats, Green Bay, Wisc.,
        University of Wisconsin - Green Bay Press.
(5)   Dubos, R. (1965) Man Adapting, New Haven, Conn., Yale Uni-
        versity Press.
(6)   Eysenck, H. J. (1967) The Biological Basis of Personality,
        Springfield, Illinois, Thomas.
(7)   Foote, N., J. Abu-Lighod, M. Foley, and L. Winnick (1960)
        Housing Choices and Housing Constraints, New York,
        McGraw-Hill.

(8)   Freedman, J. L., A positive view of population density,
      Psychology Today, Sept., 58-61, 86 (1971).
(9)   French, J. R. P., Jr., W. Rodgers, and S. Cobb (1974) "Ad-
      justment as Person-Environment Fit," in G. V. Coelho,
      D. A. Hamburg, and J. E. Adams (eds.), Coping and Adapta-
      tion, New York, Basic Books.
(10) Galle, O. R., W. R. Gove, and J. H. McPherson, Population
      density and pathology: what are the relations for man?,
      Science, 176: 23-30 (1972).
(11) Gillis, A. R., Population density and social pathology: the
      case of building type, social allowance and juvenile de-
      linquency, Social Forces, 53: 306-314 (1974).
(12) Hinshaw, M. and K. Allott, Environmental Preferences of
      future housing consumers, Journal of the American Insti-
      tute of Planners, 39 (March): 102-107 (1970).
(13) Knopf, R. C. and B. L. Driver, A problem solving approach
      to recreation behavior, paper presented at the 77th
      Annual Meeting, Michigan Academy of Science, Arts and
      Letters, Ann Arbor, Michigan (1973).
(14) Lansing, J. B., E. Mueller, and N. Barth (1966) Residential
      Location and Urban Mobility: The Second Wave of Inter-
      views, Ann Arbor: Institute for Social Research, The
      University of Michigan.
(15) Lansing, J. B., and G. Hendricks (1967) Automobile Owner-
      ship and Residential Density, Ann Arbor, The Institute
      for Social Research, The University of Michigan.
(16) Lansing, J. B., R. W. Marans, and R. B. Zehner (1970)
      Planned Residential Environments, Ann Arbor: Institute
      for Social Research, The University of Michigan.
(17) Lawrence, J. E. S., Science and sentiment: overview of re-
      search on crowding and human behavior, Psychological
      Bulletin, 81: 712-720 (1974).
(18) Leyhausen, P., The sane community - a density problem?,
      Discovery, 16: 27-33 (1965).
(19) Loo, C., Important issues in researching the effects of
      crowding on humans, Representative research in Social
      Psychology, 4: 219-226 (1973).
(20) Mandell, L. and R. W. Marans (1972) Family and Individual
      Participation in Outdoor Recreation: A National Study,
      draft report prepared for the Bureau of Outdoor Recrea-
      tion, U. S. Dept. of the Interior, Ann Arbor, The Insti-
      tute for Social Research, The University of Michigan.
(21) Marans, R. W. and W. Rodgers (1974) Toward an Understanding
      of Community Satisfaction, A. Hawley and V. Rock (eds.),
      Metropolitan America - Papers on the State of Knowledge,
      National Academy of Sciences.
(22) Marans, R. W., S. J. Newman, J. D. Wellman, and J. A. Kruse
      (1975) Living Patterns and Attitudes of Water-Oriented
      Residents, Ann Arbor, The Institute for Social Research,
      The University of Michigan.
(23) Maslow, A. H. (1954) Motivation and Personality, New York,
      Harper and Row.
(24) Michelson, W. (1969) Analytic sampling for design informa-
      tion: a survey of housing experience, in H. Sanoff and
      S. Cohen, Proceedings of the 1st Annual Environmental De-
      sign Research Association Conference.

(25) Michelson, W. (1970) Man and His Urban Environment: A
     Sociological Perspective, Reading, Mass.: Addison-
     Wesley.
(26) Mitchell, R. E., Some implications of high density housing,
     American Sociological Review, 36: 18-29 (1971).
(27) Peterson, G. L. "A model of preference: qualitative analy-
     sis of the perception of the visual appearance of resi-
     dential neighborhoods, Journal of Regional Science, 7:
     19-32 (1967).
(28) Rosow, I. (1967) Social Integration of the Aged, New York:
     The Free Press.
(29) Saile, D. G., R. Borodah and M. Williams (1972) "Families
     in public housing: A study of three localities in Rock-
     ford, Illinois," in W. Mitchell (ed.), EDRA 3, Environ-
     mental Design: Research and Practice, Los Angeles,
     University of California.
(30) Schmitt, R. C. Density, delinquency and crime in Honolulu,
     Sociology and Social Research, 44: 274-276 (1957).
(31) Schmitt, R. C., Implications of density in Hong Kong,
     Journal of the American Institute of Planners, 29: 210-
     217 (1963).
(32) Southwick, C. H., "An experimental study of intragroup
     agnostic behavior in Rhesus monkeys, Behavior, 28: 182-
     209 (1967).
(33) Stokols, D., A social-psychological model of human crowding
     phenomena, Journal of the American Institute of Planners,
     28: 72-83 (1972).
(34) Stokols, D., M. Rall, B. Pinner and J. Schopler, Physical,
     social and personal determinants of the perception of
     crowding, Environment and Behavior, 5: 87-115 (1973).
(35) Weiss, S., R. Burby, E. Kaiser, T. Donnelly, and R. Zehner,
     New community development: a national study of environ-
     mental preferences and the quality of life, Research Re-
     views, The University of North Carolina (1973).
(36) Wilson, R. L. (1962), Livability of the city: attitudes
     and urban development, Urban Growth Dynamics, New York,
     Wiley.
(37) Winsborough, H. H., The social consequences of high popula-
     tion density, Law and Contemporary Problems, 30: 120-
     126 (1965).
(38) Zlutnik, S. and I. Altman (1972) Crowding and human be-
     havior, in J. Wohlwill and D. Carson (eds.), Environment
     and the Social Sciences: Perspectives and Applications,
     Washington, D. C., American Psychological Association.

URBAN EXTENSIONS IN BELGIUM:
A CASE STUDY IN THE FRAMEWORK OF
URBANIZED NORTH WESTERN EUROPE

I.B.F. KORMOSS
Professor, College of Europe,
Secretary General, NW European Physical Planning Conference,
Bruges, Belgium

HISTORICAL ROOTS OF THE BELGIAN URBAN AND REGIONAL PATTERN

As a battlefield till the very last month of the Second World War, the area
Amsterdam - Ruhr - Lorraine - Calais had been almost completely destroyed; its
urban and transportation infrastructures were especially damaged and its
economy completely disorganized. The harbour of Antwerp had, exceptionally,
been spared and this favoured the rapid rebirth of its traffic and that of
its hinterland. As a dispatching center for the relief brought by the
U.N.R.R.A. followed by the "Marshall Plan", Belgium then began a rapid climb
towards a high standard of life which could be compared, at the beginning of
the Fifties, to that of neutral countries, e.g. Switzerland and Sweden,
which did not suffer from the disastrous effects of the war.

Individual motorisation, as a natural response, in the population's mind, to
wealth is progressing very rapidly here (1) and is bringing with it, the
well known phenomenon of a suburbanisation and even the dispersion of the
habitat over the countryside.

(1)   Passenger cars in use in selected European countries
        Source : UN Statistical Yearbook 1953, Table 139 and own
                 calculation

Country	Thousand units			Per 1000 inhabitants			Per sq. km		
	1946	1948	1950	1946	1948	1950	1946	1948	1950
Belgium	86	177	274	10.0	20.5	31.8	2.8	5.8	9.0
Denmark	100	108	118	23.4	25.2	27	2.3	2.5	2.7
France	1550	1520	1600	36.9	36.2	38.1	2.8	2.7	2.9
Germany (W) x	...	283	598	...	5.9	12.5	...	1.2	2.4
Italy	150	219	342	3.2	4.7	7.3	0.5	0.7	1.1
Netherlands	47	86	139	4.6	8.5	13.7	1.5	2.7	4.3
Sweden	138	180	253	19.6	25.5	35.9	0.3	0.4	0.6
Switzerland	63	106	147	13.4	22.5	31.2	1.5	2.6	3.6
Great Britain	1818	2020	2317	37.2	41.4	47.4	7.9	8.7	10.1

x Saar excluded

177

But the Belgian countryside and especially the flat open country of Flanders,
the hills and plateaux of Brabant have ranked among the most cultivated and
populated European regions since the Middle Ages, with a very high population density as in certain areas of Italy, the Rhine valley, Bohemia and
Ireland. At the creation of the Belgian State (1830), the population of the
country amounted to 3.8 millions, as against 2.6 for the Netherlands and
6.6 for Ireland, the latter being a very populated country before the Hungry
Forties. In comparison ($\pm$ 1850) : France 35.8 millions, Austria-Hungary
30.6, Germany 29.8, Italy 25.0, Great Britain 20.8, Spain 15.2 and Russia
64.9 (of which 60.8 in Europe). (2)

When the Industrial Revolution overwhelmed the Continent in the middle of
the 19th Century, it was precisely in the new born Belgian State, rich not
only in labour but also in coal, namely in the valleys of the Samber and the
Meuse, that the best conditions for the development of heavy industry were
to be found. This heavy industry was, afterwards, to become famous far over
the State's frontiers. (3)

One of the most important consequences, and in the long run the main one,
of the first Industrial Revolution was the breaking down of the thousand
year equilibrium between city and countryside brought about by a new means
of transportation that shortened distances for both passenger and goods and
allowed heavy goods to be carried by rail rather than by   waterway and sea.
Besides its intrinsic role in the organisation of the infrastructure of the
industrial area of the Midlands, South Wales, Tyneside, the "Nord" of France,
the central spine of Belgium, the Ruhr, High-Silesia, the fringes of Bohemia,
and so on, the spatial influence of the railway is clearly felt on a broader
scale in that it changed the aspect of whole countries; in France for instance, one of the reasons for the giantism of Paris and the sclerosis of the
provinces is the radial-concentric shape of the railway network centered on
Paris. (4)

The case of Belgium is exceptional : it is the coincidence of the creation
of a State with the outbreak of the industrial and, consequently, railway
revolution : that explains why political and managerial organisation, economic development and social progress have become dominated by and even
reliant upon this new means of transportation. The principal tracks of the
network radiate in every direction, starting from Brussels (5) which has

---

(2) V. Showers, The World in Figures, J. Wiley, New York, 1973 (pp.202-204).
(3) Building of plants in Russia e.g.
(4) J.-F. GRAVIER, "Paris et le désert français", Le Portulan, Paris, 1947.
    The same phenomenon can be noticed in Hungary, Budapest is the super-con-
    centrated "railway" capital.
(5) The "Central Point" of the Belgian railway network had previously been Malines
    (cf. U. Lamalle, "Histoire des chemins de fer belges", Off. de Publ., Bruxelles,
    1953, p.26, Fig. 32, p.38). In the Netherlands, the "0" point of the railway
    network is still Amersfoort, a medium-size town and geographical center of the
    country. In Belgium, Brussels took over this role. In other countries, with a
    regionalized structure by geography and history, the railway network articu-
    lates itself around many crossings.

turned the rest of the country (with the exception of the South-East which is more eccentric) into a greater suburb of the capital, the meeting place of more than 1/4 of a million commuters.

On the other hand, this railway network was bound to serve from the beginning a great number of stations (6) a consequence of the dispersed habitat and at the same time a factor in its consolidation. The introduction of season-tickets for manual workers (the "weekly-tickets" in Sept. 1869) for only 1/6 of the price of a regular ticket and on degressive tariffs, as opposed to the regular proportional tariffs and the "social season-tickets" launched on the eve of the Second World War (cf. U. Lamalle, op.cit., pp.67-69) have encouraged on the one hand the building of houses in the cheaper countryside and on the other hand the considerable augmentation of daily journeys : "The weekly ticket brings the workman back home each evening; if it shows him the way to emigration, at least it restrains his desire to join the mob in the tentacular cities." This explains the high degree of separation, probably the highest in Europe, between home and business-place that exists in Belgium; it has been originated by the railways but also, and recently, reinforced by the individual motorisation already mentioned.

The regional and urban pattern of Belgium is also characterized by two supplementary elements of which the first represents a <u>transition</u> between the two means of penetration of space, i.e., the railway network and the road network : it is a third network, that of the "vicinal" railways system which, as its name indicates, has taken over railway techniques (rail, locomotives and very soon electric powered engines) but the tracks of which followed roads most of the time, serving the needs of the countryside. The coexistence of the three networks lasted until the beginning of the Fifties in a relative equilibrium as far as the lenght of the SNCB (Belgian Railway Company, State owned) railway tracks, standard gauge (5,034 km), "vicinal" railway tracks with small gauge (5,250 km, giving more than 10,000 km for the railway) and roads (10,900 km) are concerned (principal network : 1950 figures). Recently the "vicinal" lines were replaced by bus lines.

We must not forget to mention the second element of penetration into space, especially in Flanders at the beginning of the 20th Century; the bicycle which had the same effect as the means of transportation already mentioned i.e. the dichotomy existing between residence and work place. From 1950 onwards the bicycle has been gradually replaced by the motor-bicycle, the automobile or by private cars and buses owned by the entrepreneurs especially in the field of civil constructions or big infrastructure works.

One could say that the spatial organisation in Belgium has relied, at least in the course of the four generations from 1830 till 1950, on the railway with the consequences and interdependencies in the economic and social fields which todays evolution towards a regionalized or para-federal State must take into account. The Railway Era - which many of us had already buried in the euphoria of "everlasting growth" with its individual motorisation polluting dangerously the urban and populated environment - could have a splendid come-

(6) The number of Belgian railway stations, already diminished compared to the earlier situation, is still higher than that of the Netherlands. Head stations : 378 - Sub-stations (managed by the former) : 365 - Train stops without personal : 327. Total B : 1,070 -- Total NL : 327.

back in the Eighties in this urbanized North-West Europe in which the Belgian space occupies a central position. It could thus be useful to give, for the same 9 countries mentioned above, some indicative figures for the culminating period of the railways (Source : UN Statistical Yearbook 1953, Tables 1 and 138, U.I.C. and national railway company reports). Year 1950.

Country	Area 1,000 sq.km	Population 1,000	Lenght of line operated km	Traffic passenger-km 1,000,000
Belgium	30.5	8,620	5,034	7,047
Denmark	42.9	4,281	4,822	3,301
France	550.0	42,000	41,272	26,401
Germany (W)	245.3	47,700	30,274	30,264
Italy	301.0	46,600	21,632	19,409
Netherlands	32.4	10,150	3,200	6,228
Sweden	440.1	7,044	16,657	6,637
Switzerland	41.3	4,714	5,200	6,428
United Kingdom	244.0	50,212	31,154 ✕	32,472 ✕
For comparison :				
Japan	368.3	83,200	19,760 ✕✕	69,004 ✕✕

✕ Great Britain only
✕✕ Government railways only - Passenger cars in use 1946 : 20,000
                                                    1948 : 21,300
                                                    1950 : 25,100

THE PERSONALITY OF URBANIZED NORTH WESTERN EUROPE

Considering the minuteness of its territory and the inter-connection of its economy with that of the neighbouring countries, the case of urbanized Belgium cannot be separated from that of the neighbouring urban regions of North-West Europe. And, already, at the very moment of the inauguration of the short (22 km) track between Brussels and Malines, May 5, 1835, three flags were flying on the "0" point of the future Belgian railway network : in the East, the Prussian, in the South the French "tricolore" and in the West the Union Jack, all three symbolising the main three routes which were to join the neighbouring countries (the fourth direction, to the North, was dropped; it was indeed unthinkable at that time to fly the flag of the House of Orange ...) (cf. U. Lamalle, op.cit.).

The four cardinal points indicate indeed the major economic and political fields which meet here : if the launching of industrialization was a result of the English influence, its development and consequently the urbanization took the three other directions : one need only think of the "invasion" of Belgian border-commuters into the textile plants of Tourcoing, Roubaix and Lille; the interpenetration of the coal-fields of the French "Nord - Pas-de-Calais" and those of the Belgian Borinage and Centre; the common interests of Belgium, France and Germany in the steel field or German-Belgian in the chemical industry of the Liège and Aachen areas; the development of the harbour of Antwerp in a northern direction and its growing interest in a heavy duty canal towards the Rhine which was achieved in 1975; not to forget the

complementary nature of tourist movements along the French, Belgian and
Dutch coastline.

It is now time to mention the spatial and economic integration "avant la
lettre" i.e. the development of the European Community and, related to this,
the creation of an international association with scientific duties, the
"NW European Physical Planning Conference" the aim of which since 1950, is
"to contribute by studies and an appropriate action, to the harmonious development of the NW regions i.e. Western Germany, Belgium, France, the Grand-
Duchy of Luxemburg and the Netherlands, according to the aims of the European
unification process". (7)

These regions - the Delta, in the broader sense of the word of the streams
Scheldt, Meuse and Rhine and their hinterlands - have many common characteristics : a country with a long industrial tradition based on rich coal and
ore-fields, serviced by large-gauge canals and, as already pointed out, by
important railway networks and, recently, by the most intensively used highway networks of Europe. As regions with high agricultural yields, they have
had at their disposal a very dense and diversified urban network since the
Middle Ages whose cultural, artistic and commercial radiance could be compared to those of the historic towns of Northern and Central Italy. Finally,
the population density there, was one of the highest in Europe together with
that of the Po-Valley, of the London Basin and the Midlands, and of Lancashire,
birthplace of European industrialization. The table underneath gives the
most important population figures for the geographical area of the "Conference". Year   1971.

Country or Region	Area 1000 sq.km	Population 1000	Density inhab./sq.km
Belgium	30.5	9,651	316
Netherlands (excl. inland water)	33.7	13,269	394
Luxemburg	2.6	340	131
BENELUX	66.8	23,260	348
Nordrhein-Westfalen	34.0	16,914	497
Rheinland-Pfalz	19.8	3,645	184
Baden-Württemberg	35.8	8,895	249
Saarland	2.6	1,120	436
4 "Länder"	92.2	30,574	332
Nord	12.4	3,847	310
Picardie	19.4	1,608	82
Champagne-Ardennes	25.6	1,301	50
Lorraine	23.5	2,304	97
Alsace	8.3	1,439	173
5 "Régions"	89.2	10,499	118
TOTAL CONFERENCE AREA	248.2	64,333	259
For comparison :			
F.R. of Germany	248.6	60,650	244
United Kingdom	244.0	55,347	226

(7) Excerpt from the Rules of the Association the registered offices of which
are in Liège and its Secretariate in Bruges.

These regions radiating around Belgium represent in a relatively small geographical area a very important population mass and still more a concentration of economic wealth and commercial activities; for ex. 50 % of the total
employment of the "Six" in the energy sector, 42 % of the chemicals, 41 % of
the metallic constructions, 43 % of the oil refineries capacity and 55 % of
the non mineral-oil maritime traffic.

SOME REFLECTIONS ON URBAN EXTENSIONS IN NORTH WEST EUROPE

Concentration of population, high level of economic development, cultural and
scientific activity : all are factors of an urbanization of which the degree
is almost impossible to measure in a comparative framework because of the differences between definitions, methods and reference years of the statistical
data. If the differences between definitions of the urban environment of the
five countries are not so relevant as those on a worldwide scale (an agglomeration is considered as urban when it has 40,000 inhabitants in Corea and ...
250 in Denmark) a common denominator is still missing, concerning one of the
most important aspects : namely the size of communes, basic elements not only
on an administrative but also statistical scale. Thus, when the latest censi
took place (1970 or 1971, 1968 and 1975 in France ...) the average surface of
communes in decreasing order (sq.km round numbers) was as follows : Netherlands 37, Luxemburg 21, France 14, Belgium 13, F.R. of Germany 10. There is
then, a gap of 3.7 between the national averages of the Netherlands and the
F.R. of Germany and still more important gaps between the giant units of the
North of the Netherlands and the dwarflike communes of the "Länder" of the
German Rhineland. (8)

The creation of multicommunal conurbations is thus at the same time a statistical and operational need; but the example of the British "conurbations"
was only reluctantly followed on the Continent; first in France but with ever
changing definitions according to one census or another (1954, 1962, 1968 and
1975), then in the Scandinavian countries and in Switzerland; in Belgium also
but only for the four "Great conurbations" (Brussels, Antwerp, Liège and
Ghent), and later seven (1970 : Charleroi, Bruges, Louvain) even from an
urban morphological point of view there are at least 12 the population of
which exceeds 80,000. In the F.R. of Germany, the first official definition
(decree of the Federal Government) was given on November 21, 1968 and takes
into account only 24 "Verdichtungsräume" with more than 150,000 inhabitants
(January 1, 1967) including the Rhine-Ruhr conurbation with more than 10 million inhabitants (Greater London : 7.4, "agglomération parisienne" : 8.2). The
Rhine-Ruhr conurb. numbers 222 communes, 20 of which exceed 100,000 inhabitants, with five historic (Köln) or industrial towns (Essen, Dortmund, Düsseldorf and Duisburg) each of them numbering more than 500,000 inhabitants.

In its turn, the "urban unit" of Paris numbers 279 communes of which two
"communes" exceed 100,000 inhabitants (City of Paris : 2.6 millions and the
industrial suburb Boulogne-Billancourt 109,000). On the other hand, Greater

---

(8) The administrative reforms in progress or already executed in the "Länder"
    will greatly reduce the number of communes (4 to 10 times). The reform
    in Belgium is now the object of a passionate debate.

London, the oldest European conurbation, numbers, since the 1963 reform, the "City" with 4,234 inhabitants and 32 new "London Boroughs" the size of which varies between 332,000 (Croydon) and 140,000 (Kingston u. Thames) with an average of 230,000 inhabitants. In the eyes of the British urban planners, this last figure seems to be an optimum for the local administration of an urban region. It is to be noted that Greater London numbering more than 8.3 million inhabitants in 1951 has lost in 20 years 1 million inhabitants and occupies now the third rank in the hierarchy of the great West European conurbations, just behind "Rhine-Ruhr" (10.4 millions) and Paris (8.2).

Finally, in the Netherlands, the relatively large communal areas were more capable of absorbing the expanding cities in the existing administrative frameworks the number of which, on the other hand, has been still diminishing since the end of the war at the rate of ten/year. In 1971, 15 conurbations with more than 150,000 inhabitants could be counted here.

This short account clearly shows how irrelevant it would be to compare figures of which not only the statistical definitions but also the urban significance vary considerably from one country to another, each of them having reached a high stage of development and having at its disposal a very sophisticated administrative, statistical and scientific apparatus. It is one of the consequences of the historic, geographic, linguistic and philosophic diversity of Europe which turns it into a very rich region with a very important common heritage. As a first attempt, we have simply gathered the data provided by the latest censi (1968 for France, 1975 not being evaluated separately yet) and showing the population of conurbations with more than 150,000 inhabitants, according to the national definitions and classified in decreasing order. It gives the conurbation units of four countries and the only big city of the last one : the Grand-Duchy of Luxemburg, Luxemburg-City numbering 76,000 inhabitants only.

Conurbations numbering more than 150,000 inhabitants (1971, in 1000) located in the area of the Conference

Sources : Censi and Statistical Yearbooks of the four following
countries : B : Belgium - D : Germany (F.R.) - F : France -
NL : Netherlands

1. Rhein-Ruhr (D) .... 10,416(a)	11. Saarbrücken & Saar conur.(D) . 663
2. Rhein-Main (D) .... 2,527(b)	12. Utrecht (NL) 459
3. Stuttgart (D) 2,148	13. Liège (B) 440
4. Rhein-Neckar (D) 1,177	14. Eindhoven (NL) 341
5. Bruxelles-Brussel (B) ... 1,071	15. Karlsruhe (D) 339
6. Rotterdam (NL) 1,066	16. Strasbourg (F) 335
7. Amsterdam (NL) 1,036	17. Lens (F) 326
8. Lille-Roubaix-Tourcoing(F) 881	18. Arnhem (NL) 274
9. 's-Gravenhage (NL) 711	19. Heerlen-Kerkrade (NL) 265
10. Antwerpen (B) 673	20. Koblenz (Neuwied) (D) 260

(a) Further breakdown of Rhine-Ruhr urban region : Ruhr core area ... 4,072
Köln-Bonn-Bad-Godesberg .. 1,400ꭗ Düsseldorf 1,032ꭗ
Wuppertal .... 942ꭗ Krefeld 223
ꭗ Estimation
(b) Partly outside of "Conference" area

21. Nancy (F) 258	31. Douai (F) 205
22. Haarlem (NL) 239	32. Mulhouse (F) 199
23. Enschede-Hengelo (NL) 233	33. Dordrecht (NL) 172
24. Gent (B) 225	34. Freiburg/br. (D) 170
25. Valenciennes (F) 224	35. 's Hertogenbosch (NL) 169
26. Münster (D) 220	36. Reims (F) 168
27. Charleroi (B) 214	37. Metz (F) 166
28. Nijmegen (NL) 206	38. Siegen (D) 166
29. Tilburg (NL) 206	39. Leiden (NL) 164
30. Groningen (NL) 205	

In the preceding list, we have 39 conurbations of which 15 are located in the
Netherlands, 10 in the F.R. of Germany (more than 30 if the "Verdichtungsräume" Rhine-Ruhr, Rhine-Main and Rhine-Neckar are split up), 9 in France and
5 in Belgium, numbering in total 27.9 million inhabitants of which 2.2 must
be substracted (the larger part of Rhine-Main located with Frankfurt and
Wiesbaden in the Land Hessen) as they are not located in the geographical
area of the Conference. The 39 conurbations, or parts of conurbations, have
a total population of 25.7 million or 40 % of the population of all continental North West Europe (64,3 millions).

It is interesting to compare the quota of the urban population of the large
cities of this mixture of countries with the national figures : the share of
the cities and conurbations numbering more than 150,000 inhabitants in the
four countries is as follows : Netherlands   57.7 %, F.R. of Germany 45.5 %,
France 36.6 %, Belgium 27.7 %. Should we draw the conclusion that the
Netherlands are the most urbanized and Belgium the least ? Not at all, because if we take the 80,000 level, the share of the 12 Belgian conurbations
in the total population would be 35 % being located on only 4.8 % of the national territory, while the 15 Dutch conurbations occupy more than 18 % of
it ! In other words, urban density in Belgium is much higher i.e. 2,260
inh./sq.km for the 12 conurbations than that of the 15 Dutch conurbations :
1,250 inh./sq.km. This is one of the consequences of the three times larger
size of the Dutch communes, of which the surface very often expands into the
neighbouring countryside : such surface area is excluded from the much more
parcelled communes in the Belgian conurbations. (9)

Nevertheless it would be a mistake to restrict consideration of the urbanization phenomenon to large cities and conurbations : the rate of urbanization
is defined in France "as the proportion of the total population living in urban units : conurbations or communes with more than 2,000 inhabitants ..."
giving, then, other rates and a different ranking : France 70.9 %, F.R. of
Germany 88.2 %, Belgium 88.4 % and the Netherlands 92.4 % (more than 5,000

(9) As a comparison (and CUM GRANO SALIS because of the various definitions)
the 18 British conurbations, numbering more than 250,000 inh. each,
groupe more than 40.2 % of the total national population; in the North
East of the USA, which can be compared with the North West European Mega-
lopolis, this proportion reaches 65 % but for a level of 200,000 inhabitants.

inhabitants). (In Great-Britain, in "urban districts" : England and Wales
78.3 %, Scotland 71.0 %.)

Concerning now the spatial impact of urban development, i.e. the urban use of
land, we can site the Ruhr (10) as an example showing the most significant
changes that have taken place during the last two generations, comparing the
data for 1893 and for 1960 for the seven big items in decreasing value
(1960, %).

	1893	1960	Trend
(1) Farming areas	67.5	56.1	−
(2) Forests	20.3	15.0	−
(3) Built-up areas	3.1	14.9	+
(4) Transportation infrastructure	3.4	7.1	+
(5) Swamps, wasteland	3.9	2.9	−
(6) Water surface	1.4	2.2	+
(7) Parks, cemeteries, sporting grounds, aerodromes and military zones	0.4	1.8	+
	100	100	

It is the evolutionary trend which is especially interesting.
The following items have decreased :

- Farming areas (1/6)
- Forests (1/4)
- Swamps and wasteland (1/4) (maybe to the benefit of the 2 above)

Have increased :

- Built-up areas (5 times)
- Transportation infrastructure (2 times) (maybe more with the aerodromes
  classified under (7))
- Water surface (+ 50 % because of the building of water reserve basins)
- Sporting grounds, etc. (4 times if aerodromes are deduced)

The global result of the impact of human activities on land-use stems from
the total of the categories (3), (4) and (5) - 1893 : 6.9 - 1960 : 23.8
i.e. an increase of almost 250 % as a result of the development of urbanization, industry and transportation.

A similar rate appears in the trend of land-use in Great Britain (11) of

Year	Population	Urban land-use - %
1901	37,000,000	3.8
1951	48,920,000	7.2
1971	54,190,000	8.6
(esti.) 2001	64,500,000	11.3

(10) Siedlungsverband Ruhrkohlenbezirk, Essen, Gebietsentwicklungsplan 1966,
     Kohlhammer, Köln, p.61.
(11) Long term population distribution in Great Britain, DoE, London, 1971, 205 p.

which the index (100 = 1900) is nowadays 226 and will, according to the prognoses, be 300 at the beginning of the next century when the population index will have reached 174 only (as a result of a downward revision of the previous estimates). The gap will then considerably widen out under the influence of a development of space consumption per capita and of course by that of the rate of urbanization. The regional maximum reaches nowadays 26.1 % in the North West, 18.2 % in the South East, 13.5 % in the Midlands (a little bit behind the Ruhr) ... and the minimum in Scotland (4.7 % isles excepted). The prognoses for the year 2001 are as follows : North West : 37.8 %, South East 22 % ... and Scotland 4.7 %.

Now a document prepared but not yet published by the Belgian "Ministère des Travaux Publics" gives following figures for 1971, concerning the proportion of urban land-use : Belgium 28 %, Walloon region 20 % and ... Flanders 38 %, i.e. higher than the regional maximum in Great Britain (North West) in the year 2001 ...

QUANTITATIVE LANDSCAPE EVALUATION FOR OPEN SPACE PLANNING

Maura O'Brien-Marchand
U.S. Geological Survey, Menlo Park, California

ABSTRACT

Twenty-three small stream basins in Pennsylvania were quantitatively assessed
for open space suitability. Uniqueness Ratio was used to measure each basin's
characteristics relative to all other basins in the sample using physiograph-
ic, hydrologic, geologic, botanic, anthropologic, and historic parameters.
Wilderness Potential was used to evaluate human impact on and alteration of
each basin through measurement of air and water quality, quantity of solid
waste, road development, degree of urbanization, and aesthetic impression
evaluated in the field. General Aesthetic Impression is based on Field
Aesthetic Impression and aesthetic judgments of the scenery as viewed in
black-and-white photographs and color transparencies. Demographic information
concerning the viewers was also collected. A sum of the ranking of Uniqueness
Ratio, Wilderness Potential, and General Aesthetic Impression is proposed here
as the best assessment of open space suitability, although these components
could be weighted if desired. Results of the study support open space recom-
mendation for some areas which might not have attracted attention. Three
basins within state parks showed rankings of one, four, and ten. Wilderness
Potential, Field Aesthetic Impression, and viewers ratings of scenic quality,
especially of black-and-white photographs, exhibited a high degree of correlation, while Uniqueness Ratio showed no correlation with these variables.
Aesthetic judgment of natural landscapes based on black-and-white photographs
differed substantially from that of color slides. Stepwise regression models
show water and air quality, anthropology, and hydrology best explain aesthetic
evaluation of natural landscapes. Results of this study show no evidence that
age, sex, education, occupation, degree of involvement in outdoor activities
or conservation interest significantly influence aesthetic evaluation of these
landscape photographs, and that aesthetic judgments transgress social boundaries.

INTRODUCTION

Each day reveals new decisions concerning the use of open space, a critical
problem in an age of exploding population and on an earth whose area and resources are finite and limited with many geological hazards (Ref 1 and 2).
Unfortunately such decisions in the past have been dictated by considerations
other than the wisest possible use of land resources, in the fullest sense of
the term. Conservationists, in their attempts to preserve as many scenic areas
as possible, have sometimes failed to save any. Obviously not all areas can be
preserved in their natural state, nor should they be if we are to provide the
world as a whole with any reasonable standard of living, given the present and
projected world population. There is, however, urgent need for wild and scenic
areas to be preserved, in addition to those already safeguarded. Parks and
open space offer great aesthetic beauty, quietude, and a place to re-create
the mind, body, and spirit. Aside from aesthetics several practical consider-

ations support the concept that open space should be of high priority in land use planning: (1) open space can be urbanized, but developed areas are not readily or quickly converted to their natural state, (2) the presence of large, natural areas, with their biological complexity, constitute ecological stability in a world where man is rapidly simplifying ecosystems and thereby rendering them unstable, (3) wild areas, a special type of open space, are of great scientific value in that they provide outdoor laboratories where natural processes unaffected by man may be studied and better understood, and (4) open spaces act as recharge areas for ground and surface waters of high quality and large quantity.

This paper proposes a system by which any element of landscape may be evaluated in terms of its inherent value and its potential for preservation in its natural state as open space, a first step in a comprehensive land use plan. Three techniques - Uniqueness Ratio, Wilderness Potential, and General Aesthetic Impression - have been developed to assess the various characteristics of the landscape (fig. 1). These techniques were used to appraise the landscapes of 23 small stream basins (watersheds) in Pennsylvania for open space suitability (Ref 3). The basins were selected to include the largest possible range of land-use practices, stream sizes, landforms, vegetation, and archeological sites.

METHODS

Evaluative Techniques

The Uniqueness Ratio (Ref 4 and 5) measures how different each basin is from every other basin included in the study. It is applied only to those landscape aspects which are no a priori good or bad; rather their value attaches to how different a given basin is from the usual or the norm. Six parameters were used to evaluate Uniqueness: physiography, hydrology, geology, botany, anthropology, and history (fig. 1). These parameters were in turn evaluated by a group of more specific subparameters. The raw data obtained for each subparameter were used to assign a value on a fivefold scale, the boundaries drawn to include the full range of data variation and to encompass five approximately equivalent ranges. From the category ratings it is possible to calculate Uniqueness Ratios for each basin by subparameter. An arithmetic average of the subparameter ratios is then used to obtain parameter ratios and an overall Uniqueness Ratio for each basin. The Uniqueness Ratio is simply defined as the inverse of the number of watersheds sharing a given category. If a basin is unique, it is rated 1/1 or 1.0, if two basins share that characteristic then the ratio drops to 0.50, and from there to 0.33 with three basins sharing that category. Consequently the ratios decrease exponentially as the number of basins sharing the rating increases such that all Uniqueness Ratios range from 0 to 1.0.

Some aspects of the landscape, however, are not well described in terms of Uniqueness because they tend to have a social value connotation (Ref 6). Obviously, a uniquely polluted site is of little societal value, even if it is very different from other sites in a region. Wilderness Potential is used as a measure of human impact on and alteration of each watershed, based on factors which have definite "good" or "bad" implications: air and water quality, solid waste, road development, degree of urbanization, and Field Aesthetic Impression. A fivefold rating, with category one representing least natural conditions and category five the most, was used to calculate the Wilderness Potential as the cumulative sum of ratings divided by the highest possible sum of ratings. For

UNIQUENESS RATIO

Physiography

topography
relief
mean elevation
max. valley
depth/width ratio
drainage orientation
basin area

Hydrology

stream width
stream depth
velocity
stream load:
 -size
 -suspended
 -dissolved
stream density
stream order

Botany +-

successional stage
dominant tree species
dom. shrub sp.
dom. herb sp.
no. of tree sp.
no. of shrub sp.
no. of herb sp.

Geology

lithology
structure
geomorphic process
paleontology:
 -diversity of species
 -number of fossiliferous outcrops

Anthropology

midden or camp-sites
natural sites with mystic quality
hunting and agricultural sites

Post-1619 History

number of pre-1850 communities
number of historic sites or structures

Air Quality

visibility
odor+

Water Quality

color
acidity
nitrogen
phosphate
iron
dissolved oxygen
algal abundance

WILDERNESS POTENTIAL

Solid Waste

quantity of litter+

Road Development

miles of paved roads/basin area
miles unsurfaced roads/area
distance from population weighted center

Degree of Urbanization

land use
industry or mining
% forested area

GENERAL AESTHETIC IMPRESSION

Photographic

Black-and-white+   Color+

Field Aesthetic Impression

Field +

Figure 1. A graphic presentation of a system of quantitative landscape evaluation based on the rank of Uniqueness Ratio rank order + Wilderness Potential rank order + General Aesthetic Impression rank order.

+ subparameter evaluated at both the confluence and the highest point in elevation of the stream basin

example, if a basin receives ratings of 4, 5, and 3 then the Wilderness Potential is calculated as 4+5+3 divided by 15, the highest possible total, giving a value of 0.80. The overall Wilderness Potential is computed as the mean of the parameter ratios, and follows a linear scale ranging from near 0 to 1.0.

Field Aesthetic Impression, evaluated by the author for each basin utilizing a standardized procedure, was used as a parameter of Wilderness Potential, but because it is a rating based on aesthetics it is also treated as a component of General Aesthetic Impression.

General Aesthetic Impression of the landscape was evaluated by randomly selected respondents who based their ratings of scenic quality on black-and-white photographs and color transparencies; the overall value for this technique was computed as the mean of black-and-white evaluation, color evaluation, and Field Aesthetic Impression. A total of 181 persons evaluated the black-and-white prints, while a subgroup of 33 participants from the same groups were shown the color slides. Viewers were asked to evaluate the scenery represented by the photographs, not the photographs themselves, on a fivefold scale. Some demographic information was also obtained from the evaluators by means of a questionnaire.

Since the photographic media is a representation of the actual scenery, the quality of representation could be a possible source of bias (Ref 7 and 8). An evaluation was undertaken by a professional artist to ascertain the degree of influence of photographic quality on the scenic evaluation.

Results and Data Analysis

The 23 stream basins were compared and contrasted by the various evaluative techniques. Since the basins were chosen instead of being randomly selected, variability due to their selection may cloud other relationships. This difficulty was inferred to be less than the problems size and logistic in sampling randomly selected areas, and because a diversity of areas was desired.

The range of the Uniqueness values in this study varied over nearly the entire possible spectrum, with most of the ratios falling approximately in the 0.15 to 0.25 range. The three stream basins located within state parks all showed very low Uniqueness Ratios.

The Wilderness Potential values ranged from 0.2 to 1.0. The means tended to have high values between 0.6 and 0.7, due in part to the rather natural character of this part of Pennsylvania. All basins within state parks showed high Wilderness Potential ratings.

The value for General Aesthetic Impression ranged from 0.4 to about 0.9 with a mean value of 0.6. The photographic evaluation means were higher than the means of Field Aesthetic Impression, suggesting that photographs might tend to idealize landscape scenes in the eyes of those who view them. The Field Aesthetic ratings, however, show a wider spread of value than either of the photographic media. In comparing the various basins, basin #11 had the highest General Aesthetic Impression, while the remaining two basins within state park boundaries ranked second and tenth.

An overall system of landscape evaluation may be established by giving equal or predetermined weighting to the three techniques and computing a composite rating for each watershed. Since the means and ranges differ, a comparison was

made on the basis of rank order. The rank of the three evaluative methods is
used in finding the mean to establish an Overall Landscape Evaluation ranking.
In the overall ranking, basins within state parks ranked first, fourth, and
tenth, respectively, confirming the validity of the decision to preserve these
areas. Several basins not within park jurisdiction, however, received high
ratings by all evaluative techniques and should be considered for parkland or
designated open space.

A correlation matrix was constructed to compare several evaluative techniques
used in this study(table 1). Significant correlation (R = 0.555) occur between
Field Aesthetic Impression and viewer rating of black-and-white photographs,
accounting for 31 percent of the variance in the scores. The correlation between color and black-and-white is in the same range while that between color
and Field Aesthetic Impression is only 0.279. The color photography seems to
be accentuating the noise rather than the information between photographic
representation and Field Aesthetic Impression. Black-and-white photographic
judgments account for nearly half of the variance in Wilderness Potential
indicating that some of the characteristics are redundant with aesthetic
judgment. Aesthetics and Wilderness Potential are clearly not related to the
objective uniqueness of an area(Ref 9).

The relation between aesthetic judgment and measurable landscape characteristics (Uniqueness Ratio and Wilderness Potential parameters) was analyzed by
means of multiple stepwise regression. Here it is possible to "predict" aesthetic judgment to observe the specific contribution of each parameter to
aesthetic judgment.

Uniqueness as a global concept is not related to aesthetics in a general overall manner, however, some unique elements of the stream basins were related to
aesthetic judgment (table 2, column 1). Specifically anthropology, hydrology,
and geology interact with aesthetic judgment.

Column 2 shows the strong association between Wilderness Potential characteristics and aesthetic judgment. Almost half of the variance in aesthetic judgment based on black-and-white photographs is accounted for by water quality
(clearness, transparency). It is the absence of focus on water quality (not a
colorful feature) that makes color slides a less accurate predictor of aesthetic judgment, in this instance, than black-and-white photographs are. Apparently Wilderness and water quality are more unambiguously related in this geographic area than any other measured parameters.

With the combination of Uniqueness and Wilderness parameters we are approaching the limits of capacity to predict aesthetic judgments from any objectives,
real world variables. Multiple correlations are now reaching the order of 0.75
and accounting regularly for half or even more of the variance. Clearly, this
shows that aesthetic judgments are not heedless, subjective, emotional opinions,
but considered estimates based on measurable features of the landscape, confirming Child's findings in a cross cultural comparison of aesthetic judgments
of indigenous and Western art (Ref 10).

Water quality holds an overwhelming importance in predicting judgments in all
instances but that of color photo quality, where the transparency of the water
is apparently obscured by more colorful distractions (litter, etc.).

Factor analysis was used to determine what natural associations of variables
exist and to search for basic underlying reasons which best explain the data

Table 1. Correlation Matrix for Several Landscape Evaluative Techniques and Photographic Quality. The field techniques are based on several parameters assessed for 23 stream basins; the black-and-white photographic technique is based on evaluation by 181 persons for the 23 basins; black-and-white subgroup is a subsample of the black-and-white evaluation (above) and is the rating by the 33 persons for the 23 basins who also rated color transparencies; color transparency technique represents scenic quality evaluation as seen thru color slides by 33 persons rating the 23 basins; and photographic quality is an evaluation of photographic quality not scenic quality by one person schooled in photography and for each of the 23 basins.

	Uniqueness Ratio	Wilderness Potential	Wilderness Potential without F.A.I.	Field Aesthetic Impression	Black-and-white	Black-and-white Subgroup	Color
FIELD EVALUATION TECHNIQUES:							
Uniqueness Ratio	1						
Wilderness Potential	-.176	1					
Wilderness Potential without Field Aesthetic Impression	-.190	.987	1				
Field Aesthetic Impression	-.019	.573	.430	1			
PHOTOGRAPHIC EVALUATION TECHNIQUES:							
Black-and-White	-.056	.678	.637	.555	1		
Black-and-White, Subgroup (N=33)	-.031	.669	.612	.628	.971	1	
Color	-.128	.557	.557	.279	.532	.575	1
PHOTOGRAPHIC QUALITY EVALUATION BY ARTIST:							
Black-and-White	.032	.461	.455	.256	.703	.668	*
Color	.276	.472	.455	.329	*	*	.379

*Irrelevant

Table 2. Stepwise Regression Analysis of Aesthetic Judgments based on Photographic and Field Evaluation. As each landscape characteristic (Uniqueness Ratio and Wilderness Potential Parameters) is added to the equation to predict aesthetic judgment models, they are added cumulatively, so in column 1, A+ Geology is Anthropology + Geology.

Independent variables

Predictor → Predicted	Column 1 Uniqueness Ratio Parameters			Column 2 Wilderness Potential Parameters without Field			Column 3 Uniqueness Ratio and Wilderness Potential Parameters		
		r	R^2		r	R^2		r	R^2
Black-and-White	Anthropology	.412	17%	Water Quality	.664	44%	Water Quality	.664	44%
	A+Geology	.625	39%				W+Anthropology	.715	51%
	A+G+Hydrology	.685	47%				W+A+Hydrology	.742	55%
							W+A+H+ Physiography	.761	58%
Color	Hydrology	.388	15%	Air Quality	.539	29%	Air Quality	.539	29%
	H+Anthropology	.520	27%	A+Solid Waste	.633	40%	A+Solid Waste	.633	40%
							A+S+Hydrology	.655	43%
							A+S+H+History	.706	50%
Field Aesthetic Impression	Anthropology	.300	9%	Water Quality	.510	26%	Water Quality	.510	26%
	A+Geology	.520	27%	W+Degree of Urbanization	.539	29%	+Physiography	.538	29%
				W+D+Air Quality	.591	35%	+Degree of Urbanization	.591	35%
				W+D+A+Solid Waste	.633	40%	+Air Quality	.633	40%
							+Solid Waste	.664	44%
							+Anthropology	.692	48%
							+History	.728	53%

Dependent Variables   Aesthetic Judgments based on

distribution. Factor 1 may be defined as the aesthetic qualities of natural
landscapes, particularly as evident to the viewer of black-and-white photographs, with 69 percent of the total variance associated with it. All of the
viewer subgroups show virtually the same factor loadings as the black-and-
white total sample, indicating that there is no significant difference in aesthetic judgment by persons of contrasting age, sex, socio-economic status,
outdoor experience, or conservation interest. Factor 2 may be defined as the
areas of the basin and size of the stream and account for 8 percent of the
variance. Physiography, hydrology, and history all show strong positive loadings on this factor due to the fact that many of their subparameters vary in
response to basin size or stream discharge.

CONCLUSIONS

The Uniqueness qualities of a landscape vary independently of its naturalness
or its aesthetic appeal. Since uniqueness assesses stream basin characteristics which cannot be evaluated by other methods, its inclusion in any scheme
of landscape evaluation is of fundamental importance. Wilderness Potential,
on the other hand, correlated strongly with all of the aesthetic evaluation
methods used. Consequently it may not be necessary to determine both General
Aesthetic Impression and Wilderness Potential, since they are intercorrelated
to a significant degree. In considering the limitations of a photographic
technique and the problem of accuracy of representing a watershed with a small
group of photographs, I think that evaluation of Wilderness Potential would be
preferable in circumstances where time and funds would not allow both methods
to be used. However, black-and-white prints could be a more rapid and less
expensive means of approximating Wilderness Potential.

Aesthetic judgments based on black-and-white prints account for more of the
variance compared to color and Field Aesthetic Impression of natural landscapes. Certain variables, particularly water and air quality, anthropology,
and hydrology best explain aesthetic judgments made both by viewers of photographs and expert evaluation in the field.

It is also possible to map Uniqueness Ratio, Wilderness Potential, General
Aesthetic Impression, and Overall Landscape Evaluation by plotting values on
map overlays and contouring the data points (Ref 11). Zones or corridors of
the landscape with high uniqueness, naturalness, and aesthetic beauty can then
be easily identified on a media suitable for planning open space. Likewise,
map overlays could also be constructed for geologic and natural hazards -
areas prone to earthquakes, volcanic activity, landslides, liquefaction, fire
or flood - areas if developed would seriously threaten the safety and financial resources of an area and its inhabitants.

If the value of the landscape can be described in generally acceptable and objective terms other than monetarily, then we are approaching a system of landscape evaluation, and hence of land use planning, that could accurately reflect not only the practical needs but the aesthetic desires of the people.
It would appear from this investigation that landscapes can be objectively
evaluated through the measurement of their physical and cultural characteristics, yielding results consistent with aesthetic perception of the landscape,
which in turn are independent of socio-economic and other demographic factors.

REFERENCES

1. Brubaker, Sterling, *In Command of Tomorrow*, Johns Hopkins Univ. Press, Baltimore and London, 1975.

2. Gulliver-Dunne, Rachel, Geologic factors for open space consideration in San Francisco bay region, California, San Francisco Bay Region Study, U.S. Geological Survey, Menlo Park, California (unpub. report), 1975.

3. O'Brien-Marchand, Maura, *A System of Quantitative Landscape Evaluation*, Bucknell Univ., Lewisburg, Pennsylvania (unpub. thesis), 1974.

4. Leopold, L. B. and M. O'Brien Marchand, On the quantitative inventory of the riverscape, *Water Resources Research* 4, 709-717, 1968.

5. Dearinger, J. A. and G. M. Woolwine, *Measuring the Intangible Values of Natural Streams, Part I, Application of the Uniqueness Ratio*, Univ. Kentucky Water Resources Institute, Lexington, Research Report 40, 1971.

6. Zube, Ervin, R. D. Bush, and J. G. Fabos, *Landscape Assessment - Value, Perception, and Resources*, Dowden, Hutchinson and Ross, Stroudsburg, Pennsylvania, 1975.

7. Craik, K. H., Psychological factors in landscape appraisal, *Environment and Behavior* 4, 255-266, 1972.

8. Wohlwill, J., Factors in the differential response to the natural and the man-made environment, *Affective Response to the Outdoor Environment*, Symposium held at the Mtgs. American Psychological Assoc., Montreal, August 1973.

9. O'Brien-Marchand, M. and J. B. Juhasz, Aesthetic judgments and objective characteristics of natural landscapes (in press).

10. Child, I. L., The experts and the bridge of judgment that crosses every cultural gap, *Psychology Today* 2, 24-29, 1968.

11. McHarg, Ian L., *Design with Nature*, Doubleday, Natural History Press, Garden City, New York, 1971.

LAND-USE MAPS FOR TOWN PLANNERS

Chauth Ram Arora
University of Wisconsin-Oshkosh
Oshkosh, Wisconsin U.S.A.

ABSTRACT

Basic geologic and hydrologic information was used to produce
environmental resource maps for land-use planning in Carlisle,
Massachusetts for planners lacking technical background in
geology. Twelve environmental resource maps depicting aspects
of the geology and hydrology of Carlisle, which may affect land
use, are printed on transparent mylar with color overprint. Each
map depicts a single element of the environment, such as depth
to bedrock and ground water, land slopes, surficial materials,
flood plains, and water quality indicators.

Either a single map or a combination of maps may suggest several
possible but mutually exclusive land uses, or a sequence of
land uses. Land-use planners could, for instance, use the maps
for such specific purposes as a shopping center, housing, or a
solid waste disposal facility; or the maps may be used to locate
all areas which have favorable characteristics for particular use.

INTRODUCTION

The traditional approach to land use planning primarily considers
economic and social values. Too often insufficient regard has
been given to natural systems. However, planning based only on
economic growth may bring potentially negative liabilities. A
strictly traditional approach may lead to such results as construction on flood plains. Legget (1973) has cited many examples
in which urban development plans failed because no consideration
was given to natural systems.

A recent approach emphasizes the assessment of natural environ--
mental systems. Natural systems, suitable to land use, may
include geologic and hydrologic information. Such geologic and
hydrologic data useful to town planners are usually available
in geotechnical publications, but planners unfamiliar with geotechnical concepts and terminology cannot correctly evaluate and
use such information for planning.

Recently, many new techniques (Ian McHarg 1969, Hackett and
McComas 1969, Lutzen 1969, Scott 1972, Turner 1973) have been
experimented with to help town planners in understanding the
value of geotechnical data. Hackett and McComas (1969) have used

feasibility maps using a color coding system (Quay 1966) to define "suitable" and "unsuitable" areas for certain land use.
These techniques have had limited success in meeting the needs
of town planners for several reasons: (a) two geologists preparing such maps for the same purpose, may interpret the geotechnical data and reach significantly different conclusions;
(b) feasibility maps may become outdated if statutory regulation,
social attitude or environmental conditions change.

This author has devised and successfully used an overlay mapping
technique (Pessl 1972) in presenting geotechnical data in simplified form. Decision makers can easily understand, correctly
identify, and wisely use the geologic and hydrologic information
for planning. Maps prepared in this study use a flexible data
base and can respond to both the present and future needs of
planners.

Geotechnical data which relate to land use planning for the town
of Carlisle, Massachusetts were collected from various kinds of
sources, most of which are published (Baker and Petersen 1962)
available in unpublished form (town record, open file map by
Donald Alvord USGS) or from field and laboratory studies. In
Carlisle, environmental resource units were defined in terms of
static and dynamic values. For example, the bedrock geology,
the nature and thickness of surficial material, and land slopes
are virtually static, since the rate of change is negligible on
a human time scale (unless altered by a natural catastrophic
phenomenon such as earthquakes, volcanoes or landslides). On
the other hand, the depth-to-water table, the elevation of the
water table, and water quality components are dynamic environmental resources, because they vary from year to year, season to
season, and even from day to day.

The following static and dynamic environmental resource maps
were prepared for the town of Carlisle, Massachusetts:

Static environmental resource maps include:
  1.   Topographic and culture
  2.   Surface materials
  3.   Depth-to-bedrock
  4.   Land slopes
  5.   Bedrock geology
Dynamic environmental resource maps include:
  6.   Depth-to-water table
  7.   Elevation of water table
  8.   Well yield
  9.   Flood-prone areas
 10.   Chloride ion content of well water
 11.   Calcium ion content of well water
 12.   Iron ion content of well water

In the following pages each map will be explained as it relates
to land use planning.

STATIC ENVIRONMENTAL RESOURCE MAPS

<u>Topographic and Culture Map</u> (figure 1)
This map which shows the topography, water bodies, updated culture
and paved roads was compiled from two 7.5-minute U. S. Geological
Survey quadrangles (Westford and Billerica quadrangles, Massachusetts), and from an aerial photograph of the town. This map
was enlarged from a scale of 1:24,000 (1 inch = 2,000 feet) to
one of 1:9,600 (1 inch = 800 feet). All maps developed in this
project have the same scale, i.e., 1:9,600.
The topography of the land is shown by contour lines (lines of
equal elevations). Elevated features such as hills primarily
consist of till, flat areas are covered with outwash deposits
(gravel, sand, and silt), and low land areas have swamp deposits

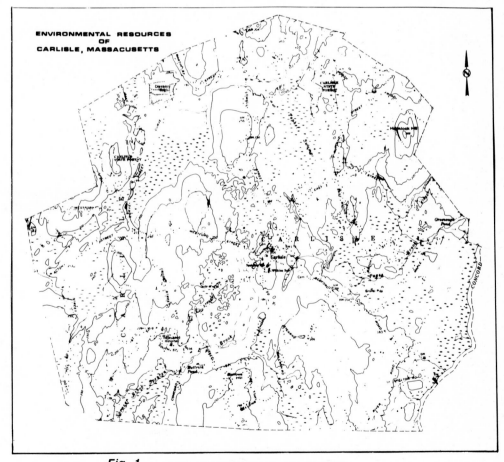

Fig. 1   **MAP OF TOPOGRAPHY AND CULTURE**

SCALE 1 inch = 800 feet

0   800   1600   2400 FEET

(silt, clay, and organic matter). Excellent deposits of gravel
and sand are located in a long narrow ridge called an esker.
The esker, in Carlisle runs in a north-south direction in the
northwest corner of the town.

The topographic and culture map was used as a base map where
the data of about 100 to 300 of various environmental resources
were analyzed.

Surface Materials Map (figure 2)
The loose surface materials of Carlisle consist of till, gravel,
sand, clay, silt and organic soils. The soil properties, hydrological, and engineering characteristics of these surface materials are of great importance in land use planning.

Till consists of a mixture of clay, silt, sand, gravel and boul-
ders which is deposited as unstratified, unconsolidated and un-
sorted material. The semi-impervious nature of till does not
provide a high yield of ground water. Furthermore, the rate of
percolation and permeability of water is low in fine textured
till. Septic systems are difficult to locate in fine textured
till, since the seasonal high water table is near the surface
and percolation rates are slow. Till is not a good construction
material, due to poor sorting. Also, the costs of trenching and
excavation are high.

Esker deposits consist primarily of sand and gravel. The soil
of esker is coarse-textured and useful for construction purposes. When underlain by relatively impervious deposits beneath the water table, they provide a very high yield of water.
Eskers are often suitable for septic systems, if there is no
danger of ground water contamination. Esker materials are good
construction materials and also the cost of excavation is low.
They are the most valuable source of roadbed construction.

An outwash deposit consists of silt, sand and gravel which was
deposited by glacial meltwater. Outwash deposits offer excellent
ground water resources, since they have a very high yield capacity and recharge potential. They are excellent construction
materials.

Swamp deposits are confined to a topographic depression. They
are poorly drained, and contain stagnant water in which organic
material may accumulate. These areas are unsuitable for septic
systems or other waste disposal. Sanitary landfill operations
should not be located within these deposits, because of the high
water table and unsuitability of the materials. Trenching and
excavation operations are difficult, owing to the high water
table.

It is apparent from the surficial map that approximately one-
fourth of the Carlisle area is covered by swamp deposits, and
approximately one-half is covered by till. The remaining area
of Carlisle is covered by sand, gravel, and silt.

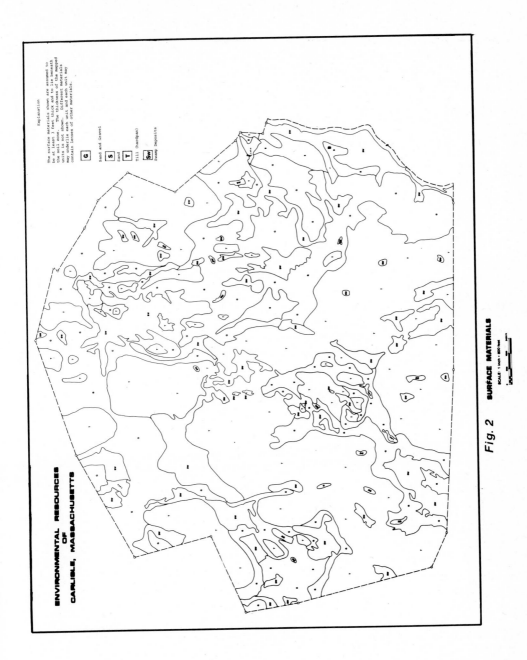

Fig. 2 SURFACE MATERIALS

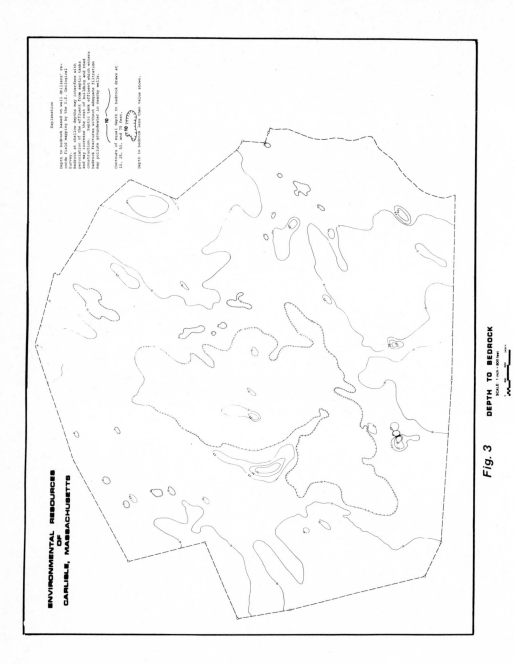

Fig. 3   DEPTH TO BEDROCK

SCALE 1 INCH = 800 feet

Depth-to-Bedrock Map (figure 3)
A depth-to-bedrock map was prepared from the available well logs,
an outcrop map (Alvord, 1973), and from interpretations of the
geological history of the area. Depth-to-bedrock is a measure
of the thickness of unconsolidated materials that overlie the
bedrock. The thickness of the unconsolidated materials varies
from zero, where the bedrock is at the land surface, to more
than 100 feet in pre-glacial valleys. Most upland surfaces are
underlain by less than 10 feet of unconsolidated materials and
have numerous exposures of bedrock. The contours of the depth-
to-bedrock map follow the northeasterly trends of the aeromag-
netic map, and the bedrock geology map. Depth-to-bedrock is an
important element to be considered in land use planning. A
shallow depth increases the cost of excavation for building and
road construction. It is difficult and expensive to install
underground municipal services in areas where the bedrock is
close to the surface. Sanitary codes prohibit waste disposal
in areas where bedrock is less than four feet below the disposal
system. Untreated or poorly treated waste water may enter fractures in the bedrock and pollute ground water supplies.

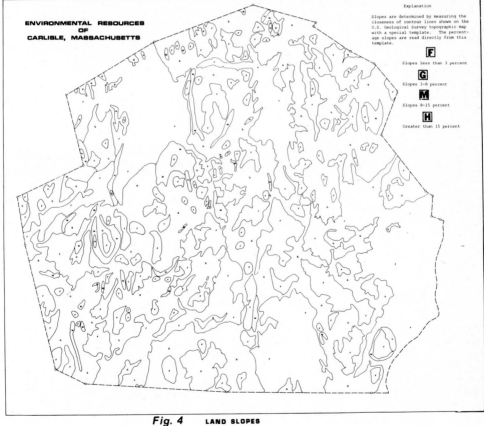

ENVIRONMENTAL RESOURCES
OF
CARLISLE, MASSACHUSETTS

Explanation

Slopes are determined by measuring the
closeness of contour lines shown on the
U.S. Geological Survey topographic map
with a special template. The percentage slopes are read directly from this
template.

F
Slopes less than 3 percent

G
Slopes 3-8 percent

M
Slopes 8-15 percent

H
Greater than 15 percent

Fig. 4   LAND SLOPES

Land Slopes Map (figure 4)
The land slopes map was developed from a topographic map. A
slope map having four classes (0-3%, 3-8%, 8-15%, and over 15%)
was produced. These slope classes were selected after a review
of a recently published slope map of Hartford, Connecticut (Baker
and Stone, 1972), and of Jefferson County, Colorado (Schmidt,
1972), and Douglas County, Colorado (Maberry, 1972).

Most of Carlisle has flat (0-3%) to gentle (3-8%) land slopes,
which do not interfere with most kinds of land use. Steep
slopes limit the usefulness of the land for most agricultural
purposes, commercial centers, interstate highways, airports,
railroads, and the building of septic systems.

Bedrock Geology Map (figure 5)
The bedrock geology of Carlisle consists of complex metamorphic
(formed under high temperature and pressure from pre-existing
solid rocks) and igneous (formed by solidification of hot mobile
material termed magma) rocks.

The map shows seven units of these rocks (nashoba formation,
Hanson, 1956) which run in a northeast to southwest direction.
One of these units is adover granite, an igneous rock, which
is solid with virtually no fractures. The other six are metamorphic rocks which are fractured and, therefore, produce more
water than granite.

DYNAMIC ENVIRONMENTAL RESOURCE MAPS

Depth-to-Water Table Map (figure 6)
The depth-to-water table map was compiled from well-record data.
The map shows the areas where the depth-to-water table is less
than and more than 10 feet.

Ground water surface levels fluctuate seasonally. When recharge
(water inflow) exceeds discharge (water outflow), storage increases, and the water level rises. Precipitation is the only
natural recharge source, and variations occur from day to day,
season to season, and year to year. The loss of water due to
evaporation is maximum during the summer. Therefore, the water
level is deepest below the land surface during late summer and
early fall, and closer to the surface in the late fall and in
early spring.

The depth-to-water table map, when compared with the topographic
map of Carlisle, indicates that the water table is typically
close to the land surface under broad valleys, and lies at
greater depths under upland surfaces. For sanitary landfill,
and other septic systems, the seasonal high ground-water table
should be more than 4 feet beneath the bottom of the depression
to be filled.

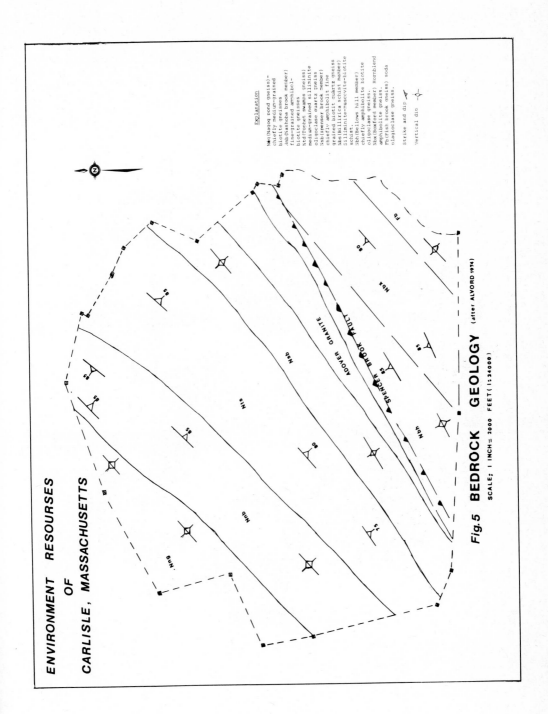

Fig.5 BEDROCK GEOLOGY (after ALVORD 1974)

SCALE: 1 INCH= 2000 FEET (1:24000)

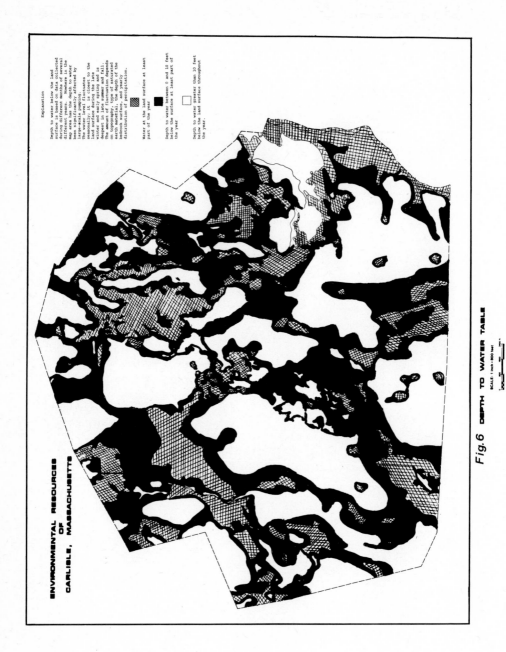

Explanation

Depth to water below the land
surface is based on data collected
during different months of several
different years. Nowhere in the
map area has the depth to water
been significantly affected by
large-scale pumping.
The water level fluctuates
seasonally; it is closest to the
land surface during the late
winter and early spring and fall.
The amount of fluctuation depends
on topography, type of saturated
earth material, the depth of the
bedrock surface, and yearly
distribution of precipitation.

Water at the land surface at least
part of the year

Depth to water between 0 and 10 feet
below the surface at least part of
the year

Depth to water greater than 10 feet
below the land surface throughout
the year.

Fig.6 DEPTH TO WATER TABLE

SCALE: 1 inch = 300 feet

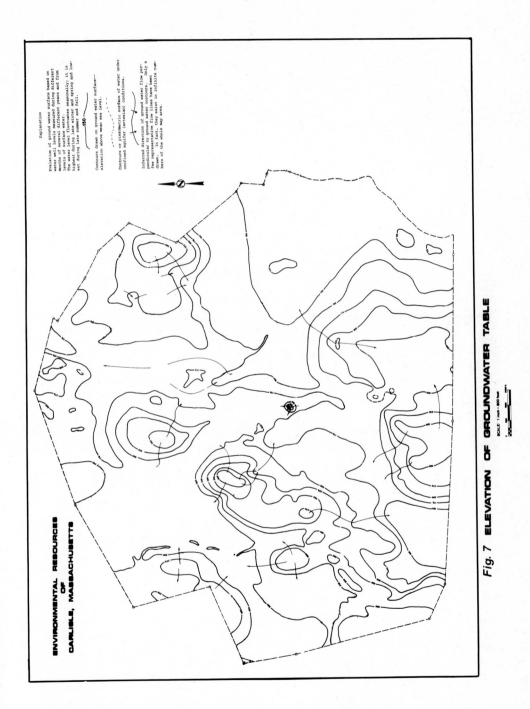

Fig. 7 ELEVATION OF GROUNDWATER TABLE

Elevation-of-Water Table Map (figure 7)
The elevation-of-water table map was compiled from data obtained
by subtracting the depth-to-water table in a well from the surface
elevation for that well. The elevation of lakes, streams, and
wetlands indicate the elevation of the water table at the land
surface. The elevation of the well site is approximate, because
the contour interval of the available topographic map is 10 feet.
Therefore, the elevation-of-water table map reflects this uncertainty. The most significant characteristic which can be
determined from this map is the ground water flow direction.
The recharge and discharge areas are also shown. Neither of
these features are readily apparent on the depth-to-water table
map.

The rate of movement of ground water is very slow, compared with
the surface water flow, in some situations as little as a few
feet per year. On slopes, ground water has a higher velocity.
Ground water moves at a faster rate through porous materials,
such as bodies of sand and gravel, than it does through less
porous till, clay, and silt. Ground water levels are higher
in non-porous surficial materials than in porous materials, such
as sand and gravel.

This relationship can be seen on the map showing the water table
elevation when it is overlain on one of the other maps, such as
the topographic map, the surface material map, or the depth-to-
bedrock map. Under surfaces at higher elevation, which in
Carlisle consist primarily of till, the water table has a relatively high elevation and a steeper slope (contours are closely
spaced). In the lowlands, where extensive sand and gravel deposits occur, the ground water table is relatively flat (ground
water contours are widely spaced apart).

Recharge and discharge areas are helpful in selecting disposal
sites. A sanitary landfill location in recharge areas may be
hazardous to the ground water quality.

Map of Well Yield (figure 8)
The map of well yield has been compiled from drillers' estimates
at the time of construction, and yield is expressed in gallons
per minute. All of the water used in Carlisle is withdrawn
from wells. Several different types of wells are in use: dug,
driven, and drilled wells. Most of the well records are from
newer wells, which are of the drilled type. There are only a
few wells which yield less than 5 gallons per minute.

From the well yield (gallons per minute) and total well depth
data (where available), the specific capacity was calculated;
the specific capacity is expressed in gallons per minute per foot.
This value was calculated for all wells and shows that deep
drilled wells do not produce as effectively as do shallow wells
driven in sand and gravel. The deepest well in Carlisle is over
700 feet deep and produces less than 1/2 gallon per minute or
about .0007 gallons per minute per foot. Several driven wells
less than 30 feet deep produce over 1 gallon per minute per foot
of well.

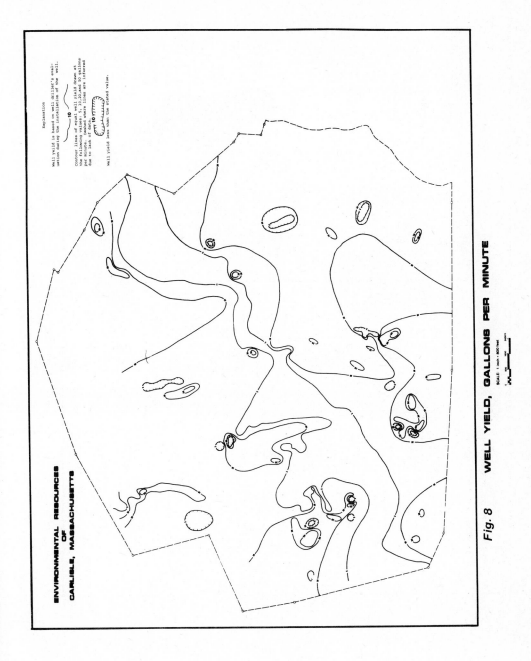

ENVIRONMENTAL RESOURCES
OF
CARLISLE, MASSACHUSETTS

Explanation

Well yield is based on well driller's evaluation during the installation of the well.

Contour lines of equal well yield drawn at the following values: 5, 10, 20 and 50 gallons per minute. Dashed where lines are inferred due to lack of data.

Well yield less than the stated value.

Fig. 8   **WELL YIELD, GALLONS PER MINUTE**

SCALE: 1 inch = 800 feet

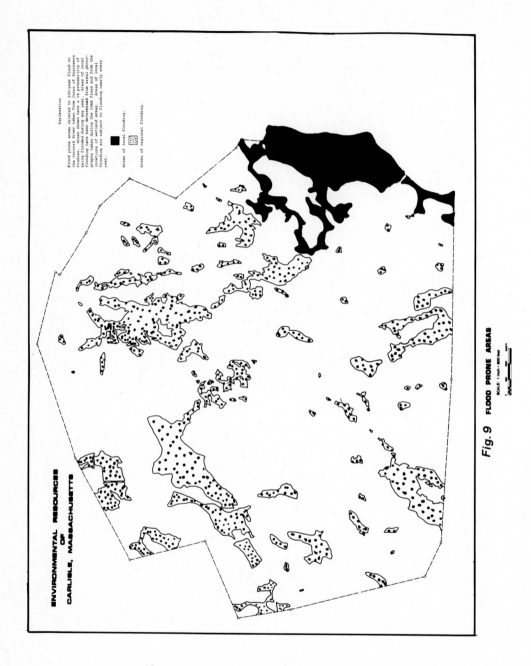

Fig. 9 FLOOD PRONE AREAS

SCALE: 1 inch = 200 feet

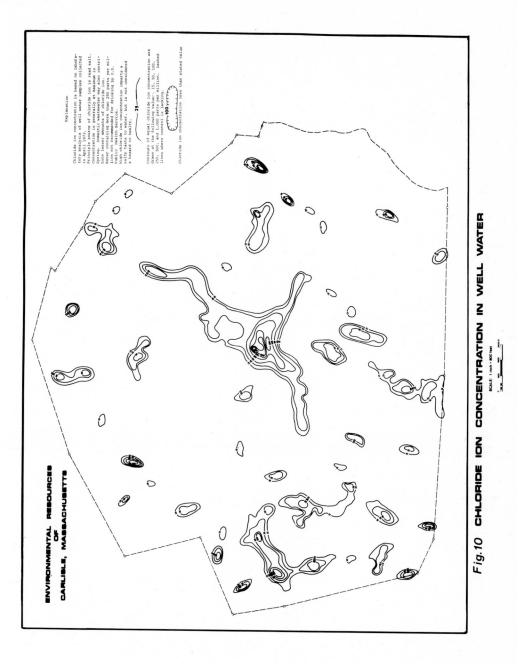

Fig.10 CHLORIDE ION CONCENTRATION IN WELL WATER

An interesting relationship between both well yield and specific
capacity and a characteristic of the bedrock geology has been
recognized. A belt of low yield (less than 5 gallons per minute) was found running from the southwest part of Carlisle,
through Carlisle village, toward the northeast. This belt has a
width of 800 to 1,000 feet with a specific capacity equal to 0.025
gallons per minute per foot. This belt coincides well with the
Adover granite that has been mapped by Donald Alvord (in edit.)
of the U. S. Geological Survey. The well yield map was prepared
without prior knowledge of the existence of the granite. Granite
is usually less fractured than are metamorphic rocks; a lower
well yield is usually found in wells drilled in granite than in
wells in metamorphic rocks.

Flood-Prone-Areas Map (figure 9)
Town planners are concerned with the frequency and magnitude of
floods. The magnitude of a flood is expressed in terms of its
ratio to the mean annual flood, and its frequency is expressed
in terms of its recurrence interval.

The flood-prone areas map of Carlisle is based on the flow which
has a 100-year recurrence interval. The map indicates areas
which have a 1:100 chance, on the average, of being flooded in
any given year. The areas shown also have about a 50:50 chance
of being flooded once during a 50-year period, and will almost
certainly be flooded once during a 100-year period.

In New England the principal cause of floods is the deep winter
snow followed by rain. The water produced by the melting snow
cannot infiltrate the ground which is generally frozen. The
second cause of flooding in New England is hurricanes.

Floods on the Concord River, which affect areas in the south-
east section of the town, are related to conditions largely outside the town and outside its possible control. In the wetland
area within the town, the conditions which promote floods are
local in nature and are, at least partly, susceptible to control
by the town.

A wetland area is one where the water table occurs at the land
surface or very close to it. The soil is frequently more per-
meable in a horizontal direction than in a vertical one. Since
the water table occurs near the land surface during most or all
of the year, wetlands cannot serve as areas for ground water
recharge; also, the low permeability of the soil in a vertical
direction prevents percolation. Since wetlands are located at
low elevations they are mostly places of ground water discharge
which has moved from higher elevations to lower elevation.
Ground water recharge in wetlands can occur only if the water
table falls. However, wetlands have the capacity to release
water horizontally to augment the flow of streams in late summer
and fall. Wetlands, then, are typically areas where ground water
is discharged by evaporation, transpiration, and base flow into
streams, rather than being areas of ground water recharge. (It

is interesting to note that the Commonwealth of Massachusetts
has several laws which protect wetlands, partly because of their
apparent importance to ground water recharge.)

Chloride Ion Concentration Map (figure 10)
In land use planning, the quality and quantity of ground water
is important. In addition, data related to the ground water
quality gives important clues to the geologic history of rocks,
as well as indications of ground water recharge, discharge, movement, and storage. In the summer of 1973 about 215 well samples
for the town of Carlisle were analyzed for chloride ion, calcium
ion, and iron ion content. The chloride ion concentration was
determined by the standard titration method. The test for calcium and iron ions were made with Perkin-Elmer atomic absorption
(303) instruments.

The concentration of chloride ion found in the ground water in
different parts of Carlisle is the result of both natural and
man-created influences. Chloride in ground water occurs naturally from the atmosphere and from the solution of chloride-
bearing minerals.

The effects of human activities on the distribution of chloride
ion concentration in the ground water of Carlisle have been most
dramatic. In 1890 the chloride content in Carlisle was between
one and two parts per million (ppm) (Motts and Saines, 1969).
But in April, 1973, due to the common practice in recent years
of salting roads to melt winter snow and ice, the ground water
along the local streets and highways was contaminated with large
amounts of sodium and calcium chlorides. Most state roads and
highways now receive from 10 to 22 tons of salt per year per
lane-mile. Town roads likely receive somewhat less. In Carlisle
chloride concentrations as high as 1,000 ppm were found in the
center of the town and about 10 ppm in areas with dead-end roads
and few houses. It was observed that the chloride values are
higher at road intersections and along well-traveled roads which
received greater applications of salt.

Another source of chloride in ground water is domestic waste-
water, when the disposal method used is an on-site disposal
system. According to Morrill and Toler (1973), about 15% of the
chloride in ground water and surface water comes from septic
systems within small watersheds.

The U. S. Public Health Service recommends that water containing
chloride in excess of 250 parts per million should not be used
for drinking.

In the town center, chloride concentrations exceeded that value,
but not in concentrations proven hazardous to health. However,
the U. S. Public Health Service does recommend that persons with
cardiovascular disease should not use as drinking water any water
with more than 20 ppm of sodium.

Map of Calcium Ion Content of Well Water (figure 11)
The presence of calcium ion in ground water is due partly to the
calcium ion in precipitation, and partly to the solution of cal-
cite or other calcium-bearing minerals in the soil or rock. In
order to dissolve any noticeable quantity, carbon dioxide is
necessary, the reaction being:

$$CaCO_3 + H_2O + CO_2 = Ca^{++} + 2HCO_3^-$$

The map shows the distribution of calcium ion in the well water
of Carlisle. The average calcium ion content is about 10 ppm,
with the lowest value being 2 ppm, and the maximum value being
about 180 ppm. The calcium content in ground water is related
directly to the local geology. The calcium content of the water
samples analyzed was directly related to the beds of calcareous
rock which run in a northeast-southwest direction through the
area.

Concentrations of calcium in excess of 60 parts per million in
water interferes with lathering and sudsing of soap, and produces
scaling in kettles and plumbing. Higher concentrations of calcium in drinking water are not considered a hazard to health.
There is no recommended limit for calcium set by the U. S. Public
Health Service. The relationship between softness of municipal
water and death rates from hypertensive and arteriosclerotic
heart diseases was demonstrated by Schroeder (1966). The softer
the water the higher the death rate.

Map of Iron Ion Concentration (figure 12)
In Carlisle, the highest iron content in ground water appears to
be associated with certain rock formations which contain iron
pyrite. For example, such iron deposits are associated with sand
and gravel. Effluent from septic systems contains biological and
chemical constituents which releases iron more readily from sand
and gravel than does normal ground water.

Iron concentration is greater where the water table is closer to
the surface. This can be confirmed in Carlisle by combining the
iron ion concentration map with the depth-to-water table map.

The U. S. Public Health Service recommends that water containing
more than 0.3 parts per million of iron not be used for drinking
water, yet iron in greater concentration is not considered a
hazard to health. A high concentration (greater than 1 ppm) of
iron is apt to produce a brownish color on plumbing fixtures and
laundered goods which is a nuisance to the domestic water user.
Also associated with iron are corrosion and encrustation problems.

APPLICATION OF LAND USE MAPS IN PLANNING

Each map presents a single element of the environment, the characteristics of which change from place to place within the map
area. A single map, such as depth-to-water table, may be used

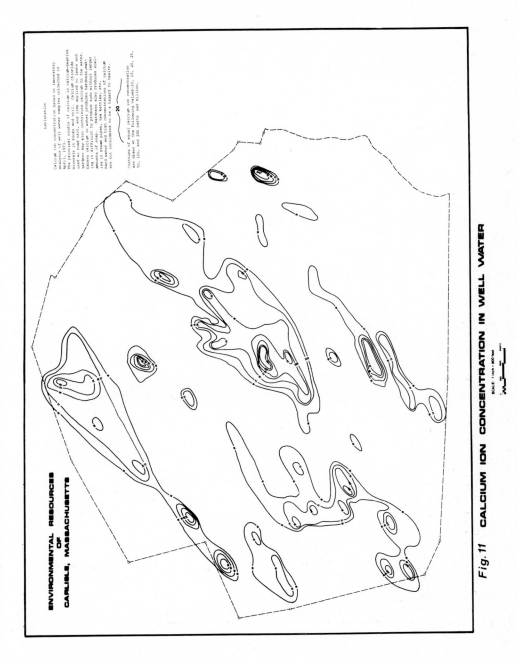

Fig. 11 CALCIUM ION CONCENTRATION IN WELL WATER

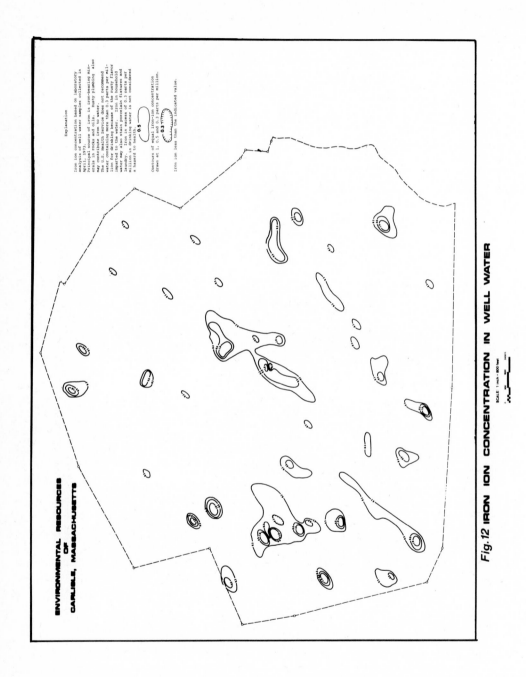

ENVIRONMENTAL RESOURCES OF CARLISLE, MASSACHUSETTS

Explanation

Iron ion concentration based on laboratory analysis of well water samples collected in April, 1973.

Principal source of iron is iron-bearing minerals in rocks and oils. Rusty plumbing also may contribute iron to water.

The U.S. Health Service does not recommend water containing more than 0.3 parts per million for drinking because of the rusty flavor imparted to the water. Iron in household water may also stain porcelain fixtures and laundry. Iron in drinking water is not considered a hazard to health.

Contours of equal iron-ion concentration drawn at 1, 0.5 and 0.3 parts per million.

Iron ion less than the indicated value.

Fig.12 IRON ION CONCENTRATION IN WELL WATER

SCALE 1 inch = 800 feet

to locate the areas of a high and low water table, whereas, a
surficial materials map may show deposits of construction materials within a planning area. Combinations of several maps may
establish all areas which have favorable characteristics for a
particular land use.

Judgment on how best to use environmental resource maps is the
province of town planners. Planners have to define the type of
facility needed, the area of land required, the funding limitations, and the limits of existing legislation. Once these guidelines have been established, the question of a proper site location for a particular facility can be solved by stacking the
appropriate environmental resource unit map transparencies on
one another. For example, a municipal ground water facility is
needed for Carlisle. Assume the town officials use the following
guidelines.

The geologic and hydrologic criteria for large yield ground water
supplies are as follows:
1. Deposits of sand and gravel over 30 feet thick.
2. Saturated zone within the gravel of adequate thickness.
3. Adequate areas of recharge.
The statutory and regulatory limitations are:
1. Water of good quality.
2. No houses within 400 feet of proposed well. (This regulatory
    minimum should be increased to about 1,000 feet to ensure
    continued protection of water quality.)
3. No major sources of contamination within the recharge area.

Transparent overlays may be prepared from the appropriate environmental resource maps. The areas on the depth-to-bedrock map,
within which bedrock lies at less than 10 feet, may be colored
solid red and placed over the town base map. Using the surface
materials map, all material other than sand and gravel may be
colored solid green. When this is placed over the bedrock-less-
than-10-feet overlay, all areas within the town, which have bedrock more than 10 feet deep under sand and gravel, will stand
out as islands within those areas which have either one or two
factors limiting ground water occurrence. Lack of major recharge
areas near the located sites would eliminate some of the "islands"
from further consideration. The water quality maps showing chloride and iron content could be used to eliminate other areas in
which water quality is unfavorable. Access to potential sites
(slope map) and possible water transmission lines (depth-to-
bedrock) may also be evaluated. Such an analysis as described
is, of course, only the first step; on-site testing within the
most favorable locations for ground water supply will be necessary.

A second example will serve to illustrate the ease with which
these maps can be used to solve sanitary landfill location
questions. First, the local requirements for a sanitary landfill
location would be defined; for example:
1. At least 50 acres of land are required.
2. Fifty acre-feet of earth cover are required.

3.   No housing development within 1,000 feet.
State and other statutory legislation limitations must be taken
into account, such as:
1.   Depth-to-water table should not be less than 4 feet.
2.   Depth-to-bedrock should not be less than 10 feet.
3.   Impervious material to insure maximum runoff from the
     completed land fill.

Areas less than 10 feet might be colored red on the depth-to-
bedrock map. On the depth-to-water table map all areas having
depth to the water table of less than 10 feet might be colored
solid blue. Land slopes greater than 8% and less than 3% might
be colored solid brown. An impervious base material is desired,
so on the surficial materials map all gravel areas might be
colored solid yellow. If these maps are placed over the base
map, potential areas for landfill will appear as clear windows.
When the criteria of 50 acres of land and no housing within 1,000
feet are applied to the open windows, all but the most desirable
sites will be eliminated. If the site study shows that such an
area does not exist in the town, the initial guidelines may have
to be modified.

The overlay mapping technique can be applied to other land-use
problems such as land-use zoning for high or low density housing,
commercial, industrial, and open space purposes. It can also be
extended to delineate specific areas which are significant because of special cultural, social, historical, or wildlife values.

ACKNOWLEDGEMENTS

My sincere thanks to Dr. D. W. Caldwell, Boston University, and
to Fred Pessl and Donald Alvord, of the U. S. Geological Survey
for their advice, criticism, and help. My appreciation is also
extended to Keith Dickinson and Steve Rosen, University of Wisconsin-Oshkosh, who read this article, and to Barbara Schiman
who helped produce the color over prints, and to Linda Busha
who typed this paper.

Funds for the project were contributed by the Ford Foundation
(Grant No. 720-0013) and matched by the town of Carlisle,
Massachusetts.

REFERENCES

Alvord, D. S., Bedrock Geology Map of Carlisle, Open file of
     the U. S. Geological Survey, Boston, Massachusetts office,
     (1973).

Baker, J. and Petersen, B., Lowell area: U. S. Geological Survey,
     Massachusetts Basic Data Reports, 3, 28, (1962).

Barker, R. M. and Stone, C. S., Natural Land Slopes, Hartford
     North Quadrangle, Connecticut: U. S. Geological Survey
     Misc. Geol. Inv. Map I-784-I, (1972).

Hackett, J. E. and McComas, M. R., Geology for Planning in McHenry County, Illinois: Illinois State Geological Survey Circ. 438, 29, (1969).

Hansen, W. R., Geology and Mineral Resources of the Hudson and Maynard Quadrangles, Massachusetts: U. S. Geological Survey Bulletin, 38, 104, (1956).

Legget, R. F., Cities and Geology, McGraw-Hill, New York, 642, (1973).

Lutzen, E. E. and Rockaway, J. D., Engineering Geology of St. Louis County, Missouri: Eng. Geological series no. 4, Missouri Geological Survey and Water Res., Rolla, Missouri, 22, (1971).

Maberry, J. O., Slope Map of the Parker Quadrangle, Arapahoe and Douglas Counties, Colorado: U. S. Geological Survey Misc. Geol. Inv. Map I-770-F, (1972).

McHarg, I., Design with Nature, The National History Press, New York, 197, (1969).

Morril, G. B. and Toler, L. G., Effect of Septic Tank Wastes on Quality of Water, Ipswich and Shawsheen River Basins, Massachusetts: U. S. Geological Survey, Journal Res., 1, 1, 117-120, (1973).

Motts, W. S. and Saines, M., The Occurrence and Characteristics of Ground Water Contamination in Massachusetts: Water Resources Research Center, University of Massachusetts, Amherst, Massachusetts, 70, (1969).

Pessl, F., Jr., Langer, W. H. and Ryder, R. B., Geological and Hydrologic Maps for Land-Use Planning in the Connecticut Valley with Examples from Folio of the Hartford North Quadrangle, Connecticut: U. S. Geological Survey Circ., 674, 12, (1972).

Quay, J. R., Use of Soil Surveys in Subdivision Design, Soil Surveys and Land-Use Planning: Journal Soil. Sci. Soc. of America and American Soc. Agronomy, 76-87, (1966).

Schmidt, P. W., Slope Map of the Evergreen Quadrangle, Jefferson County, Colorado: U. S. Geological Survey Misc. Geol. Inv. Map I-786-A, (1972).

Schroeder, H. A., Municipal Drinking Water and Cardiovascular Death Rates, Journal of A.M.A., 195, 2, 125-129, (1966).

Scott, G. R., Geologic Map of the Morrison Quadrangle, Jefferson County, Colorado, U. S. Geological Survey Misc. Geol. Inv. Map I-790-A, (1972a).

Turner, A. K. and Coffman, D. M., Geology for Planning: A Review of Environmental Geology, <u>Quarterly Colorado School of Mines</u>, 68, 3, 127, (1973).

U. S. Corps of Engineers, Flood Plain Information, Concord and Shawsheen Rivers, Bedford, Massachusetts, 50, (1968).

MEASURING THE COSTS OF AN IMPROVED URBAN ENVIRONMENT FOR LOW-COST HOUSING: THE POTENTIAL CONTRIBUTION OF THRESHOLD ANALYSIS

James T. Hughes
Senior Lecturer, Department of Social and Economic Research,
University of Glasgow, U.K.

ECONOMIC FACTORS IN THE URBAN ENVIRONMENT

The principal threat to the social wellbeing of the urban community lies in the centres of large metropolitan areas. This threat exists both in highly developed and developing countries. As the growth industries in both the manufacturing and service sectors decentralise and thrive on the periphery the income and employment opportunities available to the central city residents decline. By the same movement of commerce and the upper-to-middle-income households, the fiscal base of the central city is progressively reduced. Yet the expenditure needs to renew the outworn physical fabric of the central city and to provide incentives for the renewal of its economic health, place increasing burdens on the public economy of these areas. The problems of New York's fiscal bankruptcy is the most spectacular example of this squeeze but many other cities are surviving only by cutting back on desperately needed social investment programmes.

The combination of economic trends and political policies, which trap low-income families in the central city yet make it difficult to apply the fiscal resources to alleviate their social problems, is probably most serious for the provision of low-cost housing. Everywhere the costs of land and new construction on central sites outstrip the capacity of low-income families to pay. The alternative is to provide large subsidies from public housing agencies which frequently have their own internal financial constraints or are expected to fulfil the 'social' goals for low-income families by cross-subsidisation between middle-income and low-income families. In developing countries it is not unusual for the economic rent of "low-cost" housing to be outwith the budgets of 75 per cent of the urban population.

Although these problems are well-known and almost universally accepted as the major threat to the quality of life in large urban areas, the response of planners, economists and other related disciplines has been slow. In some respects the responsibility must lie with an ambiguous political commitment. The cost of improving the urban environment in central cities will, if they are to be fairly and realistically distributed, not only threaten the fiscal havens of suburban communities but create a significant upward shift in the demand for national investment resources. This demand will have to compete with existing claims on national savings, taxation revenue and foreign borrowing. The concentration of economic planners on encouraging more directly productive forms of investment and the frequent lack of political influence by the urban poor militate against greater diversion of resources to the urban problem.

A burden of responsibility must also lie with the professions involved in urban planning.   Whereas many of the problems cry out for a multidiscipinary approach, the professional and disciplinary barriers have remained strong.   Even where major planning teams exist, the various parts of the team may work very independently.   The author has argued elsewhere that there are significant methodological difficulties in, say the interdisciplinary cooperation of economists and other members of a planning team (Hughes and Kozlowski, 1968).   In the case of low-income housing, effective evaluation of alternative plans calls for an attention to design details and the complex structure of costs which is frequently impossible to achieve. The conventional techniques of cost-benefit analysis and project appraisal (e.g. Little and Mirrlees, 1974) are too complex for non-specialist staff and are generally geared to large scale projects.

Three major problems must be faced in achieving the goal of greater economic evaluation.   (i) The measurement of benefits which households experience in occupying houses of varying quality is a difficult exercise.   The private individual will find it difficult to evaluate the long-term benefit (often to future generations) of improved housing; he will also ignore the social or external benefits in the form of reduced disease, improved productivity, etc.   (ii) Information about the costs of alternative types, layouts and locations for housing is usually in the hands of professions and disciplines who pursue their independent functions and are often never co-ordinated either in planning procedures or in the process of housebuilding itself. (iii) Even assuming co-ordination of cost information, it is often difficult in the comparison of alternative schemes to identify where significant cost savings can occur, since many of the standards of provision and design questions are in the hands of separate professions.   Frequently also many of these detailed questions are tackled only at the design stage which follows the resolution of an overall planning strategy.

The principal components of low-cost urban housing projects are: (a) the size and quality of the dwelling structure; (b) preparation of the site and connection to central services and networks; (c) overhead costs of central networks; (d) costs of displacing or relating to existing land uses; (e) financial costs of borrowing.   There is a need to consider in considerable detail these items of costs individually, in relationship to each other and the extent to which their variation is influenced by land-use and housing planning.

THRESHOLD ANALYSIS

The main purpose of this paper is to put forward a simple quantitative technique which can help to identify decision points in the course of urban development and to provide a measurement of the relative costs of a variety of alternative schemes.   It does so within a framework which in the hands of a physical or corporate planner can act as a suitable basis for inter-disciplinary cooperation.

The technique is called Threshold Analysis.   The theoretical basis and early applications of the technique, which originated in Poland under the aegis of Professor B. Malisz, took place in the University of Edinburgh, Scotland. This work and a review of the technique to 1971 was published in 1972 (Hughes and Kozlowski, 1972).   A manual for the application of the method by planners has been issued by the Scottish Development Department (SDD 1973) in the UK and a manual for application in developing countries is to be issued by the Centre for Housing, Building and Finance of the United Nations.

The background of the theory is founded on the simple observation that towns encounter some physical limitations to their spatial growth due either to physiography or to their public utility networks and transport systems, and to existing land uses.   These limitations have been called the thresholds of urban development and on the basis of threshold analysis they can be defined either as lines on the base maps, or as points on development curves.   Analysing their impact on the physical growth of towns, it can be said that there exist discontinuity points in urban development processes resulting from limitations restricting further physical expansion of the towns concerned.   These limitations are not irremediable but can only be overcome at 'additional' – usually disproportionally high – investment costs, since they often involve major improvements of land, implementation of new infrastructure systems or radical reconstruction of existing ones.   These costs, called threshold costs, can be calculated with the help of threshold analysis.

An important inference from these observations is that the physical growth of towns is not smoothly continuous but that it proceeds in 'jumps' marked by the successive development thresholds.   Thus capital investment costs needed for the expansion of the town will change over time disproportionally to the increasing numbers of inhabitants, reflecting periods when additional lump sums must be spent in order to open successive areas for further urban development.   Thus in general the costs necessary to locate a new in-habitant in a town (C_t = total costs) are at least twofold:

    (a)   costs not connected with given location of constructive investment necessary to accommodate new inhabitants which would constitute the 'normal' costs and have to be spent in any case (C_n = normal costs);

    (b)   costs tied to existing conditions and characteristics of given land which constitute additional costs substantially varying from one location to another (C_a = additional costs).

Thus $C_t = C_n + C_a$.

This basic subdivision of costs lies at the foundations of the threshold concept and of threshold cost calculations; but it is necessary to clarify each problem further and to relate threshold analysis more closely to aspects of residential development which so far has been the main subject of its practical applications and the manuals.

It is convenient to assume that development usually starts from that part of the area where building conditions (and therefore development costs) can be regarded as NORMAL.   'Normal conditions' for the development of land, in this context, indicates land being relatively flat, having good bearing capacity of soil, being served by basic public utility networks and having direct access to an existing road system.   Thus 'normal cost' indicates cost of development on sites classified as 'normal'.   It may be noted that, in fact, this 'normal development cost' as attached to some sort of idealised land characteristics, represents the constant part of Development Cost, that is, the part which always has to be spent for a given type of development

regardless of its location (C_n).   As previously mentioned, this part of
Development Cost can fluctuate only if the type of development, its
technology or cost of labour and materials are changing.   If however normal
(or ideal) conditions of the land being developed change, then the cost of
development will rise and additional cost (C_a) representing the <u>variable</u>
part of development cost, directly depending on the location of a given
development type, will have to be introduced.   The distribution of
development cost between constant and variable costs lies at the root of
the threshold theory, and its unequivocal definition is a necessary starting
point for a full understanding of the threshold approach.   The definition
of normal cost is a matter of judgment in each application but it should be
directed towards focusing the work of economists, planners, engineers and
administrators on the significant variant elements in the structure of urban
costs.   This is not to say that there cannot be other foci of analysis,
e.g. between demographic characteristics and municipal costs (e.g. Sternlieb).

Briefly, in more economic terminology, Threshold Analysis seeks to identify
the points in residential development (in terms both of population levels
and spatial boundaries) where the physical, engineering, structural cost
factors in building may lead to a change in costs of development.   There
are two main types of discontinuity or "threshold" (T) in the cost function:
(a) a 'stepped' threshold when (see Fig. 1) investment is required, e.g. in
a new water or sewage or road network, before residential development can
continue;   (b) a 'grade' threshold (see Fig. 2) where the costs of
building each "dwelling unit" will increase, due perhaps to the site preparation required for steeper slopes or the loadbearing quality of the soil.

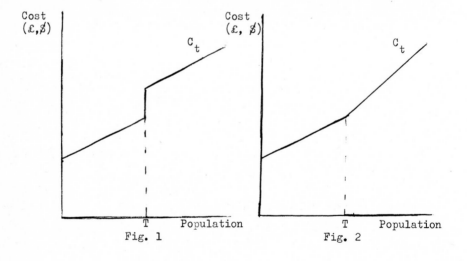

Fig. 1

Fig. 2

THE NEED TO EVALUATE RESOURCES AVAILABLE FOR IMPROVING THE URBAN ENVIRONMENT

While we may expect some improvement in the urban environment from new technology and fresh applications of existing techniques, we must also anticipate that in the foreseeable future the technical and administrative framework will be that of current urban planning. It is essential in this case to relate the desired goals of environmental change to the use of land in alternative urban forms and the investment required to service these developments.

There has been considerable interest in developing systematic planning choices, e.g. Chadwick (1971) and McLoughlin (1969), but less attention has been given to the practical problems of interdisciplinary co-operation and the basic tools with which planners will have to tackle the ambitious goals set for them. Threshold analysis is a means by which planners can test the variations in cost which will be created by alternative locations and forms of urban development and redevelopment. This section will mention a number of ways in which the method can assist rational choice. The applications are necessarily restricted by the space available but it is probably desirable to clear at least one major obstacle to its acceptance. Many planners will protest that an improved urban environment will result from an unequivocal statement of desirable standards by the planner; the planner is not concerned with saving pennies. Roland McKean (1950) typifies this as the "requirements approach" of spending agencies which is doomed to frustration in the budgetary process. Above all, the planner would be failing in his responsibility to improving the environment if he did not consider the possibility of carrying out a fixed set of goals at lower cost. Although planning may not immediately reap the benefit of the savings, in the long run savings in the use of investment resources mean a higher goal achievement for most expenditure functions.

The investigation of 'additional costs' of urban development will enable planners to identify the locations and directions of growth which will minimise threshold costs. This is the aspect of Threshold Analysis which has been given most attention in the manuals and in the published work. Since it is so well documented elsewhere, I propose to give this aspect relatively little attention. It can, however, never be repeated too often that Threshold Analysis does not claim to be the corner-stone of planning evaluation or even economic evaluation in planning. The information produced by Threshold Analysis should be brought together with other parameters in the attainment of planning goals. My claim would be that planning evaluation is so complex that it cannot be accomplished in one grand exercise. I could, I think, put forward a convincing case that such simplification of the planning process is firmly in the tradition of Patrick Geddes and the tripartite rule of Survey-Analysis-Plan.

In most of the underdeveloped and developing world, urban development cannot be constructed to high standards. There is a constant need to assess the availability of resources to plan the optimal mix of urban services which can be provided. This is not a question which can be settled 'a priori' by fixing standards for all urban areas in a region or even throughout one metropolitan region. Each major locus of development

will face differing thresholds and constraints.   Where certain areas can
be serviced by some utilities only at great expense, these services should
be economised to the greatest extent.   In other areas the topography or
sub-soil structure can bear only low-rise structures without substantial
extra cost.   It may be justifiable to divert low-rise, low density housing
to these areas to preserve superior sites for higher density development.

In view of the apparent desire to test the use of 'self-help' housing with
minimum standards as a planned alternative to squatter settlements,
Threshold Analysis could help to identify areas for these schemes.   A
problem of 'self-help' areas is that they may sterilise land which is
capable of more intense forms of development and entail a diversion of
these other forms of development to higher cost areas.   Although 'self-
help' schemes may differ widely in quantity, the ideal site would appear
to be one which did impose higher 'grade threshold' costs for low-rise
structures but which might suffer threshold constraints in the provision of
larger-scale and higher-quality services for more intensive or upper-income
development.

Many urban areas have a significant volume of spare capacity in the form of
networks which service adjacent areas and which could be easily extended or
of urban services like paved roads and water actually constructed on the
urban/rural fringe.   (As an aside, the colour slide of cattle being driven
down the paved road with street lighting installed, in a developing country,
remains vividly in my memory).   With a careful inventory it should be
possible to make much of this spare capacity effective by planning
development to utilize it, assuming there are not strong negative factors
(there is no sense in pouring good resources after bad).   It will
probably also be necessary to add selected other services which may be non-
existent or at a much lower standard.   A major reason for the sterilization
of suitable, serviced urban land in Latin-America and other areas where the
land tenure system permits is the slow development of single family plots.
To the ex-peasant the ownership of land is clearly attractive and in a time
of inflation a very rational policy.   The absorption of savings and income
to service loans and the costs of migration, however, reduce the household's
capacity to build a dwelling until it becomes better established in the
urban economy.   Meanwhile there are political pressures to provide urban
services.   It should be possible to identify areas where the infrastructure
is underutilized and, if necessary, stimulate more intensive development by
incentives and if necessary local taxation (e.g. by taxing partly developed
sites as though they were fully developed).

CONCLUSION

This paper has concentrated on the need to raise the quality of the urban
environment for the vast majority of the urban population in all countries
who cannot afford new 'low-cost' housing as currently defined.   There is a
need to relate closely developments in this category to the level and type
of urban services.   Threshold Analysis is a quantitative planning method
which will facilitate identification of the major constraints facing urban
development.   Although the main development of Threshold Analysis has been
the measurement of cost it is in a form which can be related to other
aspects of planning appraisal including qualitative aspects.   The last
section of the paper puts forward some ideas for the application of

Threshold Analysis not only to the basic problem of assessing the comparative costs of alternative urban development schemes but also to more particular aspects of a more innovative approach to planning urban development including 'self help' schemes.

REFERENCES

Chadwick, G.F. (1971) A Systems View of Planning, Pergamon, Oxford.

Hughes, J.T. and Kozlowski, J., Threshold Analysis - an Economic Tool for Town and Regional Planning, Urban Studies, 5.2 (1968).

Kozlowski, J. and Hughes, J.T. (1972) Threshold Analysis: a Quantitative Planning Method, Architectural Press, London.

Little, I.M.D. and Mirrlees, J.A. (1974) Project Appraisal and Planning for Developing Countries, Heinemann, London.

McKean, R.N. (1950) Efficiency in Government through Systems Analysis, Wiley, New York.

McLoughlin, J.B. (1969) Urban and Regional Planning: a systems approach, Faber, London.

Sadove, R., Urban Needs of Developing Countries, Finance and Development, 10.2 (1973).

Sternlieb, G. (undated) Housing Development and Municipal Costs, Rutgers University, New Brunswick, N.J.

S.D.D. (1973) - Scottish Development Department, Threshold Analysis Manual, Her Majesty's Stationery Office.

WELL-BEING IN URBAN EXTENSIONS

Morton Hoppenfeld, Dean
School of Architecture and Planning
University of New Mexico 87131

The Need for a New Way of Thinking

If we are ever to enjoy cities more humane than most are at
present, it is necessary for involved and responsible people to
understand and to clearly state over and over again that the
purpose of a city is to enhance the well-being of its citizens.
This statement of purpose seems not to be commonly shared, and
it is seldom consciously held forth as a guide for urban decision
making. Indeed, casual observance could well lead to the conclusion that other purposes, such as private economic gain,
bureaucratic maintenance, elitist esthetics, and other such 'non-
humane' or secondary purposes are being served first - in fact,
they probably are. In the face of these questionable priorities,
metropolitan areas all over the world continue to grow. They
grow because most people freely perceive that chances to improve
the quality of their own and family life are still better in the
urban areas of the world than in the small towns and rural areas.
Almost in spite of themselves, the big cities do fulfill some of
their potential to enhance life.*

Thus, urban areas continue to grow - and we must acknowledge
that they should - unless and until it can be demonstrated that
life will indeed be comparatively better in non-urban areas. It
is hard to believe that many of these cities - squalid, wasteful,
ugly, often noxious as they are - could possibly be the freely
chosen home for their residents. It is obviously a question of
alternatives. For most people, there is no real choice; the
opportunity to earn a better living, to gain an adequate education, to receive necessary health care and the like is simply
not there now, nor can it realistically be delivered in most
rural areas, in most nations.

The typical image of urban growth is amorphous and basically uncontrolled, usually following some lead: a sewer line, a highway, a transit route, or inexpensive, available land. The
typical growth pattern allows housing to set the pace - some kind
of local street pattern (usually a grid) - special streets set
aside for the random location of commercial, and later business
services, and eventually a school site designated along the road

---

*The word city as used here is meant to be synonomous with urban
metropolitan area, i.e., disregarding arbitrary urban-suburban
political boundaries.

for easy bus access. The pattern is endless as it is mindless;
it is also 'easy' for both public sector management and private
sector development. Occasional efforts to control this growth
pattern are usually merely aimed at slowing it, not necessarily
at improving quality. In this fashion, the one time natural
resources of the land are often wasted, urban activities which
might benefit users by proximity are spread apart and populations
are ghettoized by income, race, or ethnicity. Thus, socially
and economically costly conditions are built into the environment for long terms.

So long as urban expansion is thought about in the traditional
language of physical phenomena such as acres, density, building
types, miles of utilities, zoning and land use classes, etc.,
there is likely to be minimal improvement in life qualities, and
in some circumstances, it is not unreasonable to anticipate a
lowering of quality from that which may have existed before
growth was so clearly manifest.

In this rapid but random growth process the essential social
systems and institutions which are basic to urban life quality
are left to catch up as best they can. The managers of existing
community service systems, such as schools, health care, employment, recreation, comprehensive shopping, and other social
services are unlikely to have been asked sufficiently in advance
or have been brought together with the resources to plan for
their eventual metamorphasis and expansion. No systematic
public/private effort is likely to use this imminent growth as
an opportunity for the assessment of current delivery patterns
and the possibilities for improvements, even dramatic structural
changes, inherent in the eventual building of new facilities
and/or the addition of new personnel that accompany growth.
Instead, each segment of the community's life support system is
expected to respond separately to after-the-fact incremental
demands for new or traditional services, which only exascerbate
existing operational problems and daily crises. The litany of
problems resulting from today's accelerated rate and random
laissez-faire urban development is long, and need not be elaborated here. It seems obvious that this dominant, nearly universal,
growth pattern is contributing to, rather than ameliorating,
urban problems.

Is this eternal pressure for urban expansion a necessarily bad
phenomenon, carrying with it the seeds of urban, indeed societal,
destruction as some would suggest? Expansion is clearly the
manifestation of a natural human desire for a better life as
perceived in the opportunities available in the big city. The
growth of metropolitan areas is a phenomenon experienced by all
kinds of societies and accelerated dramatically in the past
thirty years with the proliferation of the automobile, major
concentrations of employment opportunities, and changes in
technologies. Is it not reasonable to observe that the connotation of badness is more a judgment as to how well we build and
maintain our cities today, than it is a judgment about urban
expansion per se?

Having thus asserted my belief in the inevitability and potential
desirability of urban growth, I must add that there are some
good and sufficient reasons to limit the size of any metropolitan
area. The holding capacity of any geographic area should have
limits. The availability of natural resources, such as water,
quality of air or other environmental, economic, convenience,
even esthetic aspects can be measured and used to determine
points of diminishing return and the desirability of growth
limitations. The numbers required to reach such growth maximums
could vary from the consciously chosen 10 million of today's
London, or the accidental 12 million of New York, down to metro
areas in the range of one million or less, provided they can
maintain a viable economic base and meet the felt needs of a
citizenry.

By choosing thus to limit the growth of certain metro areas, a
nation would be required to designate locations for the growth
of others. National policies would be required to determine the
location of basic industries, transportation networks, and other
phenomena which induce urban development. Countries such as the
United Kingdom, France, Russia, China, etc. have undertaken such
planning and have carried out such policies. If the national
interest is described in terms of human well-being, as it should
be, then that is what can best be served by such planning.

What follows is a set of ideas which I propose as valid for any
urban expansion - be it part of a national growth policy, part
of the random patterns of urban expansion that continue around
most major cities of the world (as in the new town of Columbia,
Maryland), or be it the conscious development of a new city-
metropolitan area (as in Brazilia and Milton Keynes). The ideas
are fundamental. If we accept the proposition that the basic
purpose of a city is to enhance the well-being of its citizens,
then it follows logically that:
>The fact of new growth should be viewed as leverage
>for beneficial change and the opportunity for
>creating new or improved social systems and physical
>environments. The premise offered here is tht a
>conscious and continuing planning and development
>process aimed at the building of whole but diverse
>geographically definable communities is one of the
>best means available for improving the quality of
>life for individuals, conserving scarce natural
>resources, and for beneficially altering a society
>by its commitment to the building of humane communities.

Community Development - A Better Way to Grow and Change
The alternative to random urban expansion is to channel growth
into identifiable communities, which have as their expressed
purpose for being - the enhancement of the quality of individual
and family life for its members.

The use of the word community is meant to be taken literally as
a place within which there is a sense of sharing, interdependence,
interaction, the pursuit of common life enhancing goals, and
foremost among these, the continuous building and maintenance of

such a community.*

When this purpose is elaborated upon in order to inform operational policy and design decisions, community development criteria
emerge. In other words, it is necessary to describe the expectations for an environment, as the first step toward having
that environment serve to facilitate human well-being.

We typically organize peoples' needs into categories such as:
employment (job availability, training and placement processes,
wage scales, and levels of job satisfaction); housing (conditions of crowding, cost, types, and the extent of choice);
health (levels of morbidity, access to care, quality of care,
and the extent of public sophistication and health maintenance);
and shopping and consumer services (the cost and availability of
merchandise and service, the quality of the shopping experience,
the range of choice, and the sophistication and ability of the
consumer to satisfy felt needs). One can go on to elaborate
concepts of 'well-being' in 'all' the other aspects of life -
education, recreation, governance, social services, etc. By
understanding the interdependencies and relationships among
them, a reasonable concept of wholeness can be derived to
describe the quality of present or desired well-being in a society.

Around each area of concern it would be natural for there to
emerge groupings of technicians, politicians, and 'ordinary'
people who share an interest. Other groupings of people with
common interest emerge in areas such as child care, family life,
or just plain neighboring. All of these groups interact to sort
out common and diverse needs, deciding on ways to meet them.
Leadership, management, and communication skills, all necessary
parts of a rational development process, can consciously facilitate these group formations and efforts at improving life
conditions.

In describing urban life in this fashion, and ultimately attribu-
ting to it a scale in numbers of people and amounts of interior
and exterior space necessary for their activity, plus their
geographic relationships, one is actually defining a kind of
community unique to the time, place, and people involved. In
attempting these descriptions, there will be countless opinions
and theories on how the social systems should best be organized

---

*It is necessary to note that this notion of community is
seldom pure. There are usually communities within others, as well
as those which are essentially cerebral - communities of interest,
which are unbounded. In some contemporary Sociology and cock-
tail parlance, there is a trend away from the very concept of
place-oriented communities, a glorification of the image which
a Los Angeles presents. However, there is still a dominance of
others who value a place-oriented community as the best base
from which to build socio-physical environmental quality, and
individual, as well as family, well-being.

and managed for the optimum delivery of services. Ultimately,
decisions on the design of social systems would be followed by
the design of the land and facilities required to enhance the
workings of the systems and the resultant community.

Such places can be large or small, they can be intricate and
diverse in populations and make-up, consisting of many or few
communities of interest within, and they can have varying
degrees of self-sufficiency in jobs and other life support
systems. They will change continually in response to internal
and external life conditions.

The size of each, the number and locations of their centers need
emerge from the phenomena of each metro area, but each community
should have a distinctive geographic base. The emphasis in
community design, however, should always be on the centers of
community life rather than on the edges or boundaries between
them. The centers are focal points – borne out of the juxtapo-
sition of facilities needed to provide for the social, institutional life needs of the people. By designed proximity, the
use of the facilities can be optimized and the social interaction
among institutions and individuals enhanced. The form of these
centers become the expression of the social purposes they serve.
Within these places, many diverse communities of interest will
emerge, overlap, and use the same facilities. Some people may
live in residential communities, separate from those where
their interest in work, public service, or commerce may take
them, hence the inevitability of blurred boundaries and multiple
allegiencies.

In its rudimentary terms, this is the community design and development process. It is applicable in renewing the old parts
of the metropolis as in dealing with new growth areas.
> When consciously and capably undertaken, and when
> it is participatory and learningful by its very
> nature, then the community development process is
> self-fulfilling.

Larger Political and Social Systems Can Benefit
In the pursuit of any good community, interaction with larger
political and social systems is inevitable, for in an urban
complex, only few aspects of community life will be self contained. Enlightened advocacy on the part of each community
seeking to fulfill its needs in a larger, regional context,
should ultimately improve region-wide systems and make them more
able to serve the populace through community-based structures
instead of typically less sensitive and more bureaucratic super-
governmental agencies.

Past and Present Efforts
Obviously, community planning (in the social and physical sense)
and rational development processes have not been the dominant
mode of growth in most metropolitan areas of the world. There
are, however, many efforts at building new communities and new
cities which have been undertaken in the last 25 years: the
English new towns program, the Dutch settlement of the polders,

and the building of new National Capitals, such as Brazilia and
Chandigarh. Almost every nation has had some experience with
the concepts of "new city" building. While there has been virtually no systematic evaluation of the values gained from these
projects, I believe that in each nation they are generally perceived as having succeeded in their mission.* However, most
often their missions were described in rather fundamental, if
not simplistic, terms, i.e., to relocate industry, slum dwellers
from a congested central city, or to open up and settle a hinterland. Planning process was essentially limited to the allocation of land uses and to architectural design.

Virtually all previous efforts at building new cities or pieces
thereof were more concerned with the plan and the physical
product than the planning and social system or community development process. Mostly, they were an expression of an architectural
bias, wherein concepts borne more of esthetic principle or an
economic bias dominated rather than social objective and a
balance of many pluralistic values.

We have recently lived (and continue now) through two basic
approaches to urban growth. The dominant one (at least in the
U.S.) is laissez-faire, where economics control. Concern for
well-being is an after-the-fact, catch up game played by well
meaning public servants, but with little chance of ever getting
ahead of the problem, and by politicians who thrive on uncertainty
and opportunism. The second approach is that of the planned
community-city where, because of the naive dependence on
architectural-spatial values, concern for aspects of human well-
being were rarely stated, except implicitly, in the built form
or in vague verbal generalities. In both cases, the values of
community life and enhancement of well-being have been hit or miss.

We have learned little from past experiences. There is little
empirical evidence available today upon which to base countless
community design decisions. The purposes of city building have
seldom been described in terms of human well-being, as suggested
above. The social scientists have not been much involved to
date. This means only that mostly theory and hypotheses must
suffice at present and each effort at community development must
be conceived as a learning opportunity for all involved persons
and professions, until our scientific knowledge on the subject
begins to catch up to our need to act. I have no trouble with
this fact. If our purposes are clear, if we remain conscious of

----

*The "New Towns" program in the U. S. was started much later than
in most other countries. It was aborted prematurely at the peak
of a national economic crisis, which virtually stopped all real
estate development and hit hardest at those with large front end
investment. However, the new city of Columbia, Maryland, begun
in 1963, represents a dramatic and successful example of the
principles discussed here. For a description of this community
see: Hoppenfeld, M., "The Columbia Process", pp. 34-47 in The
Architect's Yearbook 13, Elek Books, London, 1971.

the processes by which we work and understand that the sensitivity to process requires constant change in organization and
method, then, indeed, we are working in a sound direction. Most
importantly, it should be noted that learning and knowledge
building are demanding of time and money--without a conscious
'learning' effort much is lost, only to have to be rediscovered
over and over again.

Counter Opinions

Arguments have been made that the benefits of conscious community
planning and development do not warrant the investment in dollars
or human resources needed for their success. The argument is
based largely on an intractable belief in the value of a laissez-
faire approach ("we don't know enough" to tinker or plan) and a
condemnation of previous efforts at building new communities as
not having achieved their goals.

With regard to faith in laissez-faire, it must be blind; the
waste of our physical environment, the breakdown of our social
systems and the failure of cities to adequately enhance our
well-being is painfully obvious (except, perhaps, for the very
wealthy). Devaluing of existing planned communities can come
only from having unreasonable expectations on the one hand,
(they actually promised little), and on the other, a lack of
familiarity with them as real places. I believe that in most
new city (town-community) projects, the very process has forced
a level of environmental performance beyond most reasonable
expectations.

Another concern often expressed involved priorities. Those who
rightly express indignation about the wasting old cores of most
metro centers say that all resources should be applied toward
the renewal of the old city. Without seeking to diminish the
argument for renewal of the old city cores, three points must
be made: 1) A surplus of housing in the metro area is the only
solution to slums and bad housing in the core. Only a surplus
permits the poor a choice of not having to live in bad housing,
without a housing shortage, bad housing remains vacant and becomes devalued. It can then be renewed at reasonable cost without threatening other neighborhoods with overcrowding and the
blight cycle. This surplus is most readily built first on the
new lands of urban extensions. 2) When re-building old cores,
the same approach to community planning and development process
should be used, and the process itself needs continual refine-
ment. 3) There is enough financial and human resource with
which to do both, it is an issue of priorities.

The question is for the immediate future. How should we continue
to grow and change? Is laissez-faire (the economic bias) crisis-
oriented development likely to change the perceptible quality
of life in cities? Does the architectural bias suffice? The
answer to both is no. What is needed is a change in our way of
thinking about urban development: we must become planning-develop-
ment process oriented; we must articulate our social objectives
and concepts of well-being; we must accept our inadequate state
of the art and recognize the fact that we will only improve our

lives by learning - in doing over time. The important issue is
one of direction.

Urban growth and change must be viewed as having a purpose important enough to galvanize all people and their governments.
The opportunities to continually improve the social/physical
environment of individuals and families must be seized.

This process is achieved only by conscious choice, by the con-
sonant policies of appropriate layers of governments, the use of
the best available human resources a nation can recruit, and the
long term investment of public interest funds.

To build good communities will involve personal commitments by
many individuals to select a place in which to spend a significant piece of their life, because this is a time consuming
business which won't be rushed. It requires a cadre of professionals to interact with the land, the residents, and the
socio-political institutions over time, to gain feedback and to
alter courses of action.

All of these prescriptions sound too demanding, too much at
variance with our current way of working and of thinking about
urban growth and change. While calling for such a commitment,
I believe it is necessary to accept an incremental approach,
a better way of city building, even if it is not yet the best.
This allows every opportunity to be a learning experience, and
it allows for many beginnings.

A society committed to the building of good cities in the service
of man will develop the necessary human resources and choose
wisely in allocating its scarce commodities. A commitment to
build the city of man is capable of being self-fulfilling.

PLANNING AND DEVELOPMENTS IN THE DUTCH WADDEN SEA AREA

Dr. D. Eisma
Dutch Society for the Preservation of the Wadden Sea

INTRODUCTION

The Wadden Sea is a large tidal area extending from Den Helder to Esbjerg along the North Sea coast of the Netherlands, Germany and Denmark. A string of islands separated by tidal inlets forms a barrier towards the sea whereas the mainland coast nearly everywhere consists of polders closed by artificial dikes. Every tide seawater enters through the tidal inlets, while fresh water flows into the Wadden Sea coming from the major northwesteuropean rivers, the Rhine, the Ems, the Weser and the Elbe. In Roman times the Wadden Sea was still low marshland, cut by the outlets of river branches, but post-Roman floods changed this into a low tidal flat area, cut by channels and gullies, which had its greatest extension in the late Middle Ages. Up to about 1000 AD people in the flooded coastal areas lived on artificial hills ("terpen"), more or less like the Halligen which still exist in the eastern part of the Wadden Sea. Around 1000 AD however the first dikes were constructed and a large number of smaller and larger land reclamations mainly from the 16th century on has given the Wadden Sea its present form. Thus the Wadden Sea was gradually reduced to about 30% of its original size.

In the 15th and 16th centuries land reclamations had a twofold purpose: protection against the sea and acquirement of new fertile land. In the Netherlands a management system for the maintenance of dikes and the control of waterlevel in the polders was developed which was even left intact by the thorough napoleontic reorganisation of government administration at the end of the 18th century. Economically the acquirement of new land was usually only profitable in the long run, considering the cost of building dikes and water-mills to keep the waterlevel low and of digging a large number of ditches, but the protection against flooding (usually involving loss of life) was incalculable. The plans for reclamation culminated at the end of the 19th century and in the 20th century. After an abortive attempt in 1870 to connect the island of Ameland with the mainland by a low dike (which was soon destroyed by storms and drifting ice) new plans were made for a large polder between Ameland and the coast, and for the enclosure of the Zuiderzee, a southward extension of the Wadden Sea which reached into the heart of Holland. The plan for the Ameland polder was abandoned because of technical difficulties and costs but the enclosure of the Zuiderzee was eventually carried out by constructing a dike between Holland and Friesland which was completed in 1932. The resulting IJssellake was divided into five secondary polders of which the last one is still under construction. Meanwhile plans were developed within the (State) Department of Public Works for enclosure of the inlets in the south in the provinces of Zeeland and South-Holland, and for enclosure of the Wadden Sea. In this way the North Sea coast would be straightened considerably which would largely reduce the occurrence of high water levels during onshore storms. The large flood of February 1953, when nearly 2000 people died and many polders were flooded, was sufficient reason to carry out the enclosure of the inlets in

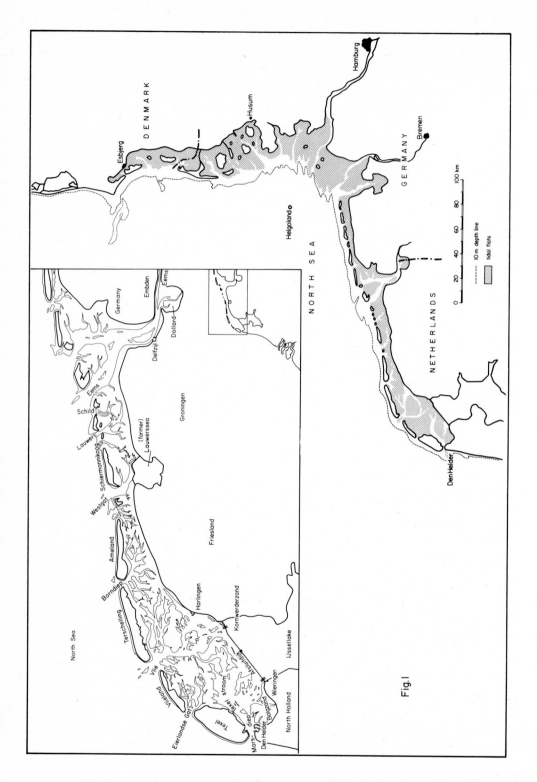

Fig.1

the south, the so-called Delta Works. The plans for reclamation of the Wadden
Sea, as well as the enclosure of the Oosterschelde in the south and the
completion of the last polder in the IJssellake (the Markerwaard) ran into
difficulties because of a growing opposition, which was due to profound changes
in the Netherlands since the early fifties.

CHANGES IN THE NETHERLANDS SINCE 1950

As is shown in Table I, the population in the Netherlands increased between
1950 and 1971/73 with about 34%. Consequently also the number of houses, public
buildings and public grounds such as sports fields increased as well as the
population density. With increasing prosperity however the average number of
people per house decreased, which in itself already meant an extra increase of
30% of the number of houses between 1947 and 1971. Also the number of cars,
mopeds and air flights increased dramatically, whereas industrial production
increased more than fourfold and the production of electricity, which involved
the construction of a dense high-tension network, increased more than three
times. To this must be added a large number of military activities (training
areas, airfields) for which no statistics are available. All this led to a
large increase of noise and to a direct increase of about 35% of the area used
for building, industrial activities, roads, canals, artificial lakes, airfields, training grounds etc., while these activities through noise, pollution
and visibility affected an area at least twice as large. Moreover the area
used for agriculture and cattle, which remained about the same because the
loss due to other activities was about compensated by the new reclamations, was
profoundly changed through re-allotment schemes which involved straightening
of roads, waterways and ditches and a complete redistribution of land: in 1973
about 41% of the agricultural area of the Netherlands was or had been involved
in such schemes. Natural areas (heaths, moors, dunes, tidal flats, marshlands)
decreased since 1950 with 33% so that in 1973 the surface of natural area per
head of the population was only 130 m^2 with 230 m^2 of forest. Considering
however that between 1900 and 1950 the surface of natural area per head of the
population decreased from 1200 m^2 to 190 m^2, due to a combination of population
increase (100%) and large-scale exploitation of natural areas for agriculture,
it was not so much because of direct loss of natural areas that opposition
against reclamation of the Wadden Sea, the Oosterschelde and the Markerwaard
emerged (although a valuable dune area had been lost because of extension of
the port of Rotterdam and a large fresh water tidal area was doomed because of
the Delta Works), but because the quality of nature (and the environment in
general) decreased rapidly, especially in wetlands, tidal areas, rivers and
lakes, and because the last remains of such areas in the Netherlands were
threatened on a large scale by the planned reclamations.

How nature in the Netherlands was affected by the developments since 1950 can
be shown by some more statistics (Table II) which indicate the decline in
number and area of distribution of a large number of plants and animals. 50
species of plants, 6 species of fish and 6 species of butterflies have
disappeared altogether, 48 species of plants have become very rare and
spectacular decreases have occurred in the number of badger, bats, porpoises,
seals, storks (316 young counted in 1939, 15 in 1972), spoonbills (reduced to
about 40% between 1955 and 1965) and sandwich terns (reduced to less than 10%
between 1956 and 1965). The decreases occurred especially in wetlands, heaths,
moors and other oligotrophic areas and were due to a destruction of nature on
a large scale with pollution, especially water pollution, as an important
factor. Increases occurred mainly in gardens and towns, fertilized grasslands
and waste areas and usually led to a strong uniformity through rapid expansion

TABLE I

Some general statistics on the Netherlands.
Source: General Environmental Statistics 1973. Netherlands Central Bureau of
Statistics, 1974.

	1947/50	1971/73
population	10.000.000	13.400.000
inhabitants per km^2	309	396
number of houses	2.100.000	3.700.000
average number of inhabitants per house	4,38	3,33
number of automobils	139.000	3.200.000
number of mopeds	55.000	1.800.000
number of airflights	74.000 (1960)	213.000
industrial production (1963 = 100)	47	200
production of electricity (kWh)	15,6 x 10^9 (1960)	49,6 x 10^9
area used for agriculture (ha)	2.505.400	2.533.300
land changed by re-allotment schemes (ha)	42.850	462.980
land being under re-allotment schemes (ha)	81.560	575.780
natural areas (ha)	264.200	176.500
natural area per head of population (m^2)	190	130
forest area per head of population (m^2)	290	230
agricultural area per head of population (m^2)	2580	1890
area of nature reserves (ha)	59.229 (1965)	79.360

TABLE II

Decrease and increase of plant and animal species in the Netherlands since
1900/60.
Source: General Environmental Statistics 1973, Netherlands Central Bureau of
Statistics, 1974.

	1970
total number of species of higher plants (Spermatophyta)	1349
number of species of higher plants that decreased since 1900	825 (59%)
number of species of higher plants that increased since 1900	20 (1%)
total number of species of mammals	56
number of species of mammals that decreased since 1950	33 (59%)
number of species of mammals that increased since 1950	3 (5%)
total number of species of nestling birds	162
number of species of nestling birds that decreased since 1960	59 (37%)
number of species of nestling birds that increased since 1960	43 (27%)
total number of species of reptiles and amphibia	22
number of species of reptiles and amphibia that decreased since 1940	21 (95%)
number of species of reptiles and amphibia that increased since 1940	0 (0%)
total number of species of fresh water fish	48
number of species of fresh water fish that decreased since 1920	33 (70%)
number of species of fresh water fish that increased since 1920	7 (14%)
total number of species of dragon-flies (Odonata)	69
number of species of dragon-flies that decreased since 1930/40	28 (40%)
number of species of dragon-flies that increased since 1930/40	0 (0%)
total number of butterflies (Rhopalocera)	90
number of species of butterflies that decreased since 1930/40	29 (27%)
number of species of butterflies that increased since 1930/40	1 (1%)

of only a limited number of species.

Added to this came a change in attitude of a large part of the population
towards government, leading to the formation of action groups and organizations
for the protection of nature and environmental quality in general. A similar
movement around 1900, in reaction to the effects of the economic expansion in
the second half of the 19th century, had led to the founding of organizations
to protect birds (1899), to prevent pollution of air, water and soil (1910)
and to acquire nature reserves (1905). Due to the effects of two world wars
and the economic crisis of the twenties and thirties, and to their rather
establishment character, these organizations had not been very effective but
the developments after 1960 gave also them a new impetus so that e.g. the
number of members of the Society for the Preservation of Nature Reserves
increased from 90.000 in 1970 to 220.000 in 1975.

THE WADDEN SEA AREA

The Wadden Sea area had been among the least affected by the economic expansion
after 1950: this is still concentrated in western Holland, the political as
well as the social and economic centre of the Netherlands since the Middle
Ages. The Wadden Sea remained therefore one of the least disturbed natural
areas but was increasingly threatened by land reclamations, either of the
Dutch part of the Wadden Sea as a whole, or of parts of it. Meanwhile the aims
of the reclamations shifted from protection against the sea and acquiring
land for agriculture to other uses such as the construction of airfields,
fresh water storage basins, military training grounds, industrial plants,
recreation projects and the replacement of the present ferry services by
connecting roads. Very little however of all these plans and proposals was
mentioned in the official planning reports.

Planning in the Netherlands in regulated by the Law of Physical Planning of
1964. Basic plans for the area under its authority are made by each
municipality which must be approved by the provincial government and the
ministry of Housing and Physical Planning. Objections can be made at each
level and by everybody. The provincial governments make regional plans,
covering part of a province, which contain the provincial guidelines for
planning in that area, and the ministry has published three planning reports
covering the whole country. These reports as well as the regional plans
explicitly contain only guidelines which can become law when incorporated in
the municipal basic plans. Besides all this there are numerous plans and
reports on all kinds of activity by government agencies and ministries covering
various aspects of municipal, regional and countrywide planning. Unfortunately
the larger water areas such as the Wadden Sea, are not covered by the Law of
1964 as they do not fall under a municipal authority but directly under the
State. Ownership rests with the ministry of Finance whereas nearly all other
ministries have some authority over activities in these areas. Another drawback
is that many aspects of planning, land (re)construction and protection of
natural and cultural values are regulated wholly or partly through other laws
which sometimes creates a complicated legal situation.

In the first planning report (of 1960) of the ministry of Housing and Physical
Planning the Wadden Sea area was designated a recreation area and (except the
island of Texel) a "problem" area, indicating that it was lagging behind in
development. A number of measures was proposed in order to stimulate
industrialization and the acceleration of public works, land re-allotment
schemes, recreation projects etc. In the second planning report (of 1966)

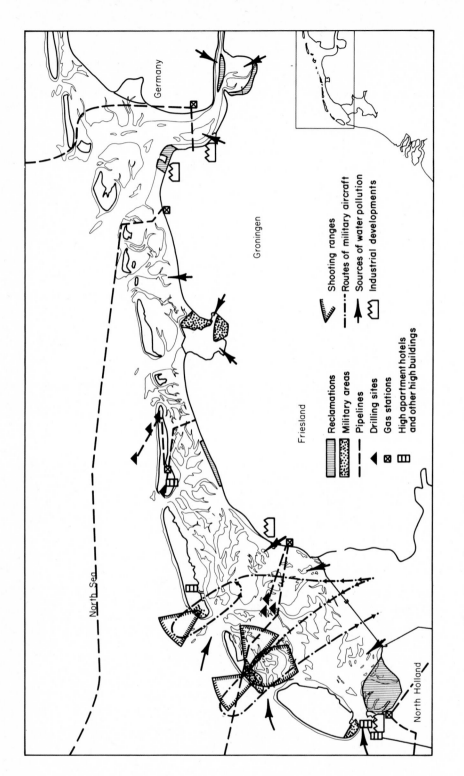

Fig. II. Main recent and planned developments in the Dutch Wadden Sea area.

awareness for the negative aspects of such a development. Elsewhere in the north part of the farmers, who value their independence, are deeply suspicious of the plans for extended national parks because they fear interference with their farming which they regard as a restriction of their traditional freedom. In order to get a better grip on what is going on in the Wadden Sea area a group of lawyers, under the auspices of the Dutch Society for the Preservation of the Wadden Sea, has made an elaborate proposal for a Wadden Council which at present is being considered by the municipalities, the provincial governments and the State government. Such a council however will only have limited possibilities. Regional plans and municipal basic plans are not available yet for the whole area and those in existence will need revision. The Wadden Sea is not included in such plans and present law makes it in some cases very difficult to stop further unwanted developments. Also the interpretation of some parts of the Law of 1964 is not firm, and fear that damages will be claimed makes that government, especially at the lowest levels, tends to give in to the stronger economic interests. Also the State government does not follow one policy - different ministeries and civil services pursue different aims - and, last but not least, the actual way in which public or private works as well as agriculture are being carried out can make all the difference whether the nature of an area remains intact or not.

In order to bridge the gaps that thus appeared between the various interests, so-called open discussions between the government, the planners, some interest groups and the general population are being held. These discussions range from simple meetings of mainly an informative character to the formation of discussion groups that work on a problem for several months. In the province of North Holland a discussion procedure was started by the provincial government with the cooperation of a number of social workers, which successfully treated the regional planning in the north of this province and especially the reclamation plans for the Balgzand in the Wadden Sea. In the province of Friesland a similar procedure was started on regional planning but this is chiefly an official action which threatens to become a paper affair producing massive reports which will hardly be read. Also in the province of Groningen such a procedure was started on the Eemsharbour - Delfzijl regional planning, together with social workers, which had more success. Also a series of discussions held in this area by the environmental organizations together with the trade unions was rather a success. Although within such discussions hardly any problems are really solved, they lead to a far better understanding of the problems and interests involved.

THE BASIC TRENDS

The conflicts that have arisen are due to mainly three causes:
a. economic expansion resulting in the promotion of usually short-term or macro-economic interests that conflict with the concept of the Wadden Sea area as a nature and recreation reserve,
b. the lack of suitable space for all kinds of activities (including military activities and recreation) in the centre of Holland so that there is an outward movement for such activities (this is also at the base of the present plan for an artificial island in the North Sea),
c. the difference in development between the Wadden Sea area (and the northern provinces in general) and the centre of Holland.
This is especially clear with regard to the harbours and industrial developments in Den Helder and the Delfzijl-Eemsharbour area. These are promoted by burgomasters (who are appointed by the minister of the interior) and by representatives of the social democratic party and the more conservative

parties alike. Procedures tend to be undemocratic with decision prepared in inaccessable committee and government meetings. This has changed somewhat for the better during the latter years but the greatest danger for the Wadden Sea area as a nature and recreation reserve is, besides waterpollution, the development of large scale projects which are incompatible with the historically small scale character of developments in the Wadden Sea area. Financial and economic interests, mainly from outside the Wadden Sea area, however promote such developments as can also be seen with the large recreation projects and apartment hotels planned on the Wadden islands: the activities of the islanders themselves will be dwarfed by these developments.

Thus the alternative for the Wadden Sea area is the promotion of small scale developments or no promotion of developments at all, which in effect means the maintenance of the traditional farming, breeding, fishing and seafaring activities. This involves a number of restrictions especially on the kind of economic activities which during the last twenty years have become the normal way of doing things. Therefore other ways will have to be found as has been done e.g. by the Dutch Society for the Preservation of the Wadden Sea in guaranteeing a small scale dairy factory project that was threatened to disappear for reasons of scale although in itself it was a viable project. Small scale recreation projects are evidently worth while (if they do not become too large in number) and other possibilities may be found in the compensation by the State for the maintenance of natural parks and extended natural parks. Meanwhile fishing, on the North Sea as well as on the Wadden Sea, is thriving on the islands but expansion is limited because of the quotation of fishing in the North Sea. Small scale workshops of various kinds may be viable alternatives: in these directions do the plans go that have the aim to preserve the Dutch Wadden Sea area as a nature and recreation reserve.

Another trend is towards internationalization of management of the Wadden Sea area. The Dutch Wadden Sea is only the western part of the Wadden Sea that reaches from Den Helder to Esbjerg. Also the German and Danish parts are threatened by industrial developments, large recreation projects and reclamations. It is the aim to keep this entire large and relatively unspoiled area intact for our posterity. It also stresses the international importance of the Wadden Sea area, for migrating birds and fish as well as for the numerous visitors from abroad. It will depend however entirely on the way present planning and management, national as well as international, will be carried out, what the Wadden area will be like in the future.

SUMMARY

After centuries of gradually reclaiming the Wadden Sea, plans were made for enclosure of the entire Dutch Wadden Sea. Also, and especially after 1960, the purpose of the reclamation plans shifted from protection against the sea and the acquirement of new land for agriculture to other aims such as the construction of airfields, industrial plants, military training grounds, etc. Meanwhile in the Dutch Wadden Sea area other activities developed such as drilling for natural gas, dredging of sand, military activities, recreation projects etc., stimulated by the economic expansion, the lack of suitable space for noisy, dangerous or polluting activities in the centre of Holland, and the general feeling in the northern provinces that the north had to be developed. Also waterpollution increased, while at the same time the quality of nature and the environment in general in the Netherlands decreased rapidly, whereas the planned reclamations threatened to destroy the last tidal wetlands. All this came in conflict with preservation of the Wadden Sea area as a nature and recreation reserve, which was strongly promoted by environmental groups, tourist- and fishery organizations and scientists, and was adopted by the State government in 1974. At present the Wadden Sea area is in a period of transition. The plans for reclamation of the Wadden Sea and most plans for partial reclamations have been abandoned. Some activities (mining, dredging, large recreation projects) are being held up or have been restricted, but other activities such as military training with aircraft and industrial development are continuing. It is considered that only small scale developments are compatible with the preservation of the Wadden Sea area as a nature and recreation reserve and with the small scale of the traditional activities in this area.

A NEW APPROACH TO URBAN WATER RESOURCES SYSTEMS OPTIMIZATION

David R. Maidment and Ven Te Chow
Hydrosystems Laboratory, University of Illinois at
Urbana-Champaign, Urbana, Illinois   61801, USA

ABSTRACT

The modern concept of urban water resources planning is to formulate the
problems as hydroeconomic systems and then to optimize the systems using
operations research techniques. A new approach to this optimization based on
state variables is developed for urban water resources systems. The application of this approach to urban hydrologic problems is outlined and
illustrated with an example. The incorporation of state variable models of
the systems into procedures for determining the design and operational
policies for urban water facilities is discussed.

INTRODUCTION

The world's urban population is expanding at an unprecedented rate. This
rate of increase in the number of urban residents coupled with the rise in
the quality of life which they expect to enjoy, has created urban planning
problems which are different and much more complex than those encountered in
the past. Urban residents are consuming more manufactured goods every year.
Although the solid and water-borne wastes so generated are constantly
increasing, the tolerance of urban residents for polluted water and landscapes is decreasing. This is but one example of the conflicts which face
urban planners today.

Systems analysis is being increasingly used as an aid in understanding and
developing solutions to complex urban problems. From the systems viewpoint,
the city may be regarded as an assembly of interrelated components. These
components include transportation, communication, energy, air, water and many
others; and likewise, each component may itself be regarded as a system. The
focus of this paper is on the urban water system, and the state variable
approach to representing and analysing this system is described. Since this
approach is of general application, it could also be used to mathematically
model other urban system components or perhaps even the whole urban or world
systems (Forrester, 1969; 1971).

One approach to visualizing the urban water resources system is shown in
Fig. 1. This approach considers the system to be made up of two kinds of
elements: location elements and transfer elements. Location elements are
the places where the water stops and undergoes substantial changes as the
result of humanly controlled processes. These elements include water storage,
water treatment, water use and waste-water treatment. The transfer elements
connect the location elements and represent the channels, pipelines, and
ground surface through or across which the water moves with relatively little
change in its characteristics. The urban water resources system is fed by
rainfall, influent streams and imported water in pipes or channels. The

receiving water environment can include rivers, lakes or oceans (Water
Resources Engineers, 1968; Orlob, 1971; Sonnen, 1971).

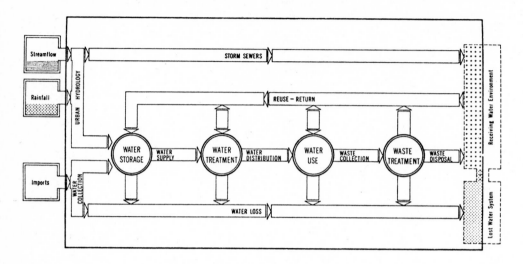

Fig. 1. The Urban Water Resources System (By
permission from Water Resources Engineers,
1968).

Among the problems of urban water resources management, systems analysis may
be applied to advantage in the determination of volumes, flowrates, and
quality of urban storm water runoff. The analysis of this problem must
account for both the spatial and temporal variations in urban water systems.
Urban watersheds vary in space since the ground surface slope and cover and
the soil type change from place to place in the watershed. The change in
hydrological characteristics with time, particularly in response to urbanization, gives rise to the temporal variations which must be considered.

For the analysis of urban storm water runoff, the system may be divided into
two parts: the surface flow and the subsurface flow. The determination of
the surface flow is primarily a hydrological problem, which includes the time
and space distribution of the rainfall, infiltration, and other abstractions,
and the overland flow on the ground surface and gutters. Once the time
distribution of flows at the sewer inlets, or inlet flow hydrographs, are
known, the determination of the subsurface or sewer flows is mainly a
hydraulic problem. This involves the translation and attenuation of the inlet
flow hydrographs to produce the flow hydrographs at the sewer outlets.

Strictly speaking, the urban water system should be mathematically formulated
as being distributed in space and time. Such a formulation is so complicated
however that it appears to be too difficult to solve using the computers
currently available. Accordingly, the spatial variation is sometimes ignored
and the system is treated as being "lumped" or concentrated at one point in

space. Some spatial variation may be introduced by dividing the watershed
system into subareas which are each considered to be lumped, then linking
these lumped system models together to produce a model of the entire system
(Chow, 1962; Chow, 1964; Tholin and Keifer, 1960; Watkins, 1962; Tierstrep
and Stall, 1969; Papadakis and Preul, 1972; U.S.E.P.A., 1971; Yen and Sevuk,
1975; Chow and Yen, 1975).

STATE VARIABLE MODEL

State variable modeling is capable of describing systems which are linear or
nonlinear, time-variant or time-invariant, deterministic or stochastic, and
with multiple inputs and multiple outputs. Continuous-time or discrete-time
formulations are feasible. A deterministic model is one for which a given
known input to the model always produces the same output. A stochastic model
is one for which the output is a function of both known and random inputs.

The condition of the system at any time t is considered to be completely
described by the values of a group of state variables, $\{x_1(t), x_2(t), \ldots,$
$x_n(t)\}$ which constitute the state vector $\underline{x}(t)$. These state variables could
represent, for example, the volumes of water or the amounts of prescribed
pollutants contained in various parts of the system. At this time a group of
input variables $\underline{u}(t) = \{u_1(t), u_2(t), \ldots, u_p(t)\}$, which have known values
are exerting a controlling influence on the system. These variables may be
natural inputs such as rainfall, streamflow or non-point waste loads or they
may be humanly controlled variables such as interbasin water transfers,
reservoir releases or point source waste loads.

Responding to these inputs, the system is producing outputs $\underline{y}(t) = \{y_1(t),$
$y_2(t), \ldots, y_r(t)\}$, which may be flows of water or waste-water constituents.
In water resources systems, the state variables are usually expressed in
volume or mass units while the input and output variables are volume or mass
flow rates.

The relationship over time of the input, state, and output variables is
described by two equations: the "state equation" and the "output equation."
The state equation, Eq. 1, expresses the evolution of the state of the system
over time in response to the inputs, and comprises a set of linked, first-
order, ordinary differential equations.

$$\underline{\dot{x}}(t) = A\underline{x}(t) + B\underline{u}(t) \tag{1}$$

In Eq. 1, $\underline{\dot{x}}(t) = \frac{d}{dt}[\underline{x}(t)]$ which is the vector of state variables, each
differentiated with respect to time, $\underline{\dot{x}}(t) = \{\dot{x}_1(t), \dot{x}_2(t), \ldots, \dot{x}_n(t)\}$, and A
and B are matrices:

$$A = \begin{bmatrix} a_{11} & a_{12} & \cdots & a_{1n} \\ a_{21} & a_{22} & \cdots & a_{2n} \\ \cdot & \cdot & & \cdot \\ \cdot & \cdot & & \cdot \\ \cdot & \cdot & & \cdot \\ a_{n1} & a_{n2} & \cdots & a_{nn} \end{bmatrix} ; \; B = \begin{bmatrix} b_{11} & b_{12} & \cdots & b_{1p} \\ b_{21} & b_{22} & \cdots & b_{2p} \\ \cdot & \cdot & & \cdot \\ \cdot & \cdot & & \cdot \\ \cdot & \cdot & & \cdot \\ b_{n1} & b_{n2} & \cdots & b_{np} \end{bmatrix}$$

The purpose of the matrix format is just to simplify the notation.

The output equation, Eq. 2, describes the production of outputs from the state and input variables:

$$\underline{y}(t) = C\underline{x}(t) + D\underline{u}(t) \tag{2}$$

where C and D are matrices:

$$C = \begin{bmatrix} c_{11} & c_{12} & \cdots & c_{1n} \\ c_{21} & c_{22} & \cdots & c_{2n} \\ \cdot & \cdot & & \cdot \\ \cdot & \cdot & & \cdot \\ \cdot & \cdot & & \cdot \\ c_{r1} & c_{r2} & \cdots & c_{rn} \end{bmatrix} \; ; \; D = \begin{bmatrix} d_{11} & d_{12} & \cdots & d_{1p} \\ d_{21} & d_{22} & \cdots & d_{2p} \\ \cdot & \cdot & & \cdot \\ \cdot & \cdot & & \cdot \\ \cdot & \cdot & & \cdot \\ d_{r1} & d_{r2} & \cdots & d_{rp} \end{bmatrix}$$

The way in which Eqs. 1 and 2 represent the system is shown in Fig. 2. From Fig. 2 it may be seen that the time rate of change of the system's state, $\dot{\underline{x}}(t)$, is formed as the sum of the modified inputs $B\underline{u}(t)$ and the modified current state $A\underline{x}(t)$. Matrix A is the most important of the four system matrices because it represents the proportion of the current system state, $\underline{x}(t)$, which is contributing to changing that state. This state feedback has a major role in determining the future behavior of the system. The elements of matrix B are scalars and represent the proportion of the value of each of the input variables that affects each of the state variables. The rate of change of the state, $\dot{\underline{x}}(t)$ is integrated with the current state to produce a new state. The outputs, $\underline{y}(t)$, are formed by combining the state which has been scaled by matrix C with a direct contribution from the inputs, $D\underline{u}(t)$. The elements of C and D are scalars which represent respectively the proportions of each of the state and the input variables which produce the outputs.

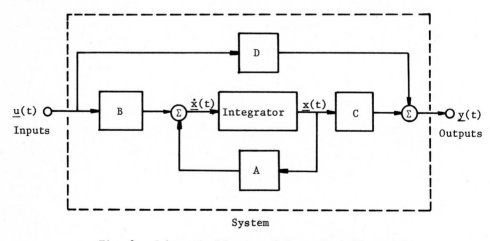

Fig. 2. Schematic Diagram of State Variable Model

The behavior of urban water systems often changes with time. For example, as urbanization proceeds, the proportion of the watershed area which is impervious increases, and the relationship between storm rainfall and runoff changes. This time-variant behavior can be incorporated into state variable models by making some of the elements of the matrices A, B, C, and D, functions of time. The urban water system may also respond in a nonlinear manner. Nonlinear response occurs when changes in the system's inputs do not produce linearly proportional changes in the system's outputs. These effects may be accounted for in state variable models by making some of the elements of the matrices A, B, C, and D functions of the current system state (Muzik, 1974).

While most water resource systems operate in continuous time and are therefore able to be described by a model of the form of Eqs. 1 and 2, for digital computation purposes, the time horizon must be discretized into stages. In discrete time, the analogous model is given by Eqs. 3 and 4:

$$\underline{x}(k+1) = A\underline{x}(k) + B\underline{u}(k) \tag{3}$$

$$\underline{y}(k) = C\underline{x}(k) + D\underline{u}(k) \tag{4}$$

where the subscript k is the stage index.

In application, the input sequence $\underline{u}(k)$ is known for the period of analysis made up of K stages, $k = 1, 2, ..., K$. The initial state of the system $\underline{x}(1)$ is also known. The computations are performed recursively from stage to stage. Beginning with $k = 1$, Eq. 4 may be used to calculate $\underline{y}(1)$ and Eq. 3 to calculate $\underline{x}(2)$. Proceeding to the next stage, $\underline{y}(2)$ and $\underline{x}(3)$ may be calculated using $\underline{x}(2)$ and $\underline{u}(2)$ and so on.

To extend the discrete time model of Eqs. 3 and 4 to incorporate probabilistic inputs, a vector of random variables $\underline{w}(k) = \{w_1(k), ..., w_m(k)\}$ is defined. This vector is usually considered to be independently, normally distributed with zero mean and unit variance. These variables are joined to the matrix equations to produce a stochastic discrete time state variable model as shown in Eqs. 5 and 6.

$$\underline{x}(k+1) = A\underline{x}(k) + B\underline{u}(k) + G\underline{w}(k) \tag{5}$$

$$\underline{y}(k) = C\underline{x}(k) + D\underline{u}(k) \tag{6}$$

APPLICATION TO URBAN WATER RESOURCES SYSTEMS

Three purposes for which state variable modeling could be used in urban water resources systems analysis are now described. For each of these purposes, the state variable model mathematically represents the behavior of the system in order that the effects of alternative planning strategies may be evaluated.

Hydrologic Modeling

Hydrologic models may be employed to represent the production of streamflow in response to rainfall. Two types of models may be distinguished by the time scale over which they are applied. For the determination of peak rates of urban storm water runoff, a short time scale measured in minutes or hours

is usually appropriate. A much longer time scale, measured in weeks or
months, is needed when the long term average volume of streamflow is of concern such as in studies of storage for urban water supply. State variable
modeling may be used for either of these time scales. Generally, the
deterministic form of Eqs. 1 to 4 is more applicable to the shorter time
scales while the stochastic form of Eqs. 5 and 6 is more suitable for the
longer time scales.

In the formulation of deterministic, state variable models of storm water
runoff, some available hydrologic concepts may be used as a basis. Usually
the conservation of mass principle is used in combination with one or more
relationships linking the level of storage of water in the system to the inflows and outflows. Examples of these relationships include the linear
reservoir and Muskingum models described by Chow (1964) and Manning's
equation (Muzik, 1974). State variable models are lumped and can consider only
one independent variable, usually time. As mentioned earlier, some spatial
variation may be introduced by dividing the watershed into subareas, each of
which is described using the state variable method, then linking these
subarea models together using the common format to reproduce the response of
the whole watershed.

Once the state variable model has been formulated, the values of the
parameters in the model must be chosen so that the model response or output
matches that of the actual system as closely as possible. This parameter
fitting may be accomplished by two main approaches, depending on whether
suitable historic records of rainfall and streamflow are available for the
watershed or not. If the records are not available, the model parameters
must be related to physical characteristics of the watershed such as slope,
type of vegetation, and proportion of impervious area. If the records are
available, the optimum parameter values may be found as those which give a
close fit between the model and the observed system response. Multiple
regression, linear programming, and direct search methods may be used for
these purposes (Chow and Kulandaiswamy, 1971; Himmelblau, 1972).

Automatic Control

State variable modeling was originally developed for the design of automatic
control systems (Athans and Falb, 1966). An automatic controller, such as
that for an aircraft, continuously receives information on the current state
of the system. This information is modified and sythesized; then signals are
emitted from the controller for the guidance of the system. For the controller to be able to anticipate the response of the system to its actions, it
must be linked to a mathematical model of the system itself. This mathematical model is formulated using the state variable approach.

A number of automatic control schemes for water systems have been suggested.
Young and Beck (1974) formulated a state variable model for dissolved oxygen
and biochemical oxygen demand in a river and then employed this model in the
determination of a control scheme for sewage effluent discharges to the river.
Fan, et al. (1973) applied the Pontryagin maximum principle to find control
strategies for biological waste treatment using a state variable model of a
continuously stirred tank reactor.

Dynamic Programming

Dynamic programming and discrete differential dynamic programming are two effective methods for optimizing water resource systems, particularly those involving staging and scheduling of activities (Chow and Cortes-Rivera, 1974; McBean and Loucks, 1974; Mays and Yen, 1974; Chow, Maidment and Tauxe, 1975). These methods have the ability to account for the nonlinear, sequential decision characteristics generally exhibited by problems of planning and operation of urban water resources projects.

In dynamic programming, the procedure is to break down the optimization problem into stages, each stage being a step in time or space. The computations are performed stage by stage, each stage using the results of the immediately preceding one. An important aspect of this procedure is the state transformation equation. This equation must be written for each stage to express the output values of the state variables as a function of the input values of these variables and the values of the decision variables. The state transformation equation is, therefore, the mathematical model which represents the physical behavior of the system in dynamic programming.

State variable modeling may be used to formulate this state transformation equation. This approach is particularly useful when the stochastic nature of the inflows to the water resource systems is considered. An autoregressive time series model, commonly employed to describe the inflows, can be written in state variable form and combined with a deterministic, state variable model of the behavior of the system itself. Thus the output values of the state variables at each stage are treated as random variables whose probability distribution is a function of the decisions chosen, the stochastic inputs and the initial values of the state variables. Chow et al. (1975) have developed an optimization scheme based on stochastic dynamic programming with a stochastic, state variable transformation equation and applied it to determine the operating policy for a multiple purpose reservoir.

AN EXAMPLE

The formulation and application of a hydrologic model in state variable format is illustrated with the following example. The model is of the storm rainfall-runoff process and produces direct runoff as output given the rainfall as input.

The formulation used is adapted from Chow and Kulandaiswamy (1971) and illustrated with data from the U.S. Army Corps of Engineers (1954). These data comprise the rainfall hyetograph and streamflow hydrograph for the storm of April 4-5, 1941 on the 247-square mile Wills Creek watershed near Cumberland, Maryland. The storm duration of 65 hours is divided into hourly stages, k, $k=1, 2, \ldots, 65$. The model has one input variable, $u(k)$, the volume of effective rainfall in stage k; one output variable, $y(k)$, the volume of direct streamflow in stage k; and three state variables, $\underline{x}(k) = \{x_1(k), x_2(k), x_3(k)\}$. The formulation is given in Eqs. 7 and 8:

$$
\begin{bmatrix} x_1(k+1) \\ x_2(k+1) \\ x_3(k+1) \end{bmatrix} = \begin{bmatrix} 1 & 1 & 0 \\ 0 & 1 & 1 \\ -\alpha_1 & -\alpha_2 & -\alpha_3 \end{bmatrix} \begin{bmatrix} x_1(k) \\ x_2(k) \\ x_3(k) \end{bmatrix} + \begin{bmatrix} 0 \\ 0 \\ 1 \end{bmatrix} u(k) \qquad (7)
$$

$$y(k) \quad = \quad [\alpha_1 \quad \alpha_4 \quad \alpha_5] \quad \begin{bmatrix} x_1(k) \\ x_2(k) \\ x_3(k) \end{bmatrix} \qquad (8)$$

Several methods may be used to choose the optimum values of the five parameters, α_1, α_2, ..., α_5. Chow and Kulandaiswamy (1971) used a linear
regression approach employing a watershed storage function which is a linear
combination of the parameters and derivatives of $\underline{x}(k)$ and $y(k)$. A linear
programming approach to the same problem was developed and its results were
very close to those obtained by the linear regression. It is concluded,
however, that the linear regression is an easier approach to implement
because of the problems with negative parameter values in the linear programming formulation.

Direct search methods, such as the relaxation method and the steepest descent
method, may be also used to find optimum parameter set. To apply these
methods the following objective function is formulated:

$$\min F = \sum_{k=1}^{K} [y(k) - y_r(k)]^2 \qquad (9)$$

where $y_r(k)$ is the actual streamflow. An iterative scheme is employed
whereby a parameter set is chosen, the model response and the value of the
objective function are computed, and then a new parameter set is chosen,
using the search method, until a satisfactory solution is obtained. It is
found that the relaxation method is superior to all other approaches. This
method consists of freezing all parameters except one, allowing this one to
vary and then freezing it and releasing the next one, and so on. A
comparison between the modeled streamflow and the actual streamflow is shown
in Fig. 3 for two methods of fitting the parameters. The model itself is
computationally very efficient since the simulation of one storm hydrograph
took only 0.04 seconds of IBM 360/75 computer time for this example.

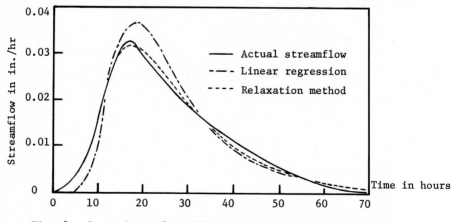

Fig. 3.   Comparison of Results of Parameter Fitting Methods

SUMMARY AND CONCLUSIONS

The modern concept of water resources planning is to formulate water resources problems as hydroeconomic systems and then to optimize the systems using operations research techniques. A new approach to this optimization based on state variables is developed for urban water resources systems. The application of this approach to urban hydrologic problems is outlined and illustrated with an example. The incorporation of state variable models of the systems into procedures for determining the design and operational policies is also discussed.

It appears that this new approach has considerable potential for application to urban water resources systems. The basic format of the model is general enough that it seems to be capable of representing a wide range of the types of systems encountered, yet simple enough that it does not have excessive computer or data requirements. It may be however, that since the state variable mathematical format is so general, there may be easier ways to formulate models of specific phenomena. The storm rainfall-runoff process, for example, has been used to illustrate state variable modeling of a hydrologic system. It is possible that this process may be more readily analysed with the well known unit hydrograph concept for some simple cases instead of going through the more elaborate procedure of matrix representation.

State variable modeling was originally developed for the design of automatic control schemes in fields such as the aerospace industry. It is anticipated, therefore, that the application of state variable modeling for this purpose in urban water resources systems will develop as the use of automatic control of urban water facilities becomes more widespread.

The incorporation of stochastic state variable models into dynamic programming procedures for the determination of system design and operational policies is also promising. This approach directly imbeds the stochastic nature of the water resources system inflows within the dynamic programming and provides a way of accounting for some of the uncertainties in the behavior of the system as well as optimizing the expected net benefits from it.

ACKNOWLEDGEMENTS

The work upon which this paper was based was supported in part by funds provided by the U.S. Department of the Interior under the Water Resources Research Act of 1964, P.L. 88-379, Agreement 14-31-0001-4080, OWRT Project B-084-ILL. Computer services were provided by the Digital Computer Laboratory of the University of Illinois at Urbana-Champaign.

REFERENCES

Athans, M., and P. L. Falb, Optimal control, McGraw-Hill, New York, (1966).

Chow, V. T., Hydrologic determination of waterway areas for the design of drainage structures in small drainage basins, Eng. Expt. Sta. Bull. No. 462, Univ. of Illinois, Urbana, Ill., (1962).

Chow, V. T., Handbook of applied hydrology, McGraw-Hill, New York, Chapters 14 and 25, (1964).

Chow, V. T., and G. Cortes-Rivera, Application of DDDP in water resources planning, Res. Rep. 78 (UILU-WRC-74-0078), Univ. of Illinois Water Resource Center, Urbana, Ill., (1974).

Chow, V. T., D. H. Kim, D. R. Maidment, and T. A. Ula, A scheme for stochastic state variable water resource systems optimization, Res. Rep. 105 (UILU-WRC-75-0105), Univ. of Illinois Water Resources Center, Urbana, Ill., (1975).

Chow, V. T., and V. C. Kulandaiswamy, General hydrologic system model, Jour. Hydr. Divn., ASCE, 97(HY6), 791-803 (1971).

Chow, V. T., D. R. Maidment, and G. W. Tauxe, Computer time and memory requirements for DP and DDDP in water resource systems analysis, Water Resources Research, 11(5), 621-628 (1975).

Chow, V. T., and B. C. Yen, Urban stormwater runoff determination of volumes and flowrates, Municipal Environmental Research Laboratory, Office of Research and Development, U.S. Environmental Protection Agency, Cincinnati, Ohio, (1975).

Fan, L. T., P. S. Shah, N. C. Periera, and L. E. Erickson, Dynamic analysis and optimal feedback control synthesis applied to beiological waste treatment, Water Research, 7(11), 1609-1641 (1973).

Forrester, J. W., Urban dynamics, M.I.T. Press, Cambridge, Mass., (1969).

Forrester, J. W., World dynamics, Wright-Allen Press, Cambridge, Mass., (1971).

Himmelblau, D. M., Applied nonlinear programming, McGraw-Hill, New York, 111-121 (1972).

Mays, L. W., and B. C. Yen, Optimal cost design of branched sewer systems, Water Resources Research, 11(1), 37-47 (1975).

McBean, E. A., and D. P. Loucks, Planning and analysis of metropolitan water resource systems, Tech. Rept. No. 84, Cornell Univ. Water Resources and Marine Sciences Center, Ithaca, New York, (1974).

Muzik, I., State variable model of overland flow, Journal of Hydrology, 22(3/4), 347-364 (1974).

Orlob, G. T., The urban water system-technical aspects, in <u>Treatise on Urban Water Systems</u>, ed. by M. L. Albertson, L. S. Tucker, and D. C. Taylor, Colorado State Univ., Fort Collins, Colo., 48-63 (1971).

Papadakis, C. N., and H. C. Preul, Univ. of Cincinnati Urban Runoff Model, <u>Jour. Hydr. Divn, ASCE</u>, 98(HY10), 1789-1804 (1972).

Sonnen, M. B., The urban water system - economic aspects, in <u>Treatise on Urban Water Systems</u>, ed. by M. L. Albertson, L. S. Tucker, and D. C. Taylor, Colorado State Univ., Fort Collins, Colo., 64-90 (1971).

Tholin, A. L., and C. J. Kiefer, The hydrology of urban runoff, <u>Trans. ASCE</u>, 125, 1308-1379 (1960).

Tierstrep, M. L., and J. B. Stall, Urban runoff by Road Research Laboratory method, <u>Jour. Hydr. Divn, ASCE</u>, 95(HY6), 1809-1834 (1969).

U.S. Army Corps of Engineers, <u>Unit Hydrograph Compilations</u>, Civil Works Investigation, Pt II, 1-4, Office of the District Engineer, Washington District, Washington, D.C., (1954).

U.S. Environmental Protection Agency (USEPA), Storm water management model, <u>Water Poll. Control Res. Ser.</u> No. 11024, 1-4, USEPA, (1971).

Water Resources Engineers, Inc., Comprehensive system engineering analysis of all aspects of urban water ... a prefeasibility study, prepared for the <u>American Society of Civil Engineers, Urban Water Resources Research Program</u>, 121 p. (July 1968).

Watkins, L. H., The design of urban sewer systems, <u>Road Research Technical Paper</u> No. 55, Dept. of Sci. and Ind. Res., London, (1962).

Yen, B. C., and A. S. Sevuk, Design of storm sewer networks, <u>Jour. Env. Eng. Divn, ASCE</u>, 101(EE4) 535-553 (1975).

Young, D., and B. Beck, The modelling and control of water quality in a river system, <u>Automatica</u>, 10(5), 455-467 (1974).

ENHANCING THE VISUAL ENVIRONMENT

Kevin Lynch
Department of Urban Studies and Planning
Massachusetts Institute of Technology, U.S.A.

Despite this title, one must speak of the whole sensory environment: smell, sound, and feel, as well as look. This "sense" of the world is fundamental to our well-being, and is direct and immediate in its effect. Through our senses we interact with what surrounds us. Sensing is being active and alive. Sense quality links directly to many psychological, social, and economic issues.

There is no ideal form for a settlement, any more than there is an ideal culture. But there are underlying criteria, based on our human nature, and these include sensory criteria. The first, most obvious, is that people be able to see, smell, feel, hear well. Smog and noise are restrictions on sensing. Sense deficiencies or overloads can prevent our functioning, or cause organic damage, disturb our comfort or reduce our efficiency. Many organic processes are affected by sense conditions: motor actions of the body, body temperature and rhythm, breathing, eating. All social communication, and each everyday action, depends on sight and sound, smell and touch. The deaf, blind, handicapped, aged have their special requirements, in addition. A good environment is one in which people can sense well, act competently, and feel at ease. More, it encourages us to look sharply and hear acutely, to take delight in our luminous, odorous, sonorous world.

If one set of sensory concerns deals with the direct action of our senses, another refers to perception as it develops with experience, using and constructing a mental image of place and time. People must be able to identify the place they live in, and to connect it with other places in their region. Each small group needs a visibly secure and remarkable home territory (as well, perhaps, as a waste or "wilderness" where they may feel free), and also a sense that an entire region of potential action is comprehensible and accessible to them. Places should reinforce the image of time, as well: make the present vivid, and connect it to past and future. People delight in distinctive times and places, and in being able to link them to the great ranges of time and space.

Still further, a landscape is a medium of communication. Its messages affect our performance, cognition, and development, as well as our emotional and esthetic satisfaction. There can be too little information or too much; it can be legible or incom-

prehensible. There can be good opportunities for direct human
intercourse, or a lack of them. Along with the social milieu,
the spatial setting is the ground for human development. It
stunts or drives that growth by the richness of the information
it affords, the challenge of its contrasts, and the room it
makes for experiment and expression.

But the deepest meaning of any place is its sense of connection
to human life, and to the web of living things. "Liveliness" is
enhanced by place identity, and by a visible fit with biological
and social process. It is heightened where people leave sensible
traces of their presence and activity; if things express their
function; if there is a threshold intensity and mix of movement
and activity; if there are evident signs of belief and values.
We also wish to perceive the natural context of our being: the
animals and plants which live around us, the elementals of rock,
earth, fire, air and water, the celestial bodies, the cycles of
growth and decline. Too many existing settlements have a way of
separating us, sensibly, from other people and other living
things.

These criteria seem to be general. For the most part, they
refer to simple and obvious qualities. They touch on bodily
health, psychological balance, and social function. They are
based on how well-being arises as men, biologically limited and
endowed as they are, actively interact with their surroundings.
From this point of view, a good settlement supports and extends
our senses, helps us to build a powerful image of space and
time, communicates a rich and coherent array of information, and
conveys a deep intuition of life.

World settlement patterns are moving consistently toward large,
relatively low density, metropolitan regions, whose parts are
increasingly specialized by function and inhabitant. Landscape
elements within these broad regions seem surprisingly similar
from one country to the next: endless small house suburbs on the
urban peripheries; massive, oppressive housing projects; crowded
but vital squatter settlements; central slums and "grey areas";
vast industrial zones; depopulated small towns and city centers;
extensive single-crop rural extractive regions; and special
areas for leisure and entertainment which are alternately
crowded and deserted. In the developing nations, the current of
migration sets toward the great centers of employment, unless
restrained by strong national policy. In the developed countries, there begins a counter-movement to the small towns, and
the favored landscapes that promise a better quality of life.

These changes have marked consequences for the sense of our environment. Air pollution degrades sight and smell; mechanical
noise floods our hearing. The city climate is more uncomfortable and debilitating. Biological rhythms are upset. We use
our bodies less, and idle our senses. Identification with
place and time is disturbed as populations move. A home ground
is more difficult to define, in a mass housing project. The
vast metropolitan regions resist translation to a clear mental

image. Human communications are more fragmented; we are more
isolated from other living things. There are fewer special
places left--of great beauty, or sanctity, or significance.

Yet these new regions are not impossible habitats. They offer
countervailing advantages: more material goods, better health
and immediate comfort, the chance to break out of old molds,
the stimuli for personal growth. In their sensory aspects they
have their compensations, too: a flood of new sights and new
information; a mix of people; better interior environments;
physical and mental access to extended, complex regions; the
ability to reach and enjoy fine countrysides for leisure; the
opportunity to own and control a very visible home territory.
There are even new sensory pleasures: the night lights of the
great city, the jet trail in the evening sky, fast motion along
a good highway, the sights and smells of the urban markets, new
urban ceremonies.

Indeed, it is likely that the optimum sensory conditions for
human beings will eventually be found in just such extensive
urban regions: areas of moderate density and diverse character,
whose low rise structures, clustered in open settings, make up
the predominant fabric, but are embroidered with more compact
and intensive centers. There one might enjoy the pleasures of
civilized life, along with the delights of that savanna landscape in which our sensory and cognitive apparatus apparently
evolved. In addition, such extended patterns seem to have
important advantages of other kinds: of cost, resource deple-
tion, social communication, local control and enterprise, wide
acceptance. But we began by warning ourselves about prescribing
universal solutions. Like it or not, we are committed to the
urbanized region, over much of the world, and must make it
humane.

Thus it is most disturbing that the possibilities of this new
regional pattern are not being exploited. The areas of unregu-
lated growth are patently formless. They lack diversity and
open space. They are often at such scattered densities as to
incur serious social costs. But the deliberately designed new
places are also sensibly deficient in many ways. New towns,
housing estates, redeveloped areas, and industrial zones fail
to meet the elementary criteria outlined above. They are
splendid only in plan. The rapid rate of urbanization makes it
difficult to achieve humane settings, but so also does our deni-
gration of sense quality as if it were a triviality, and the
alienation of the user from the creation and management of
places: treating urban regions as if they were buildings to be
designed by one mind and managed by one remote agency, whether
for profit, or political control, or smooth, technical operation.

What we have built must be rebuilt, renewed, made denser and
more diverse. The fundamental strategy is to create that strong
local identity which is fitted to local circumstance and to the
memories and values of local people. Thus we should put local
areas into the hands of their occupants, and give them the means

of managing them. Simultaneously, the complex urban region must
be made comprehensible and accessible to all its residents,
since the promise of the new pattern is an ability to live at
once in a great society and also in a secure local place.

Beyond this strategy of local control and regional management,
we must at last grant the importance of sensory quality. Sense
is not a whimsical or mysterious realm, but one simple, basic
dimension of a satisfactory setting. Sensory criteria can be
made a normal element in programming any new settlement, or
rehabilitating an old one. Completed areas should be evaluated
to see how they work and feel, and what their inhabitants think
of them. In fact, they can do it themselves. The sensory
quality of a region can be monitored, as an input to policy,
just as its traffic, its economy, or the cleanliness of its
waters can be.

Conservation is a critical public action, but it must be
directed away from the preservation of special isolated places
toward the discovery and conservation of sensory quality and
local history throughout the living environment. Public con-
servators might be instituted, to identify and enhance those
qualities wherever people are. Every place that people inhabit
has valuable and memorable elements. Diversity and rich identity is built out of these existing values.

From this point of view, it would be advantageous to moderate
the rate of growth of the urban settlements. It is difficult
to create humane places, and to see them firmly placed in local
hands, given the present rate of spatial changes. Public investment in the existing village, or in the inner urban neighborhood, will reduce urbanization and abandonment alike. Thus
we would have a chance to enhance the quality of each new
place, new and old.

Conservation, and the retardation of growth, are only partial
answers. With few exceptions, the settlements of the past were
hardly joyful places, at least for the majority. We have new
opportunities, some knowledge, and, at times, a new will to act.
We could make the far-spreading, urbanized countryside, which is
the new human setting new evolving, into a homeland deliberately
fitted (for the first time in history) to man's sensory, emotional, cognitive, and social nature--just as we know that a
good chair, or a fine story, can be made to fit our nature. We
can imagine such regions, where one might see things clearly,
hear human voices and natural sounds, walk and sit at ease,
reach centers quickly, feel secure and yet stimulated, remember
and foresee--and this at work and while travelling, as well as
inside the home or in the park.

To achieve this will require environmental experiments, where
novel spatial features are tested by people who learn to
respond to those features in novel ways. Indeed, the quality
of the sensory environment is by itself of no importance. The
interaction between person and place is the key. Educating

people to observe, understand, and use their surroundings, in deeper and more fulfilling ways, can be as strategic as operations on the environment alone. The landscape is a magnificent learning place.

We need more research on environmental perception, cognition, and behavior. We also have a rather small understanding of how to manage sensory quality, particularly at the urban and regional scales. But, while such knowledge is urgently needed, we know something already. Nor is sense quality as abstruse a subject as it has been made out to be. It is everyone's experience. What we lack is a public realization of how deeply the sense of places affects the quality of life.

For a lengthier discussion, see:

Sense and Region, The MIT Press, Cambridge, Mass. (early 1976).

"The Possible City," Technology Review, January 1968.

And, as an example of sensory analysis at a regional scale:

"Temporary Paradise: A Look at the Special Landscape of the San Diego Region" (with Donald Appleyard), The City Planning Department, San Diego, California, 1975.

A METHODOLOGY TO DETERMINE THE ASSETS AND LIABILITIES OF AN EXISTING URBAN RESIDENTIAL AREA FROM THE POINT OF VIEW OF ITS INHABITANTS

Thomas Martineau
Research Architect
Battelle-Columbus Laboratories
Columbus, Ohio, USA

ABSTRACT

This paper presents a methodology which permits the analysis of existing urban areas for the purpose of determining requirements for growth and change from the point of view of the areas' residents.

The methodology relies on data gathered from the residents of a given urban residential area. These data provide information about the frequency of occurrence of certain urban activities from the point of view of the residents, and also information about the importance of such activities to those residents. This act of placing frequency and importance of urban activities side by side allows the development of "assets" and "liabilities" of an urban area as these are perceived by those who live in that urban environment. On the basis of these assets and liabilities, plans can then be developed to further enhance the assets and to alleviate the liabilities as the urban residential area in question changes and grows.

This methodology is innovative primarily because it seeks and relies upon the expressed needs and preferences of those who use the urban environment being studied. Secondarily, the methodology presents an approach to urban modeling which assumes each urban area to be unique in its personal interrelationships and priorities for growth and change.

INTRODUCTION

A considerable gap exists between our ability to shape, manipulate and control the urban environment, and our ability to do this wisely. As the problems of our urban environment increase in both complexity and size, and as our growing technological capacity permits us to increasingly bring more vast, rapid and sweeping change upon the urban environment, it becomes urgently necessary for us to develop tools which aid in the making of intelligent decisions for planned environmental change.

The success or lack of success of an urban environment in promoting or enhancing the well-being of its inhabitants must necessarily be determined by those persons whose well-being is at stake. No amount of planning expertise or other long-term experience qualifies a non-resident to presuppose or to predetermine the success or failure of an urban environment in promoting the well-being of that environment's inhabitants. Instead, the planning professional's role is most aptly carried out when he seeks to determine the degree to which a given urban environment fulfills the desires and life-styles of its residents, and when he subsequently uses his expertise to plan for environmental changes which will strengthen those environmental attributes that promote well-being and which will remove other attributes that hamper or counteract such well-being.

267

Conditions of the Past

Human settlements have in the past had the chance to evolve in a slow process
of growth and change which permitted a more positive symbiosis between environment and man and which thus resulted in a more likely state of well-being of
the inhabitants of urban environments. This condition was primarily fostered
by the slow expansion of populations, the general stability of mores and life-
styles, and a more characteristically rigid social structure. In this slower
pace, it was easier to respond to the wishes and needs of urban residents, i.e.
it was easier to obtain a match between the expectations of urban dwellers and
the fulfillment of these expectations in the man-made environment. The only
significant obstacle to the attainment of maximum well-being was at that time
our relative lack of technological capacity to build urban systems free from
major hazards to safety, health, and comfort.

Conditions of the Present

At the present time, the conditions are essentially reversed. First, we are
no longer blessed with the past's conditions of gradual, slow and linear
change. Populations are expanding and shifting rapidly, mores and lifestyles
are broadening and increasingly subject to redefinition, and the stratifi-
cations of urban society are in a state of flux and form nearly infinite
varieties of social structure. Under these conditions of rapid and often
exponential change, it becomes difficult to create environments which can
best fulfill the requirements for the well-being of their inhabitants. Thus,
from the point of view of growth and change, it is less likely under present
conditions to obtain a match between the expectations of urban dwellers and
the fulfillment of these expectations in the man-made environment. Second,
our presently awesome technological capacity to construct large-scale and
permanent urban systems in a short time often helps to compound and to
accentuate our lack of ability to respond favorably to the rapid and multi-
faceted changes in urban society: as a result, we now have the capacity to
build more, larger and more monumental unsuccessful human settlements in a
shorter period of time than ever before.

This development has now brought us a new challenge: to develop tools for
intelligent planning which are of equal sophistication to our technological
tools of construction.

DEVELOPMENT OF AN URBAN ACTIVITY MODEL

In response to the conditions of the present as described above, I have
developed the initial structure, contents and function of an Urban Activity
Model with the capacity to assess the assets and liabilities of urban residential areas from the point of view of the persons living in those urban
residential areas.

This "Urban Activity Model" has thus far been employed in analyses of two
communities, to determine how well or how badly each community fulfilled
the needs, desires and life-styles of its residents. The results of these
analyses have shown themselves to be of potential benefit to the making of
future planning and design decisions for each urban area under study. In
addition, a comparison of results from the two analyses has begun to point
toward a number of possible trends, which, if confirmed, may lead to the
development of urban theory and to resultant predictive capabilities in the
Model.

Short-Term and Long-Term Potential Benefits of Using the Model

It was recognized early in the development of the Urban Activity Model
that it would likely need to evolve from being somewhat primitive and
unsophisticated to becoming a more versatile and comprehensive instrument
over a long period of time. It was also recognized, however, that this
evolution of the Model must be permitted to occur as a result of repetitive
uses of the Model in the actual analysis of existing urban areas, i.e. that
the Model would be simultaneously a tool for analysis as well as a tool for
learning. The decision was made, therefore, to consciously build into the
Model the capability to evolve. This was done by placing the three main
components of the Model--structure, contents, and function--in a relationship
which would permit the Model to grow and to change on the basis of its own
feedback from analyses of existing urban areas, as well as from externally
introduced information.

Figure 1 illustrates the Model's outflow and inflow of information
and it also shows the potential short-term and long-term benefits of using
the Urban Activity Model. Each analysis of an existing urban area is of
direct short-term benefit to the urban area under study, and new knowledge
gained as a result of several analyses of different urban areas may, over
time, result in a modification and improvement of the Model's components of
structure, contents and function.

The Structure of the Urban Activity Model

The structure is the first component of the Urban Activity Model. It consists of two basic concepts--Selfhood and Totality--which are the governing
precepts of the Model's contents which make up the second component.

The concept of Selfhood is expressed in terms of several criteria for selfhood which deal with the importance of the individual in the context of the
larger urban community. Alienation from others, and alienation from the
purposes of life, is not likely to be conducive to a person's interest in
shaping a more suitable environment; in fact, it is likely to bring about in
people a reduced concern about anything which happens to them or to their
environment. Thus, a primary condition to the well-being of individuals
must probably be a positive and conscious contribution to the individual's
sense of belonging, participation and importance in the community at-large.
The above, and most likely other dimensions not yet considered, define the
meaning of Selfhood for the purposes of the Urban Activity Model. The
individual criteria for selfhood are thus briefly explained as follows:

Age Group Involvement: The urban environment must provide for the fulfillment
of needs and the exercise of activities by all age groups.

Involvement of Others: The urban environment must permit and encourage the
interaction of individuals, an involvement which fosters mutual recognition
and acknowledgement. This must not only occur between people of the same
age, but also to some degree between people of different age groups.

Time Period Influence: The urban environment must make available a choice
among a variety of activities during all seasons, days of the week and hours
of the day as a prerequisite for the full involvement of all age groups and
for the optimum interaction among people.

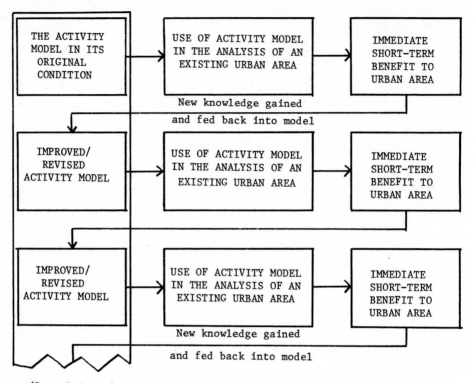

(Repetition of the above steps must occur several additional times,
but the exact number depends on the quality of the feedback obtained.)

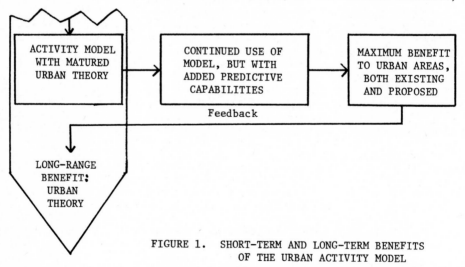

FIGURE 1.   SHORT-TERM AND LONG-TERM BENEFITS
OF THE URBAN ACTIVITY MODEL

Continuity, Stability: The urban environment must exhibit and present itself as an element of continuity and stability in order to allow people to identify with their environment,and in order to permit them to develop a clear set of expectations from their surroundings.

Identification, Orientation, Stimulation: The visual configurative appearance of the urban environment contributes considerably to selfhood in the fact that it brings one to identify oneself with a place, and, in turn, to become identified with a place. Urban environments which provide exciting, pleasant and memorable visual stimuli, and provide for orientation and place-finding, are likely to also contribute to a person's attainment of selfhood.

In addition to the concept of selfhood, as briefly described above, the concept of Totality is also a part of the Model's structure. The realization of selfhood through interaction with others takes place in a background, or setting, which consists of a totality of interdependent human activities. This means, for example, that work cannot be fully understood without leisure, family without community, privacy without interaction, and production without consumption. It means, in fact, that no single factor of urban life can be understood, evaluated or judged by itself--for the quality of every facet of urban life is affected by the qualities of every other facet. This entirety, this wholeness of urban life, is expressed in the Urban Activity Model in terms of six Urban Activity Categories which reflect many of the varied activities which people carry out in pursuit of their daily lives:

> 1.00 Consumption-related activities
> 2.00 Celebration and congregation-related activities
> 3.00 Work-related activities
> 4.00 Service-related activities
> 5.00 Recreation and relaxation-related activities
> 6.00 Communication and learning-related activities.

The Contents of the Urban Activity Model

In the development of the Model's contents, the Model's structure was literally as well as figuratively "filled in". By analogy with the human body, the skeletal structure was used to affix functioning as well as functional elements to create a dynamic, rather than static, entity. In order for the contents of the Model to be truly functional, they had to be expressed in terms of a series of measures of performance, i.e. statements which presupposed a certain condition, and whose validity could be rated from the point of view of the residents of urban areas. This procedure of developing the Model's contents was necessary if the Model was to function as a means to measure the responses of people in analyses of existing urban areas.

Since such required measures could not be stated in predetermined quantities, a different method of gauging performance had to be employed: a benchmark level of performance would be stated in terms of what people should be able to do, or of what should be, in the urban environment, from the author's point of view. Thus the Model contains a series of positively-written Performance Statements. These Statements, captioned below, were generated from the six Urban Activity Categories and they each represent individual measures of the values expressed in the Criteria for Selfhood.

It must be re-emphasized at this point that both the structure and contents of the Urban Activity Model are flexible and subject to gradual evolution.

These Performance Statements are therefore <u>not</u> inviolate standards. Instead,
they are merely benchmarks against which people may be able to express what
may be suitable or unsuitable, worthwhile or worthless, to their daily lives.
Below is a list of the Performance Statements as it is currently constituted:

Urban Activity Category 1.00: Consumption-Related
   Activities.

1.01 Children are able to perform errands for adults at
     nearby shops and stores.
1.02 Children are able to set up makeshift roadside stands
     to sell lemonade, cookies, etc. to passers-by.
1.03 People are able to reach grocery stores by public
     transportation.
1.04 People are able to drive to a variety of shopping
     areas to do their grocery shoping.
1.05 People are able to shop for groceries on their way
     home from work (or have someone else do this for
     them).
1.06 People are able to walk to necessary grocery stores.
1.07 People are able to window shop.
1.08 People are able to reach a variety of larger depart-
     ment stores by public transportation.
1.09 People are able to reach a variety of larger depart-
     ment stores by driving to them.
1.10 People are able to find parking when driving to
     shops and stores.
1.11 People are able to eat in outdoor restaurants
     during the warmer seasons of the year.
1.12 People are able to dine in a variety of restaurants
     in the larger area of the community.
1.13 Local establishments provide catering/take-out
     services.

Urban Activity Category 2.00: Celebration and Congregation-
   Related Activities.

2.01 People are able to partake in a variety of programs
     which bring many people together in the larger area
     of the community (e.g. concerts, theater, athletic
     events, etc.)
2.02 People are able to partake with other community
     members in a seasonal schedule of activities (e.g.
     art shows, caroling, picnics, festivals, etc.)
2.03 People are able to discuss concerns about the
     community with friends at meeting places provided
     for this purpose.
2.04 Children and adolescents are able to partake in the
     activities of community youth groups.
2.05 People are able to partake in community activities
     with older people.
2.06 People are able to partake in community activities
     with younger people.
2.07 People are able to partake in community activities
     with people of the same age.

Urban Activity Category 3:00: Work-Related Activities.

3.01 People are able to walk to and from work.

3.02 People are able to use public transportation facilities to go to and from work.

3.03 People are able to comfortably drive to and from work.

3.04 Children are able to attend day care facilities.

3.05 Children are able to find small jobs in the community.

3.06 Older people are able to find small jobs in the community.

Urban Activity Category 4.00: Service-Related Activities.

4.01 Garbage collection occurs frequently and sufficiently without major disruption of traffic or sleep.

4.02 All sidewalks and roads are well-illuminated at night.

4.03 All sidewalks are regularly cleaned by the people in the community.

4.04 All roads are regularly cleaned by the municipality.

4.05 All sidewalks are regularly repaired and maintained by the municipality.

4.06 All roads are regularly repaired and maintained by the municipality.

4.07 People are able to get action on complaints and requests through political channels in the community.

4.08 Ambulances respond quickly and reach their destinations without delays.

4.09 Fire equipment responds quickly and is able to reach an emergency without delays.

4.10 All laws and ordinances are satisfactorily enforced.

4.11 The community's sidewalks are adequate to handle all pedestrian traffic.

4.12 The community provides local outpatient health care.

4.13 The community provides legal aid services.

4.14 The community has an adequate number of practicing physicians to handle all patients.

4.15 The available hospital facilities adequately serve the needs of the community.

4.16 The public schools provide satisfactory education for the children of the community.

4.17 The community provides adequate automobile service facilities.

4.18 The community provides adequate laundry and dry-cleaning facilities.

4.19 The community provides adequate off-street parking for all vehicles.

4.20 Hotels, motels and other overnight accommodations are placed conveniently from the residences.

Urban Activity Category 5.00: Recreation and Relaxation-Related Activities.

5.01 People are able to watch traffic and other people from benches or from similar observation places in the community.

5.02 People are able to partake in a variety of indoor and outdoor recreational activities throughout the year within the larger area of the community.

5.03 The community provides for quiet relaxation, especially on weekends.

5.04 The community provides for boisterous, outgoing recreational activities.

5.05 Playgrounds and other recreational areas for children allow for play which is without interference from children of other age groups.

5.06 Children are able to safely ride bicycles in the community.

5.07 People are able to enjoy safe walks in the community.

5.08 People are able to enjoy walks which are visually stimulating.

5.09 The community provides adequately for the keeping of pets without their becoming a nuisance.

Urban Activity Category 6.00: Communication and Learning-Related Activities.

6.01 Elementary schools are located within walking distance from the community residences.

6.02 Children are able to walk to school safely.

6.03 The community is free from persistent foul or annoying odors.

6.04 The community contains a number of characteristic, identifiable smells.

6.05 The community contains places of lively activity.

6.06 The community is free from dominant visual clutter and ugliness.

6.07 People are able to orient themselves easily with the help of signs and symbols when looking for a particular place or places.

6.08 People are able to view exhibits in museums, galleries, etc. in the larger area of the community.

6.09 The community provides adequate library facilities.

The Function of the Urban Activity Model

The Urban Activity Model's primary function is its use in the analysis of existing urban residential areas. A secondary function of the Model is the development of urban theory as a result of a series of analyses of existing urban residential areas. (Refer to Fig. 1 and the previous discussion of the short-term and long-term benefits of using the Model.)

As a result, the Model has the immediate capacity to aid in the analysis of existing urban residential areas, while it also has the future potential capacity of evolving the knowledge gained from a series of such analyses into urban theory. Because the Model has thus far only been employed in the analysis of two existing urban residential areas, little is presently known about the Model's capability to derive such theory. However, sufficient information is available at this time to illustrate the manner in which the Model is employed in analyzing existing urban areas, and to point toward some of the potential of the Model as a tool for learning about human settlements.

Analysis of Existing Urban Areas by Questionnaire. A questionnaire, based on the previously identified Performance Statements was constructed and administered initially in two urban communities in the States of New York and Maryland. This questionnaire is a direct outgrowth of the Model's structure and contents, and it constitutes the Model's functional part in the analysis of existing urban areas. The questionnaire is made up of two parts: the first part contains the Performance Statements with two rating scales after each statement. Each rating scale has values from zero to four, within which the respondent is asked to give his valuation (1) of the frequency of occurrence in the community and (2) of the importance to him, of the activity described in the Performance Statement in question. The numerical order of the performance statements was scrambled in order to randomize the sequence of responses to each urban activity category. The second part of the questionnaire asks the respondent to give some personal data, to identify landmarks and places of activity in his community, and to describe major attributes and problems of his community. Consideration was given in the design of the questionnaire format to allow easy transposition of results onto data processing cards. Figures 2 and 3 on the next page illustrate a sample page of Part I and the page containing Part II of the questionnaire.

As is shown in Fig. 2, each respondent is asked to react to the performance statements by rating two values: frequency and importance. This dual measure is applied in keeping with the previously stated idea that the Urban Activity Model cannot, at this point, presume to be rigidly prescriptive about what is good for the well-being of urban dwellers, and that it must instead be capable of learning from the expressed desires of urban dwellers, and allow such feedback to be considered in future modifications to the Model. Thus the questionnaire allows the Model to become a tool for learning about urban areas, because it determines not only the degree to which a certain activity does or does not occur in a particular urban setting; it also determines the relative importance of this activity to the respondents from this urban area.

The Urban Activity Questionnaire as a Generator of Assets and Liabilities. While it is beyond the scope of this presentation to show the precise and detailed numerical relationships and statistical parameters employed in obtaining the questionnaire's results, it must be pointed out that five distinct relationships among frequency and importance form the basis for the development of assets and liabilities of existing urban residential areas.

First, frequency and importance may both be rated significantly high. This indicates that a particular activity not only occurs frequently, but that it is of commensurate importance: a desirable quality, which for the purposes of this Study is termed a first order asset.

Second, frequency and importance may both be rated significantly low. This indicates that the particular activity not only occurs infrequently, but that it is equally unimportant. This is also a desirable condition, termed a second order asset.

Third, frequency and importance may be rated significantly high and low, respectively. This indicates that an oversupply exists beyond the expressed importance. For example, a high frequency-low importance rating on the statement "People can use day care facilities" would indicate that such facilities are known to be available, but that the need for them is for one or another reason less than that for which has been provided. While this relationship between frequency and importance describes conditions of oversupply, they are nevertheless non-destructive and therefore termed third order assets.

URBAN ACTIVITY QUESTIONNAIRE

Ⓐ THIS HAPPENS IN YOUR COMMUNITY: Ⓑ ITS IMPORTANCE TO YOU IS: REMARKS:

PART I: FOR EACH STATEMENT PLEASE CHECK THE APPROPRIATE BOX UNDER ITEMS Ⓐ AND Ⓑ (zero is lowest, four is highest) ►

never...always   none.....great
0 1 2 3 4   0 1 2 3 4

▼ THE STATEMENTS BELOW WERE DELIBERATELY TAKEN OUT OF THEIR NUMERICAL ORDER

2.03 You can discuss concerns about the community with friends at meeting places provided for this purpose

4.15 The available hospital facilities can adequately serve the needs of the community

4.16 Children can obtain satisfactory education from the public schools in the community

4.07 You can get action on complaints and requests through political channels in the community

1.08 You can reach a variety of department stores by public transportation

3.06 Adults can find small jobs in the community

5.07 You can enjoy safe walks in the community

6.03 Your community is free from persistent, annoying odors

1.02 Children can set up makeshift roadside stands to sell lemonade, cookies, etc. to passers-by

URBAN ACTIVITY QUESTIONNAIRE

PART II

① your age: ____ years

② sex: M □ F □

③ marital status: M □ S □

④ including yourself, the number of people in your household: _____

⑤ your approximate total family income per year (for statistical purposes only): $ _____

⑥ the length of time you have resided in this community : ____ years

⑦ do you rent or own your place of residence? rent □ own □

⑧ how many vehicles does your family operate ? cars ____ other ____

⑨ Do you live near some easily identified place or landmark? If so, please name it or describe it in the space below:

Please name the places where you and your family shop for groceries:
_____

Please name the places where your family shops for other items:
_____

Please name some of the places where you meet and socialize with friends, relatives, aquaintances and others:
_____

Please name the places or buildings where you and others in your family are working:
_____

Of the following persons, check those who KNOW YOU by name:

local politician □   restaurant owner □   car service man □
local policeman □   local doctor □   teacher □
trash collector □   local lawyer □   president of local society □

Please name some of the places you and your family go to for recreation, relaxation, enjoyment and the like:
_____

What physical and other characteristics of your community do you find most attractive? (use back of sheet if necessary)
_____

What should be changed or improved in your community? (use back of sheet if necessary)
_____

THANK YOU FOR YOUR INTEREST AND COOPERATION

FIGURE 2 and FIGURE 3. PARTS I AND II OF THE URBAN ACTIVITY QUESTIONNAIRE

Fourth, frequency and importance may be rated neither high nor low, but near the median of both scales. Such an ambiguity must be further investigated, but because of its generally harmless characteristics, it is termed a fourth order asset.

Fifth, frequency and importance may be rated low and high, respectively. This signifies the only destructive or harmful condition, in that a lack of provision for the activity exists in the face of high importance to the respondents. This is a potentially or actually harmful condition, a liability.

Figure 4 on the following page summarizes the five conditions as described above. For each of the two analyses of existing urban residential areas thus far performed, these assets and liabilities were listed and further analyzed by subcategories of (1) age groups; (2) marrieds versus singles; (3) males versus females; (4) income groups. These tabulated results, once obtained, had a dual usefulness: first, they provided significant input for the future planning and programming for the urban areas analyzed; second, they provided some clues as to possible trends of development and the relationship between the environment and those who live in that environment.

In the subsequent description of the results of the analyses of the two urban residential environments which have been performed to date, significant variations among results were evident when subcategories were examined. Age, sex, income and marital status have in a number of instances accounted for significant deviations from the responses by the total population sample. Such data are valuable in the effort to consider the interests of people according to the previously described criteria for selfhood.

Statistically, and because of the strongly positive wording of the Performance Statements, one may expect a preponderance of first order assets and liabilities in the results of an urban activity analysis performed with the use of the urban activity questionnaire. Because of the larger number of first order assets and liabilities, these are put in rank order in order to identify which liabilities are the worst and which first order assets are the strongest. This rank ordering permits one subsequently to establish priorities for an existing urban area with respect to the alleviation of liabilities and the maintenance or perpetuation of assets.

Assets and Liabilities Lead to Action Program. Based on this information about priorities, and considering other political, financial and logistical input, one may then establish an action program for the urban area in question. Such an action program may identify programming, planning and design actions in a prescribed sequence over a period of time.

TWO EXAMPLES OF URBAN ACTIVITY ANALYSES
BY USE OF THE URBAN ACTIVITY MODEL

The Urban Activity Model has thus far been employed in the analysis of two existing urban residential communities of an outwardly opposite character: Lansingburgh, in the State of New York, and Bowie, in the State of Maryland.

Description of Lansingburgh, New York

The community of Lansingburgh (pop. approximately 20,000) is located north of the center of the City of Troy, whose total population of 62,000 includes that of Lansingburgh. The site of Troy and Lansingburgh is bounded by the

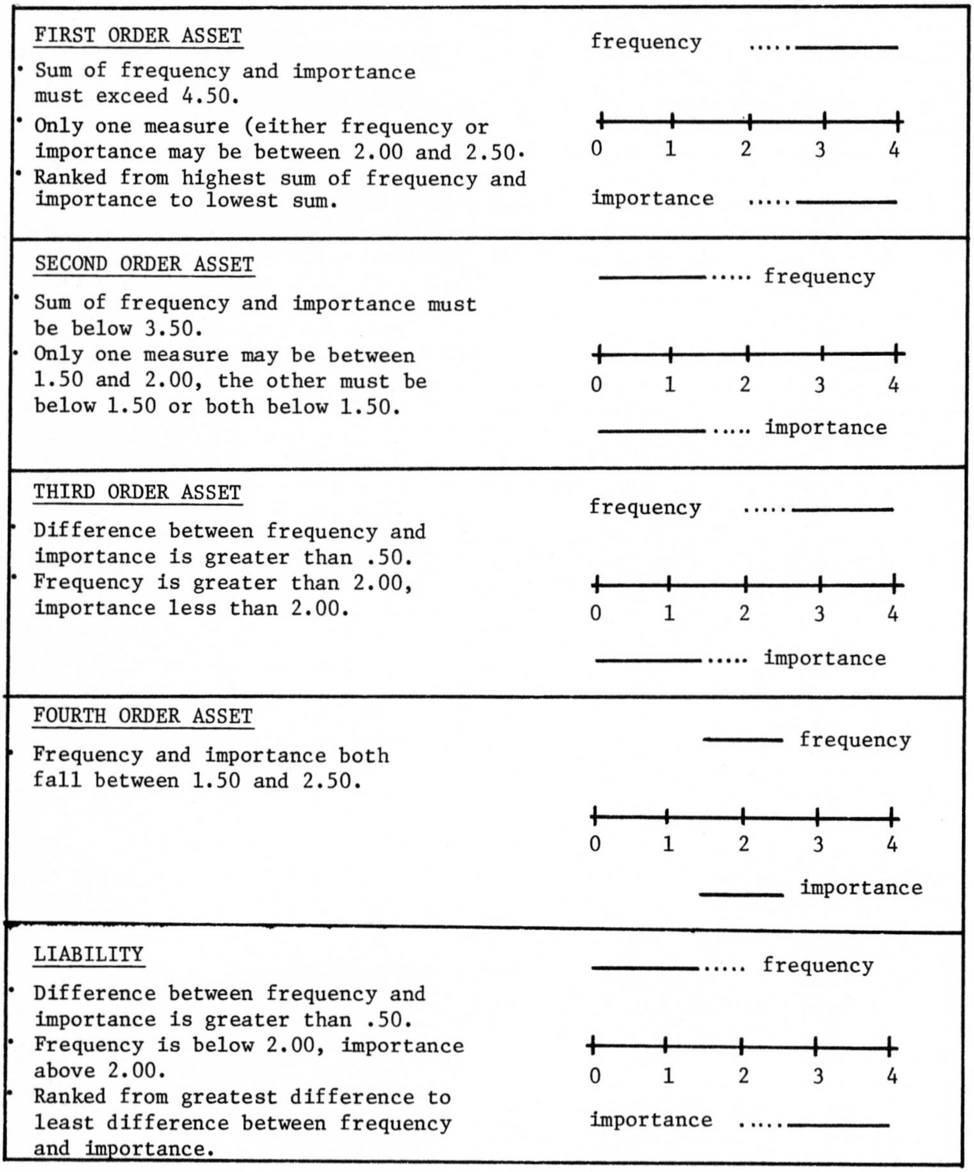

FIRST ORDER ASSET	frequency ..... ————
• Sum of frequency and importance must exceed 4.50.	
• Only one measure (either frequency or importance may be between 2.00 and 2.50·	0 1 2 3 4
• Ranked from highest sum of frequency and importance to lowest sum.	importance ..... ————

SECOND ORDER ASSET	———— ..... frequency
• Sum of frequency and importance must be below 3.50.	
• Only one measure may be between 1.50 and 2.00, the other must be below 1.50 or both below 1.50.	0 1 2 3 4
	———— ..... importance

THIRD ORDER ASSET	frequency ..... ————
• Difference between frequency and importance is greater than .50.	
• Frequency is greater than 2.00, importance less than 2.00.	0 1 2 3 4
	———— ..... importance

FOURTH ORDER ASSET	———— frequency
• Frequency and importance both fall between 1.50 and 2.50.	
	0 1 2 3 4
	———— importance

LIABILITY	———— ..... frequency
• Difference between frequency and importance is greater than .50.	
• Frequency is below 2.00, importance above 2.00.	0 1 2 3 4
• Ranked from greatest difference to least difference between frequency and importance.	importance ..... ————

FIGURE 4.   NUMERICAL PARAMETERS AND RANKING OF
ASSETS AND LIABILITIES

Hudson River to the West, and to the East it occasionally overflows up a
steep grade, approximately one-half mile from the riverfront. As a consequence, Lansingburgh has expanded generally northward, following a rectangular
grid pattern of streets. Several parks and open spaces are contained within
this grid, but the riverfront is undeveloped for recreation. The City Government of Troy, including police, fire protection and municipal services, has
jurisdiction over Lansingburgh. Lansingburgh's Public Schools and its Public
Libraries are, however, separate from those of Troy. Lansingburgh was founded
200 years ago on farmland owned by the Lansing family. This founding preceded
the founding and development of Troy by approximately 50 years. Eventual
circumstances, having to do particularly with the construction of the New York
State Barge Canal and the consequent changes in navigation of the Hudson River
lead to a more strategic position of Troy, to its faster growth, and to
Lansingburgh's incorporation into Troy's boundaries. Lansingburgh's past is
rich with the history of the past two Centuries, especially the Revolutionary
and Civil War periods, and Herman Melville lived there for a few years of his
life. Lansingburgh became primarily a fashionable residential community
supportive of Troy. Some stately town houses and mansions are in evidence
from this time, and the character of the community is dominated by large two-
story single and two-family homes. A number of secondary industries have
since moved into Lansingburgh, taking such forms as dry cleaning plants and
automobile dealerships. On the whole, however, Lansingburgh remains an
integral residential community, containing many of the essential commercial,
educational and recreational facilities.

Description of Bowie, Maryland

The large part of Bowie, Maryland is a 12-year old community of approximately
40,000 inhabitants. It consists of approximately 9,000 single-family dwellings,
stretched out over a rolling countryside near the center of a triangle between
Washington, Baltimore and Annapolis, whose industry and commerce it generally
supports as a bedroom community. These homes were built by Levitt and Sons,
Inc., of Levittown fame, who also built the roads and set aside areas for
shopping centers, schools and churches, as well as for some later constructed
recreation areas (pools and tennis) with private membership. The roads are
arranged in a random, spiderweb-like pattern which sometimes follows the
contours of the land, with the advantage of avoiding uniformity, monotony
and drag-racing, but which makes it often difficult to orient oneself.
Fifteen years ago, Bowie was a small village with a railroad freight yard and
a cement factory, and with some farmland. Nearby was an all-black Teachers
College and a regional race track for horse racing. This old part of Bowie
is presently a mere appendage, the Teachers College is integrated and the
race track is flourishing.

The respondents to the questionnaire were less homogeneously grouped than in
Lansingburgh: there were no low-income groups (income below $8,000 per year),
no single adults represented in the sample.

Assets and Liabilities of Lansingburgh

The questionnaire survey of Lansingburgh was accomplished during February of
1971. The tallying of questionnaire results was performed manually in order
to demonstrate that although automated data processing systems were available
for this purpose, communities with limited financial resources could afford
nevertheless to have such a survey performed by less expensive means.

Liabilities Listed in Order of Priority. Because of the limited space available for this presentation, only fhe first five of a total of 21 Performance
Statements which were identified as liabilities are listed below. Liabilities
are those Performance Statements which the respondents rated to be of high
importance to them, but which did not in their opinion occur frequently
enough, or were not in their opinion available enough, in accordance with
this ascribed importance. These items are listed in order of their relative
priority, beginning with the liability which showed the greatest difference
between the frequency and importance ratings.

1. 4.05 All Sidewalks are Regularly Maintained and
         Repaired by Your Municipality
2. 5.07 You Can Enjoy Safe Walks in the Community
3. 4.06 All Roads are Regularly Repaired and Maintained
         by Your Municipality
4. 6.07 Your Community is Free from Dominant Visual
         Clutter and Ugliness
5. 4.14 Your Community's Practicing Physicians can
         Handle all Patients Adequately

First Order Assets Listed in Order of Priority. Once again because of space
limitations, the following list contains only the first five of those Performance Statements which were identified to be first order assets by the
respondents to the Lansingburgh urban activity questionnaire. (A total of 36
Performance Statements were rated as first order assets.) This means that the
respondents rated these items to be of high importance to them, and that they
did in their opinion occur frequently enough, or that they were in their
opinion available enough, in accordance with their ascribed importance.
These items are listed in order of their relative priority, beginning with
the first order asset which received the highest importance and frequency
ratings.

1. 1.04 You (or Someone Else in Your Family) can Drive
         to a Variety of Shopping Areas to do Your
         Grocery Shopping
2. 4.09 Fire Equipment Responds Quickly and can Reach
         an Emergency Without Delay
3. 4.16 Children can Obtain Satisfactory Education from
         the Public Schools in the Community
4. 1.09 You can Reach a Variety of Department Stores by
         Driving to Them
5. 3.03 You (or Someone Else in Your Family) can Com-
         fortably Drive to or From Work

Second, Third and Fourth Order Assets. Because of the limited space, the
list of the Performance Statements rated in this fashion cannot be presented.

Summary. In general, residents reacted favorably toward their community,
many stating that they especially welcomed the double benefit of being able
to live in an urban area, but within easy reach of the countryside. They
were also fond of the generally residential character, with enough commercial
facilities that could be reached on foot. Of primary concern, however, were
such items as the quality of municipal services and the nature of the political
structure, zoning of commercial establishments, noise, facilities for
youngsters of all age groups; furthermore a strong rift between lower income

and higher income families appeared to be present. Fig. 5 shows in some
greater detail the pattern of responses to a few selected Performance Statements by subcategories.

Assets and Liabilities of Bowie

The following assets and liabilities form a basis for the development of a
program of planning, programming and design actions by the community of
Bowie. This action program must deal with (1) alleviating the cited liabilities in order of their respective priorities, and (2) maintaining current
assets and strengthening others, also in order of their respective priorities.

Liabilities Listed in Order of Priority. Because of space limitations, the
following list contains only the first five of a total of 11 of those Performance Statements which were identified as liabilities by the respondents
to the Bowie urban activity questionnaire. The liabilities are listed in
order of priority, with the worst liability listed first.

1. 4.15 The Available Hospital Facilities can Adequately
        Serve the Needs of the Community
2. 6.04 Your Community Contains a Number of Character-
        istic, Identifiable Smells
3. 6.09 You can View Exhibits in Museums and Galleries
        in the Wider Area of the Community
4. 4.11 Your Community's Sidewalks can Adequately Handle
        all Pedestrian Traffic
5. 4.13 Your Community Provides Legal Aid Services

First Order Assets Listed in Order of Priority. The following list contains
the first five of a total of 42 of those Performance Statements which were
identified to be first order assets by the residents of Bowie. These items
are listed in order of their relative priority, with the highest ranking
asset listed first.

1. 4.09 Fire Equipment Responds Quickly and can Reach
        an Emergency Without Delay
2. 4.08 Ambulances Respond Quickly and can Reach an
        Emergency Without Delay
3. 1.04 You can Drive to a Variety of Shopping Areas
        to do Your Grocery Shopping
4. 4.16 Children can Obtain Satisfactory Education From
        the Public Schools in the Community
5. 4.01 Garbage Collection Occurs Sufficiently and
        Regularly Without Disruption of Traffic or Sleep

Second, Third and Fourth Order Assets. Because of the limited space, the
list of the Performance Statements rated in this fashion cannot be presented.

Summary. As evidenced by the great number of first order assets as compared
to the minimal number of liabilities, Bowie is in general a well-balanced,
young, suburban type of City. Primarily noticeable is the considerable
amount of satisfaction which the residents seem to express toward their
City Government. In present times, this is surely the exception rather
than the rule.

Six areas of liability, however, are identifiable as follows: (1) A hospital

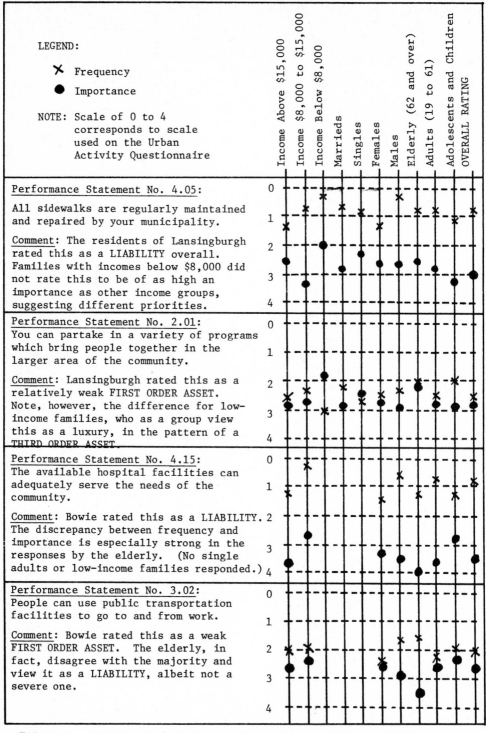

FIGURE 5.   SELECTED RESULTS OF THE BOWIE AND LANSINGBURGH ANALYSES

facility nearby or in Bowie is required, and perhaps some local health care
facilities in conjunction with such a major hospital could be constructed in
some areas within Bowie; (2) More consideration must be given to facilities
and activities for adolescents and also for elderly people; (3) Improved
public transportation facilities and systems are required for both commuting
and shopping; (4) More caution and planning are perhaps advisable to avoid
uncontrolled development of commercial facilities at the outskirts of Bowie;
(5) More police protection appears to be desired by the residents; (6) Some
concern, although not blantantly evident, has been voiced about a lack of
communication between the residents of the City, especially between neighbors.
This was noted mostly by adolescents who responded to the Urban Activity
Questionnaire.

Figure 5 shows in some greater detail the pattern of responses to a few
selected Performance Statements by subcategories.

A COMPARISON OF LANSINGBURGH AND BOWIE

Although it is too early to draw significant conclusions as to trends or
urban theory from the analysis of a mere two urban communities, a comparison
of the results of the two questionnaire surveys tends to point toward the fact
that, in spite of the different environments represented by these two communities, the residents of both communities seem to place the same importance on
the same things. The indication of this comes from the manner in which the
residents of both communities rated the Performance Statements of the urban
activity questionnaire.

Twenty-five of the Performance Statements were rated as first order assets
by the residents of both communities, which means that a high importance
rating was indicated by all respondents. Twenty other Performance Statements
were rated as first order assets by the residents of one community and as
liabilities by the residents of the other, which once again means that the
respondents from both communities had to place high importance on these
statements. In addition, four Performance Statements were rated as liabilities
by both communities, again indicating that the respondents felt these issues
to be highly important. As a result, 49 of the 64 Performance Statements
in the questionnaire were rated to be of high importance by the respondents
from both communities, despite the differences in environments and population characteristics. This points out, perhaps, that the originally
developed 64 Performance Statements are strongly indicative of what people
seem to prefer in their urban environments, but it is too early to conclude
from this information that the value systems of both communities are perhaps
completely independent of the physical makeup, the population characteristics
and the histories of each community.

At best, the information thus far obtained may justify the formulation of a
hypothesis for future testing. This hypothesis would state that for any
given urban community in the United States, regardless of the character of
that given community, the criteria for the well-being of that community's
residents are largely the same as the criteria for any other urban community
in the United States.

This hypothesis merely hints at some of the knowledge which may perhaps be
developed by the pursuit of the type of inquiry illustrated in this presentation.

CONCLUSION

The research work outlined above shows the development of a procedure or methodology for determining some of the social and physical requirements of an urban community, with the dual purpose of providing immediate infor- mation for future community planning and long-term information for the formulation of hypotheses and subsequent urban theory. Perhaps the most important aspect of this methodology is that it can be an integral part of the age-old and larger process of planning, programming and design which occurs, consciously or not, in every urban area.

The process of analysis of existing urban areas, along the lines described herein, must be constantly refined and repeated with a larger number of urban communities. The results of such analyses must then be examined for similarities and differences, and for identifiable trends which may lend themselves to the formulation of hypotheses and subsequently to the develop- ment of theory.

While nothing I have written here will ensure able environmental planning and design, the chances for it must surely increase as our knowledge increases. As certainly as there appear to be no substitutes for creativity, there must be replacements for our lack of understanding and dearth of knowledge.

THE IDENTITY OF THE CITY AND ITS CAPACITY FOR CHANGE

Jan Tanghe, architect and planner
Groep Planning, Brugge, Belgium
Senior Lecturer at the Faculté Polytechnique at Mons.

THE HISTORIC TOWN IS ESSENTIAL FOR THE QUALITY OF LIFE

It is irritating to be obliged to re-state a principle that we had unanimously agreed upon, namely, that the building is an integral and subordinate part of the town and landscape. It is equally disappointing to see that this principle, which is so simple at first sight, is rarely kept to. To this another distressing fact must be added: the enormous and concentrated volume of built-up areas within towns and the peripherial growth of suburbia that has taken place during the XXth century.

We may well wonder if we are not confronted with the most extensive urban disintegration ever known to history. This urban disintegration is nothing less than the physical and spatial expression of the transmutation of an agrarian and pre-industrial society into a tecnological civilisation.

The reasons for this disintegration are well known. There is the general conflict between 'unlimited economic growth and the 'environment'. To begin with there is the immediate conflict between the 'environment' and the 'technological industrialisation' (mass production) on the one hand, and between 'environment' and 'mobility' (communication and intercommunication) on the other. Secondly, there is a particular conflict between the 'urban environment' and the 'growth of urban activities and the scale of the town'. This growth is often dictated by economic principles and decisions (frequently in relation to false needs), rather than by the town's physical capacity for change.

I should like here to develop a townplanning approach that would allow a precise evaluation of the town's capacity for change through its physical and spatial characteristics rather than through the interaction of economic and financial implications. The capacity for change of historic towns has until recently always been done and must continue to be done on the basis of the philosophy of the continuity of the urban identity both in time and space.

This philosophy is not synonymous with a conservative and outdated policy, but rather with a progressive attitude and an awareness based on the conviction that urban culture and the continuity of the physical structure of the town are not opposed to the aspirations of the man of today. 'Yesterday is tomorrow' said André Malraux.

Any interruption of this continuity, either because of war (Rotterdam) or undue preoccupation with business affairs and cupidity (Brussels), provides us with the undeniable proof of the town's downfall and the consequent degradation of the quality of life. This brings us to a first hypothesis, namely, that there is no fundamental opposition today between the needs, and the inspirations of the human habitat, and the structures of historic towns, in so far as we adapt them to the life of today. It is therefore necessary to consider their rehabilitation as an impor-tant and integrated element in town and country planning policy.

THE REHABILITATION OF TOWNS AND THEIR CAPACITY FOR CHANGE

There are 3 fundamental conditions regarding the macro-structures for carrying out an integrated policy of urban rehabilitation, namely:
a) The region in which the historic town stands must have econo-mic stability;
b) The region must be able to dispose of a Structure Plan which makes a policy of adaptation possible;
c) The national, regional and local authorities must have a total rehabilitation policy and a subsidy policy in regard to rehabili-tation in general.

The economic stability depends on the quality of the industries, offices and shopping amenities, the demographic policy and hou-sing, the character of the social amenities, the transport poli-cy, and potential for change, be it for growth or compression, inside the towns of the region. These elements are interdepen-dent and must be evaluated in a regional Structure Plan. The in-terrelation between the urban nucleus, the agglomeration and the rural area is essential in order to carry into effect a policy of continuity and rehabitation of the historic city.

In what concerns the historic city, the policy of continuity must also be expressed by an urban Structure Plan that takes into con-sideration a number of fundamental objectives. This urban plan will be subject to the main lines laid down by the Regional Plan.

1. All decisions concerning the continuity of the urban structu-res is a political decision. 'The problem which arises as soon as one wants to develop a given space, is the choice of objectives, and no scientific knowledge can determine this. 'The finality of urban planning is philosophical and political'. (1)

Any political decision concerning rehabilitation will only be socially acceptable in so far as the users and inhabitants of the town are well informed and understand the principles of the policy tha is being followed. And, in the same way, the politician must have a good grasp of the real needs and aspirations of the inha-bitants.

(1) Françoise Choay, Metropolis Interview Paris (July 1974)

On the other hand it would be a great mistake to think that cultural considerations prompt the general public to take care of
their urban and architectural heritage. The real reason why public opinion prefers to keep its district or neighbourhood, as
it is, rather than demolish it, to leave the countryside untouch-
ed, rather than build a motorway, is a psycho-social and economic
one. The public reacts against anonymity and against the inhuman urban scale, against pollution and noise, against what has
been done in the name of progress. The identity of the historic
city and its physical structure fulfil the psycho-physiological
(2) needs of the inhabitants better than the anonymous disparity
of many of our new neighbourhoods.

Conservation, whose only aim is to beautify, based on the extremely odious taste of would-be aesthetic enthusiasts, which in no
way fulfils any social or human needs, is just as fatal to the
policy of continuity as the demolition of the heritage. This is
because it is fundamentally a question of adapting the town to
the real needs of the man of today.

2. The use of buildings is, therefore, an essential aspect, for
the function and aesthetic character of buildings always go together. Their relationship is essential in the creation of satisfactory environments where the twofold aspect of function and
aesthetisme is concerned. (3). Every effort must always be made to
adapt the functions of the buildings to modern life.

3. A policy of continuity can only be brought about if it creates
conditions favourable to the self-rehabilitation of buildings and
finds new uses for them that are perfectly justifiable. This
means that every integrated rehabilitation policy must include
utilisation of all sites, in all the neighbourhoods and in the
whole city. Not only must one know and appreciate the financial
value of the land, but one must be equally well aware of its possible use, and that of the buildings, for the needs of tomorrow.

4. Traffic is a derived function from urban activities. Only by
controlling urban functions can one control its traffic, while at
the same time respecting the rigour of the town's physical
structure. This can only be done by limiting private traffic and
actively encouraging public transport. Traffic is essential for
the general vitality of the town.

5. Housing has an important spatial impact on the town. But the
functional aspect is even more important because the residential
function is essential for the life of the town.

---

(2) Michel Didisheim, A+ n°1 Bruges sauve l'honneur Brussels,1974.
(3) A.A.Wood, Thème du congrès sur le patrimoine architectural
        européen, Responsabilités des pouvoirs locaux et participa-
        tions des citoyens Amsterdam 1975.

6. It is permissible, indispensable even, to restore both large and small monuments as well as the town's appearance. Nevertheless, a policy of continual care of the urban and architectural heritage would put a stop, in the end, to all restoration. This would finally be a great economy and make possible the restoration of certain urban functions and services, as well as the social and economic rehabilitation of the town.

There must also be some policy concerning the construction of architectural replicas, though these are seldom acceptable because they devalue the original.

7. The policy concerning the architectural conception of new buildings is fundamental because the architecture of today is as much a part of the urban scenery as the historic. We have to be capable of intelligently integrating an architecture, that is the expression of the times in which we live, into the structure of our cities.

Among the objectives stated above, there are two ideas which appaer fundamental. On the one hand we see that the re-use of urban structures - buildings as well as urban spaces - are essential for continuity. On the other hand the life of the city has a number of common-needs which create the necessity for constant change: Change in continuity.

Town-planning finally comes down to solving the problem between the shell, which is the town, and the social animal living inside this shell. Until now a laissez-faire policy has evolved unilaterally without worrying about the impact of the economic need on the urban structure. This state of affairs far from solving the problem, has, since the war, violated the character of the towns and has diminished their quality.

On the contrary, I think that the city's potential for change should first be based on the physical and spatial appraisal of the city. This would then allow for the sort of possible or desirable changes, in the city even if it means that other structures derive from it, such as a pattern of decentralisation on the regional level.

It is equally true that a historic town may be in danger through lack of essential activities in such a way that supplementary needs and, consequently, specific changes (expansion or compression) become indispensable.

The crucial question is to find a balance between the capacity of the town for change and the needs of the life of the town. In other words, it means evaluating the town's dispositions for change while maintaining its character and even improving it, if possible.

The experience of the last few decades has proved that the estimates of financial and economic needs were often over-estimated.

The 'quartier nord'of Brussels is a flagrant example. The majority of financiers and economists openly admit that their estimates can only be approximative.

A methodology based on the extrapolation of economic data which risks great fluctuations in the estimates of floor space, has always had very unfortunate effects on the character and face of the town and equally bad effects on the quality of the habitat for the population. One is therfore perfectly justified in suggesting a method of town appraisal by analysing and evaluating the urban character of a city. From this its capacity for change and the potential of supplementary space and floorspace can be deduced and be allocated to the necessary need for changes.

This theory has already be defended by Ray Worskett and I agree with him in saying that we must not worry unduly because this method of analysis and evaluation gives a very crude result.(5)

We have been able to examine and test this method in Bruges since 1972. We are gradually beginning to see that the needs for change can most of the time, be absorbed either by the existing empty or wrongly used buildings, or they can give place to rehabilitation or re-structuring in derelict areas.

The degree of fluctuation of this method of town appraisal differs very little in the end from the financial and economic method of determining the supplementary needs of floorspace. It has, however, the great advantage of being more pragmatic and flexible, and beside this, it does not violate the urban identity.

On the other hand, a laiser-faire policy based on fincancial and economic estimates and in the absence of any policy concerning building limitations gives rise to a systematic degradation of the town and this gives free rein to an appreciable rise in the value of building land and consequently of a general increase of the scale of the town.

This brings us to a second conclusion, namely, that any adaption of the town to its real needs can only be done if those concerned are fully aware of the physical capacity for change of the town, and of the importance of the town's physical appearance. This does not exclude the basic hypothesis that any living organism must change.

THE VISUAL AND PHYSICAL ASPECTS OF THE URBAN SITE AND ITS USE

The establishment of a methodology for assessing the quality of the urban site in order to determine   the town's degree of physical capacity for change, is necessary if the problem stated above is to be solved.

This means establishing a number of parameters
which define the morphological character of the town.   There are
two pairs of parameters.

Urban Volumes and Spaces
a) Urban volumes: the buildings and important technical infrastructures: bridges, traffic lights and signals etc. and the
whole of the soft townscape: trees etc. their shape material and
colour.

b) Urban spaces are the spaces between buildings; the hard and
soft townscapes, their shape, material and colour.

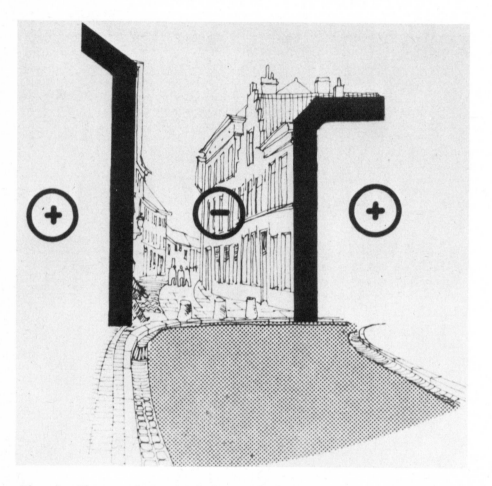

Fig. 1. The morphological face of the town is a single projec-
        tion in one only vertical or horizontal urban facade.

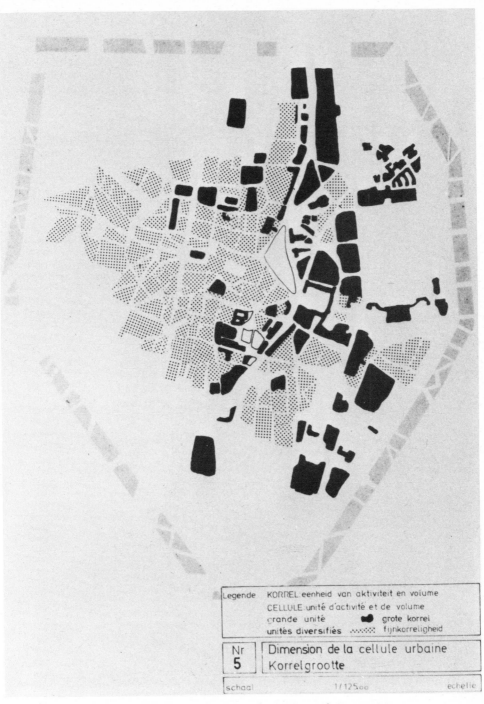

Legende KORREL eenheid van aktiviteit en volume
CELLULE unité d'activité et de volume
grande unité   grote korrel
unités diversifiés   fijnkorreligheid

Nr 5 | Dimension de la cellule urbaine
Korrelgrootte

schaal   1/12500   echelle

Fig. 2. The structure and scale of Brussels.

The Use of Urban Volumes and Spaces
a) The activities within the buildings and the functions within
the urban neighbourhoods.
b) The use of urban spaces; the character and the bustle of the
pedestrian precincts, the quality and quantity of the traffic
both public and private, their physical and visual impact on the
townscape.

Urban Volumes and Spaces
There is no distinction here, either, between architectural volumes and urban spaces. The morphological face of the town is a
single projection in one only vertical or horizontal urban faca-
de of private and interior space that we call architecture or positive volumes on the one hand, and the exterior and public space, that we call urban space or negative space on the other.
fig. 1.

Three morphological characteristics are common to both volumes
and spaces. These are: form, material and colour.

The form of the buildings and other urban volumes is determined
by several characteristics:
a) The first is the 'scale', or the 'relationship to the whole'.
The scale is influenced by the idea of 'unity' and 'contrast'
and is an architectural concept that helps orientation and perception within the urban structure. The 'scale' is a range or a
scale of relationships, a hierarchy of values, of a house in a
street, of a street in a town, of a town in the landscape. fig.2.

Fig. 3. The skyline of Bruges.

b) The second characteristic, the 'skyline' is analogous to the concept of the scale.

The skyline is a visual summary of the urban identity. It is a constant that can rarely be improved upon. Ghent, with its three towers, is an example of this. When Henry Vande Velde's University Library tower was added, it gave rise to much discussion. The addition since then of innumerable multi storey buildings has completely annihilated the identity of this once extra-ordinary town, simply because the hierarchy of values has been falsified: one does not put a typist at the same height as the weather-cock on the belfry or the cross on a cathedral spire. fig. 3.

c) The third characteristic is 'the shape and rythm' of the roofs. The slope of the roofs is important in determining the visual identity of the town. What is more subtle and difficult to grasp is the rythm of the roofs, and the creativity necessary to harmonise new possibilities with the urban unity. fig. 4.

Fig. 4. The roofs of Bruges.

d) The fourth characteristic concerns the 'width and rythm of the urban plots and facades'. The structure of ancient towns is principally determined by the shape a..d dimension of the plots. According to the size of the plot, the town is either a town of houses' or a 'palatial town'. The horizontality or verticality of the town's architecture is dictated by the width of the plots In the same way, their depth is indirectly responsible for the height of the roofs.

e) The fifth characteristic concerns the 'alignment' of the plots along the streets and squares. It is essential to keep the alignment unchanged. Nevertheless certain corrections have to be made, as for example, in the rue du Pépin in Brussels. fig. 5.

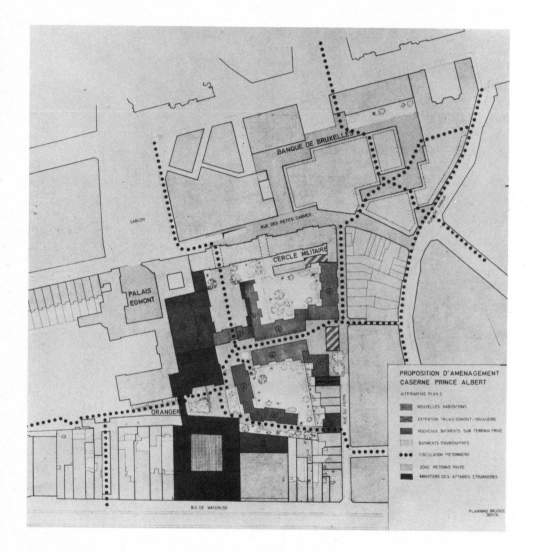

Fig. 5. The rue de Pepin in Brussels
         (Townplanning proposal for Brussels, Groep Planning).

Fig. 6. The hard townscape

f) The last characteristic concerns the architectural expression
and the character of the townscape. The identity of the town is
more than the some of the characteristics named above. It dicta-
tes the architectural expression that is to be given to the changes in the city structure. The character of the town determines
the language and the mood of its architectural particules, thus
by composing (not by adding) streets and squares as well as parts
of the town or even the whole town can be created, restructured,
ameliorated and enhanced. The relationship between the hard
parts of the town is called the hard townscape. fig. 6

Similarly the character of the town is also determined by the
trees, canals and rivers, and the general topography of the site.
The relationship between them creates the soft townscape. fig. 7.
The correlation between both townscapes as well as between the
public and private space, the exterior and interior, the positive
and negative finally constitues the identity of the town. fig.8.
It is therefore of the greatest importance to understand and describe with great exactitude the relationship between the architecture and the urban space of the town in order to crasp the exact
meaning of the town's identity.

Fig. 7. The soft townscape

Fig. 8. Bruges

Use of Urban Volumes and Spaces

It has already been said that the correlation between the function and the shape of the buildings is so important that it is not possible to appraise the physical and spatial urban value without at the same time evaluating the activity within the buildings, nor the functions within urban areas.

An examination of the use of buildings will chiefly investigate the meaning of the activities: their vitality, their influence on the traffic, in how far they are a source of animation, their need to expand, their noise and pollution level, the relationship, harmony and/or complementarity with other activities. Another aspect of the use of buildings concerns the relationship with the structure of the buildings and the structure of the neighbourhood. The examination of the use of urban space, i.e. streets, squares, parks, canal sides, is principally concerned with quality of such urban possibilities as entertainment and information of strolling about, of shelter, amenity, convenience and enclosure for the old and visitors, games for children, the amenities of life for the inhabitants, especially for the women in regard to shopping. At the same time it concerns the improvement of street structures, the means of passing through public parks and public buildings. It provides serial vision and creates the act of relationship (4). Efforts must be made to improve the verdant areas, and in a watering-place to ensure easy access to the water and see that full use is made of whatever form it takes, canals, rivers, etc. This can be done by encouraging sailing, fishing and walks along the edge of the water.

In regard to the traffic and means of transport, it is imperative that the town traffic should be judiciously restricted; this also applies to rehabilitated areas so that they may be seen at their best, and that their upkeep may be ensured.

It is for the local authorities to decide to what extent they are prepard to let private cars and other vehicles circulate. It is for them to fix the maximum number of vehicles to be allowed to park in the area in question. The unsightly character of moving or stationary vehicles, the noise and vibrations harmful to ancient buildings and their use, the speed of the traffic, the security and various interests of both pedestrains and cars, the question of upkeep, public transport, the supervision of parking places, these are probably the principal points to take into consideration (3).

CONCLUSION

From this extended form of townscape appraisal a series of essential points can be considered in order to answer the fundamental question of the capacity of the town for physical change. This means, chiefly, evaluating the physical and spatial limits and possibilities of the urban structure.

The first consideration deals with the possibilities for the development of waste land within the historic city, namely, the
size and density of the development and the need to limit or extend it.

Obviously, a study of the site will clarify the choice. In this
way it will be possible, while taking into account the options
of the regional structure plan, to make a choice either of trans-
ferring the development away from the centre, but within the
agglomeration, or outside the latter, as an inducement for other
activities in the region.

At the same time an extended appraisal of urban waste land sites
may point to a policy for decentralising its undertakings within
the city. This would be either because the programme was over-
loaded, or because the scale of the building is to important, or
again because the obvious thing to do was to re-use the large
existing and empty buildings within the city.

So this decentralisation policy may be carried out by putting up
new buildings, either in different part of the town, or in one
or several definite areas so as to improve access, or to revita-
lise or to increase density in one or other neighbourhood.

A second consideration concerns the rehabilitation of derelict
buildings or of slum areas. This means either improving the
existing buildings and sites, or increasing or diminishing the
quantity of the floor and spaces.

These two considerations have a very important influence on the
quality of the town and the townscape. When translated into an
economic quantity these considerations give us an idea of the
size and importance of the supplementary floor surfaces.

A strong conservation and town & country planning policy can list
a number of sites and buildings such as the 'secteurs sauvegar-
dés' in France or the 'listed buildings' in G.B.. This has a
twofold consequence: on the one hand the capacity for adaptation
and change is restricted and the investment of funds is strongly
discouraged; on the other, the total value of the townscape, and
of the town in general is greatly increased. This may attract
abundant investments for the whole urban area.

Consequently, it is of the greatest importance to elaborate a
land policy and a policy limiting the built-up volumes without
which all activities and business investments will go towards the
outside of the town, leaving a very inactive and unattractive
centre.

It can at once be seen that a policy of urban rehabilitation based on an estimate of the town's capacity of change, taking into

(4) Gordon Cullen:Townscape,The architectural Press London 1961.

account the physical and spatial criteria, is impossible without
a town and country planning policy for the whole agglomeration
or region. As was said at the beginning, it is a choice of political objectives: in other words, it is impossible to have a twofold policy. In our country, remembering the weak demography and
the dense urban structure, it is not economically possible on
account of the quality of life, to opt for a rehabilitation policy of towns, both historic and others, without at the same time
developing a complementary policy of compression in regard to the
agglomeration and the region.

Any serious rehabilitation policy must of necessity be an integral part of the town & country planning policy. Here the same
land objectives concerning the town services and public transport are essential.

A subsidy policy for rehabilitation must be established as soon
as it becomes clear that the regional land policy and the building limitation policy based on physical and spatial appraisal
make it impossible to introduce economically viable activities
in rehabilitated historic buildings, which are socially indispensable, and necessary for the livelyhood of the community. In
other words the difference between what is economically desirable and physically inacceptable must be made up by grant and
subsidy (5)

I think I may conclude by saying that the town's capacity for
change can be evaluated by an analysis and an appraisal of the
town's physical and spatial characteristics and their use.

That this qualitative assessement can be translated quantitavely
into supplementary floor space. That this result must be paral-
lelled with the complementary economic financial and social ap-
praisals.

Our experience in Bruges has proved two important and conclusive
points. First, that the estimate of the supplementary floorspace obtained by the analysis and evaluation of the urban character compare very favourably with the estimate obtained by the
financial and economic approach. Secondly, inspite of a very
bad national town & country planning policy, which makes it impossible to control or limit the buildings that are put up
either in the agglomeration or in the region, around Bruges (and
in relation to the city), we have been able, by strictly applying, the method explained above, to establish the fact that
Bruges was the only Belgium town where the value of land and
building property increased during the year 1975; whereas in the
majority of other Belgian towns the value decreased, or in a few
cases, remained stable. (6).

---

(5) Roy Worskett 'Great Britain Progress in conservation'
     Architectural Review, London (January 1975).
(6) de Sagher 'Discussion Pannel in Ghent' 10.12.1975.

I intended with this article to raise up a number of problems of the character and identity of the historic town and its repercussions on the general town and country planning policy.
I preferred this rather incomplete approach which surely raises many questions than being comprehensive.

WELLBEING IN CITIES AND THE FUTURE

Yona Friedman

Wellbeing in cities is a difficult concept to define, because the necessary criteria for its definition are, necessarily, subjective ones: either individually subjective (like esthetical or emotional criteria) or group-subjective ones (like socio-economic, biological, cultural criteria etc). In this paper I have no intention to make value judgements concerning such criteria, but I will try to consider how to help the future users of a town (individuals or groups), who have to establish for themselves what kind of wellbeing he would prefer for himself and what kind could he attain.

It is evident that town-users' wellbeing cannot be achieved with certainty by an expert, or by a planner. There is no known method of communication which could guarantee good understanding between the planner and the future user of his plan. This lack of communication between decision makers and those for whom decisions are made is the root of most aspects of actual crisis. The planner's role has practically always been that of a regulator who was supposed to produce a framework in which the aims of one group of people could coexist, without conflict, with the aims of another group. As such, a regulator never succeeded to solve this problem satisfactorily, for none of them, and the different parties generally began to have a direct dialogue, without middlemen. In the near past, experience showed that such direct negotiations between parties were fruitful, provided that all parties were previously sufficiently informed about all the possible alternatives, and about the specific risks implied by each alternative. From this point of view, the architects' role and the future users' role might both become very different today. Thus, decision making should belong, by right, to the user, and the task of the planner should be reduced to that of a facultative technical adviser.

After examining who has to determine the character of the urban environment in respect of the wellbeing of the inhabitants, let us look what the different possible ways to act are.

Manmade environment in towns is an ordered environment. This order has the goal to lead to the wellbeing of the users. The ordering can be done in different ways:

a) functional ordering, based on a preconceived way of use
b) esthetical ordering, based on a preconceived taste
c) minimal ordering, based on least constraints (laisser-faire)
d) multifunctional ordering, based on models which can be adapted to all unforeseeable ways of use.

The first three orderings are well-known. We shall thus consider, in this

303

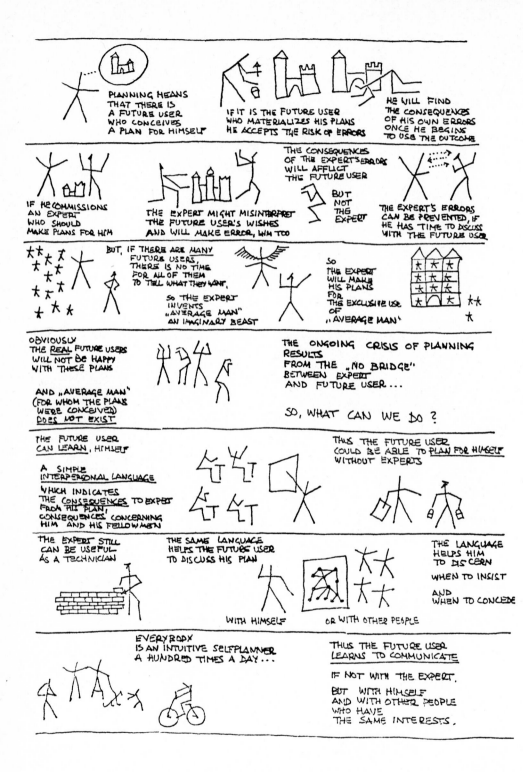

PLANNING MEANS
THAT THERE IS
A FUTURE USER
WHO CONCEIVES
A PLAN FOR HIMSELF

IF IT IS THE FUTURE USER
WHO MATERIALIZES HIS PLANS
HE ACCEPTS THE RISK OF ERRORS

HE WILL FIND
THE CONSEQUENCES
OF HIS OWN ERRORS
ONCE HE BEGINS
TO USE THE OUTCOME

IF HE COMMISSIONS
AN EXPERT
WHO SHOULD
MAKE PLANS FOR HIM

THE EXPERT MIGHT MISINTERPRET
THE FUTURE USER'S WISHES
AND WILL MAKE ERROR, HIM TOO

THE CONSEQUENCES
OF THE EXPERT'S ERRORS
WILL AFFLICT
THE FUTURE USER

BUT
NOT
THE
EXPERT

THE EXPERT'S ERRORS
CAN BE PREVENTED, IF
HE HAS TIME TO DISCUSS
WITH THE FUTURE USER

BUT, IF THERE ARE MANY
FUTURE USERS,
THERE IS NO TIME
FOR ALL OF THEM
TO TELL WHAT THEY WANT,

SO THE EXPERT
INVENTS
„AVERAGE MAN"
AN IMAGINARY BEAST

SO
THE EXPERT
WILL MAKE
HIS PLANS
FOR
THE EXCLUSIVE USE
OF
„AVERAGE MAN"

OBVIOUSLY
THE REAL FUTURE USERS
WILL NOT BE HAPPY
WITH THESE PLANS

AND „AVERAGE MAN"
(FOR WHOM THE PLANS
WERE CONCEIVED)
DOES NOT EXIST

THE ONGOING CRISIS OF PLANNING
RESULTS
FROM THE „NO BRIDGE"
BETWEEN EXPERT
AND FUTURE USER...

SO, WHAT CAN WE DO?

THE FUTURE USER
CAN LEARN, HIMSELF

A SIMPLE
INTERPERSONAL LANGUAGE

WHICH INDICATES
THE CONSEQUENCES TO EXPECT
FROM HIS PLAN,
CONSEQUENCES CONCERNING
HIM AND HIS FELLOW MEN

THUS THE FUTURE USER
COULD BE ABLE TO PLAN FOR HIMSELF
WITHOUT EXPERTS

THE EXPERT STILL
CAN BE USEFUL
AS A TECHNICIAN

THE SAME LANGUAGE
HELPS THE FUTURE USER
TO DISCUSS HIS PLAN

WITH HIMSELF

OR WITH OTHER PEOPLE

THE LANGUAGE
HELPS HIM
TO DISCERN

WHEN TO INSIST

AND
WHEN TO CONCEDE

EVERYBODY
IS AN INTUITIVE SELFPLANNER
A HUNDRED TIMES A DAY...

THUS THE FUTURE USER
LEARNS TO COMMUNICATE

IF NOT WITH THE EXPERT,

BUT WITH HIMSELF
AND WITH OTHER PEOPLE
WHO HAVE
THE SAME INTERESTS.

paper, the fourth one primarily.

If a planner or an architect has to adapt his plans to unforeseeable
scenarios because these scenarios happen to materialize more often than
foreseeable ones (this is the origin of the dissatisfaction of users with
planners and architects), we have to examine some of these scenarios.

a) Scenario of the "Poor World".

The principle of the impossibility of communication within a large
organization (like a state, for example) implies that, in case of crisis,
such an organization is unable to act. Survival (or wellbeing) of people
depending upon a large organization - those who got "abandoned" by it
because it was unable to act - cannot be guaranteed by others than themselves. For example, no government was able to organize supply while
the "petrol crisis" was going on, or during certain periods of the second
world war.

It is easy to analyse the phenomenon of the inability to cope with a
situation for such organizations: they rely on "wise men's councils" who
pass a solution on paper, but are unable to implement it. We don't
lack such "wise men's councils" who know how to settle a crisis, but their
solutions <u>have to</u> be slow because of the communication difficulties; thus,
in case of sudden scarcity the measures they take are ineffective.

International organizations, like W.H.O. or F.A.O., consider that our
world, with its growing overpopulation, inevitably enters into a period
of scarcity (food, energy, housing etc), and that the "impoverishment"
of the world is too fast increasing to be slowed down: "wise men's
councils" have no time left to act through the usual channels of communication.

Within large organizations
transmission paths are too
long and transmission too
slow:

the organization cannot react
fast enough in case of crisis.

This impoverishment might develop relatively slowly from one year to
another, but its rhythm is far too fast to put the brakes on, as the "wise
men's councils" contemplated doing. On the other hand, once the "Poor
World" materializes itself, it might last for a long time, and getting back
to the present "normal" situation seems very improbable.

We have thus to presume that a new phenomenon will emerge: small groups
might organize themselves and will be able to secure a better chance of

survival by using a simpler and less dependent technology. These groups
or communities will try to produce the largest part of their food, their
tools, etc., without depending on other groups.

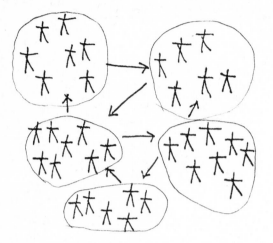

People who got "abandoned"
by large organizations try to
form small groups to secure
their survival.

This would mean a sort of autarchy, thus a relative independence on
transportation, devised labor, commerce etc. The "Poor World" scenario
would imply a complete reorganization of urban environment: "urban
villages", decay of large urban centers, construction and repair of
buildings by self-help me thods, space allocation and arrangement decided
and executed by the users themselves, urban agriculture (growing food
within the town), etc. Certain activities might even change their actual
"privacy" into "public" (for example, eating, sleeping, bathing etc).

Urban agriculture could
provide an important
part of the necessary food.

If transportation stops
craftsmanship can continue
but factories close down.

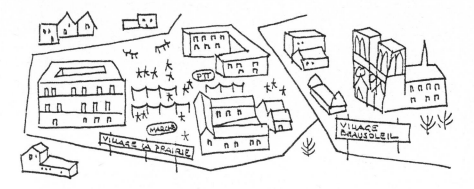

The "urban villages" appear:
they are parts of the town which became completely autonomous.

In case of scarcity these communities try to secure services which
decayed with the large organizations.

b)   Scenario of "Intermittent Poverty".

If the scenario of the "Poor World" shows a gradual and definitive transformation of the present social and urban pattern, there is a not less
possible alternative of "intermittent poverty": sudden crises which don't
last long, but last long enough to be considered seriously. There are many
examples of such "quakes": the monstrous blackout in eastern U.S.,
general strikes that last for months, epidemics, longwearing transportation breakdowns etc.

Such "quakes" can be, if not eliminated, at least reduced in their impact,
if urban environment is conceived to be able to cope with them.

c)   Scenario of "Urban Insecurity".

This scenario can happen at the same time as the other ones, or it can
happen all by itself: it consists in a deterioration of public security in
streets, subways, homes, in increasing violence, in street battles etc.

There are many new phenomena accompanying this state of facts: fenced
or walled neighborhoods, security patrols and voluntary militias,
checkposts and guard towers. Urban villages surrounded with ramparts
are surely no science fiction for the near future.

No research is done, at the present time, to find architectural solutions
which could cope with situations such as those described by these scenarios.
Obviously, architectural solutions would not have the effect of escaping
the scenarios, but at least they could make life easier in critical conditions.
This could not be said about present urban environment which is conceived
on the basis of a hypothesis of affluence. How would a building like the
World Trade Center work in a poor world? How could public security in
New York or in Los Angeles work? How could Paris or Milan be
provided with food in the case of "intermittent poverty"?

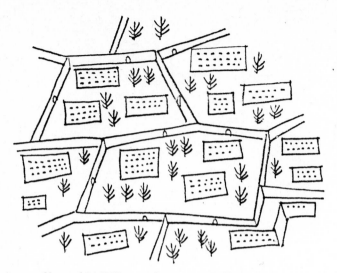

The big city cannot
guarantee for its
inhabitants
their personal
security.

The urban village can
do it if it fences in
itself and does not
permit any transit.

Recycling of buildings, for very different conditions, is the touchstone of
urban environment. Roman basilicas, churches, markets were recycled
in very various ways during the centuries. At the same time, the
Pyramids were unusable for the last 5000 years. How are buildings going
to be recycled today if scenarios, such as the ones described above, might
happen?

USERC ENVIRONMENT RESOURCES AND URBAN DEVELOPMENT WORKSHOP

Edward A. Wolff, Past President, United States
Environment and Resources Council, NASA/Goddard
Space Flight Center, Code 950, Greenbelt, Mary-
land 20771

The United States Environment and Resources Council (USERC) held a workshop in the Washington, DC area from November 12-14, 1975. The objective of the workshop was to obtain an interdisciplinary view of the impact of various urban development alternatives on the environment and resources. The workshop was attended by sixty participants organized into ten panels that considered urban development, energy, communications, meteorology, water resources, public health, in-situ sensing, remote sensing, socioeconomic problems, and science technology and government.

The urban development panel provided information on possible and probable future strategies of human settlements to provide information for use by the other panels. The in-situ and remote sensing panels provided information to the others on the tools and information that could be made available to assist the panels in measuring the success of efforts in their fields.

All of the panels endeavored to provide common information in terms of their discipline including a description of a successful human settlement (and the good and bad features of human settlements), the anticipated likely future state of human settlements, the differences between the likely and the desirable future states, possible strategies for reducing these differences to make future human settlements more successful, and the improvements that can be expected from such strategies.

The urban development panel presented eight possible urban development techniques including abandonment of cities, benign neglect, micro-revitilization, transcendental solutions, satellite communities, growth centers, new towns in town, and free standing new cities.

It was generally concluded that a successful human settlement was one that maintained a high quality of life while conserving energy and resources. It was felt that the successful human settlement would give the residents a maximum freedom to choose among the available living environments and work opportunities. This freedom, however, seems to be highly dependent on the availability of energy and resources and the utilization practices which impact the environment.

The workshop participants felt that the future state of human
settlements will depend greatly on the decisions that are taken
today regarding energy and resource utilization. The quality of
life in future human settlements will depend on the ability of
urban and land use planning to take advantage of the knowledge
available in the various environment and resources disciplines
and to take advantage of the technology and tools that are
available.

The urban development approaches that appeared most desirable
were micro-revitilization, new towns in town, free standing new
cities, and growth centers. These appear to be more efficient
in their utilization of energy and resources. They are also
more efficient in terms of other utilities, distribution systems,
transportation and communications. The alternative of eliminating cities and dispersing the population appears extremely
wasteful. The alternative of change without deliberate action
(benign neglect) is the antithesis of the concept of applying
our knowledge for the solution of problems. The approach involving transcendental change in human behavior could provide
workable solutions but was regarded by the participants as relatively unlikely to occur with sufficient intensitiy in a free
society. The satellite communities concept was seen as being
desirable only in so far as the satellites could be configured
as compact, high-density, areas in close proximity to the urban
core. The free standing city was seen as a rare opportunity to
apply our knowledge for the solution of urban problems, but the
participants were not sure the institutions could meet the
challenge.

The energy panel concluded that energy has been too inexpensive
because its costs have not properly reflected true replacement costs for renewable resource utilization. They felt the
movement to effectively utilize energy should embrace all forms
of energy not just petroleum. Human settlements should strive
to become energy self-sufficient on renewable non-polluting
sources in such a manner that each settlement has political control of its energy supply system.

The communications panel identified several areas where communications could be used to conserve energy and resources including
the substitution of communications techniques for transportation
of people and information.

The meteorology panel recommended that construction standards
and zoning be developed taking full account of meteorology for
optimization.

The water resources panel recommended that water be priced to
include all costs and to induce efficient use. Total water management means consideration of surface water, ground conservation, recharge, reuse, waste use, and weather modification.

The sensor panels called attention to the data flow feedback cir-
cuit of human settlements where in-situ and remote sensors are

used to monitor the urban environment, the measured information
is used in mathematical models to present the measurement of the
habitation system to the political decision makers so that proper decisions can be made to assure a desirable human settlement
in terms of environment and resources. The sensor panels pointed
out that advanced sensor technology is presently available for
immediate implementation to signfiicantly aid in optimizing urban
development, but this technology is not being properly utilized.

The science, technology and government panel recommended
increased and improved efforts in the forecasting of technological occurrences that will affect human settlements and the assessing of the potential impact.

One of the important features of the workshop was the interdisciplinary interactions that occurred between the various panels.
The energy panel discussed the interaction with transportation,
communications, meteorology, water quality, in-situ and remote
sensing, and economics. The communications panel examined its
interaction with energy, meteorology, in-situ and remote sensing, transportation, land use, social and economic problems,
and science-technology and government. Similar interactions
occurred between the other panels.

The general conclusion of the participants was that this type of
interaction needed to be continued in depth in the future, and
that the efforts of thr workshop were only a small beginning.